Investment, Employment and
Income Distribution

Aspects of Political Economy
Series Editor: Geoffrey Harcourt

Published

A. Asimakopulos, *Investment, Employment and Income Distribution*
Pat Devine, *Democracy and Economic Planning*
Richard M. Goodwin and Lionello F. Punzo, *The Dynamics of a Capitalist Economy*
Marc Jarsulic, *Effective Demand and Income Distribution*
Peter Nolan, *The Political Economy of Collective Farms*
Bob Rowthorn and Naomi Wayne, *Northern Ireland*
Christopher Torr, *Equilibrium, Expectations and Information*
Warren Young, *Interpreting Mr Keynes*

Forthcoming

Grazia Ietto-Gillies, *Causes and Effects of International Production*
Ravi Kanbur, *Risk Taking, Income Distribution and Poverty*
Jose Salazar, *Pricing Policy and Economic Development*
Ian Steedman, *From Exploitation to Altruism*

Investment, Employment
and
Income Distribution

A. ASIMAKOPULOS

Routledge
Taylor & Francis Group

NEW YORK AND LONDON

First published 1988 by Westview Press

Published 2018 by Routledge
605 Third Avenue, New York, NY 10017
2 Park Square, Milton Park, Abingdon, Oxon OX14 4RN

First issued in paperback 2022

Routledge is an imprint of the Taylor & Francis Group, an informa business

Library of Congress Cataloging-in-Publication Data

Asimakopulos, A., 1930–
    Investment, employment, and income distribution.
    (Aspects of political economy)
    Includes bibliographies and indexes.
    1. Saving and investment. 2. Employment (Economic
theory) 3. Income distribution. 4. Keynes, John
Maynard, 1883–1946. 5. Kalecki, Michał.
6. Robinson, Joan, 1903–   . I. Title. II. Series.
HB843.A84 1988   339   88-20709

Typeset in 11 on 12½pt Plantin by Photo·Graphics, Honiton, Devon

ISBN 13: 978-0-367-15320-5 (pbk)
ISBN 13: 978-0-367-00333-3 (hbk)

To the memory of the late J. C. Weldon

Contents

Preface

Most of the articles reprinted in this collection were based on material developed for my students in order to assist them in understanding the theories of Michal Kalecki, John Maynard Keynes and Joan Robinson. Each article is self-contained, but together the articles provide an introduction to the important contributions of these three economists that also makes clear the interrelations between their theories. The treatment of their theories in these articles is sympathetic, but not uncritical. Some slips are pointed out, unstated assumptions are brought to light, and the limitations of particular analyses are discussed. Other teachers have also found some of these articles to be useful for their students, and this book will make them more readily available.

Many of the articles gratefully acknowledged the assistance obtained from the comments of colleagues and friends, and these acknowledgements are repeated in the relevant chapters. But special mention should be made here of four people.

Geoff Harcourt has played an important role in my career from the time in the late 1960s when our paths crossed again, 12 years after we had first met as research students in Cambridge. A mutual friend sent him a copy of my manuscript dealing with Robinson's growth model, and Geoff promptly accepted it for publication in the *Australian Economic Papers*. He has always been more than generous with his time in reading, commenting on, and encouraging my writings (and those of many others). This book would not exist, and many of its articles would not have been written, were it not for Geoff's endeavours.

The paper on the incidence of taxation was written as a result of my interest in introducing government economic activity into the framework of my Robinsonian growth model, and John Burbidge's interest in writing a Ph.D. thesis on the incidence of taxation. This paper was the result of a genuine collaboration and I look back with very fond memories to the rapid exchange of ideas that resulted in a truly joint product.

My wife, Marika, has been a constant source of support for my research. She reads all my manuscripts before they are sent for typing, and her comments on style have helped improve the final product. The task of standardizing the reference format for this book has fallen on her, and she has compiled the master reference list, as well as taking charge of the index and assisting with the proofreading.

This book is dedicated to the memory of the late Jack Weldon, a former teacher, colleague and close friend, who died at the end of February 1987. His was a formidable intellect, and I was privileged to be associated with him over a long period of time. Jack's availability for checking out an analytical construction, or to explore some confusion in the economics literature, as well as the excitement he could convey about economic theory, and his constant encouragement, helped guide my research efforts and writings. We wrote several articles together that dealt with models of economic growth and the treatment of technical progress, as well as the theory of public pension plans and intergenerational transfers. My publications have all been influenced by him.

Acknowledgements

The essays in this volume were first published in the following journals and collections, and the author and publisher are grateful for permission to reprint them here:

'The short-period incidence of taxation' (co-authored with J. B. Burbidge). *Economic Journal* 84, June 1974, 267–88.

'A Kaleckian theory of income distribution.' *Canadian Journal of Economics* 8, August 1975, 313–33.

'Keynes' theory of effective demand revisited.' *Australian Economic Papers* 21, June 1982, 18–36.

'Anticipations of Keynes's general theory?' *Canadian Journal of Economics* 16, August 1983, 517–30.

'Kalecki and Keynes on finance, investment and saving.' *Cambridge Journal of Economics* 7, September–December 1983, 221–33.

'Joan Robinson and economic theory.' *Banca Nazionale del Lavoro Quarterly Review* 151, December 1984, 381–409.

'Keynes and Sraffa: visions and perspectives.' *Political Economy: Studies in the Surplus Approach* 1, No. 2, 1985, 33–50.

'Kalecki on the determinants of profits' in G. Fink, G. Pöll and M. Riese (eds), *Economic Theory, Political Power and Social Justice: Festschrift Kazimierz Laski* (Wien: Springer-Verlag, 1987).

1

Introduction: Kalecki, Keynes and Robinson

The articles in this collection are mainly based on lecture material that I prepared in an attempt to explain, and to expand on, various aspects of the writings of Michal Kalecki, John Maynard Keynes and Joan Robinson. Robinson's writings were very important in this process, because it was through them that my approach to the theories of Kalecki and Keynes was reached. Her writings contain penetrating expositions of their theories, as well as attempts to use these theories as the foundations for a theory of accumulation.

Robinson was also an important personal 'intermediary' between Kalecki and Keynes – they each had close intellectual relations with her rather than with one another. It was through her that Kalecki first made contact with Keynes's Cambridge circle after the publication of *The General Theory* in 1936. Kalecki had a leave that year, financed by a Rockefeller Foundation Fellowship, the first part of which he spent in Sweden. He then went to England in mid-April, where he attended seminars at the London School of Economics (Patinkin, 1982, p. 93). It appears that Robinson had not heard of Kalecki before she received a letter from him that September. She recalled, in her 1976 Michal Kalecki Memorial Lecture at Oxford, that 'I received a letter, evidently from a foreigner visiting England, who said that he was interested in my article ['Disguised unemployment' *Economic Journal*, June 1936] as it was close to some work of his own' (Robinson, 1980b, p. 186). Robinson was clearly very impressed by her first meeting with Kalecki that took place soon after her receipt of this letter. In a letter to him dated September 16, she wrote '. . . I cannot delay to tell you what a pleasure it is to me to be arguing with someone who is making an advance upon Keynes instead of endlessly disputing with people who have not understood the elementary points' (Patinkin, 1982, p. 94).[1]

The intellectual and personal friendship that started from that first meeting continued until Kalecki's death in 1970. Robinson's attachment to Kalecki, even in those early days, is evident in her comment in a brief letter to Keynes, after she had accompanied Kalecki when he gave a paper at Keynes's Political Economy Club. She had written: 'Thank you so much for being kind to my Pole' (Keynes, 1973b, p. 140). The relations between Kalecki and Keynes were much more formal, and the written record largely consists of correspondence concerning articles that Kalecki had submitted for publication to the *Economic Journal*. (Parts of this correspondence will be examined below, because they shed some light on the differences in the approaches of these two theorists.) Robinson's comments on Keynes's reactions to Kalecki indicate the wide gulf between the two, even though certain aspects of their theories are very similar.

> When Kalecki came to Cambridge in 1936, we told Keynes about him, but he was not much impressed. His own ideas were in full spate (he was thinking about rewriting the *General Theory* in a completely different way) and he had not patience with anyone else's. . . . Keynes did not sympathize with Kalecki's political presuppositions and by background and temperament they could not have been further apart. I commented on this once, saying 'oil and vinegar would not mix'. Some critic objected that they are mixed every day, but that needs constant stirring. Neither of these two characters was easy to stir. However, Keynes took the trouble to get a research project set up to provide Kalecki with a job. (This was just before the war and nothing much came of it.). (Robinson, 1980b, p. 187)[2]

In spite of personal differences, and some differences in the questions they addressed and in the type of formulations they used, there are important similarities between the theories of Kalecki and Keynes. These differences and similarities make them complementary and thus suitable as joint bases for further work. Much of Robinson's work can be seen in this light, as a continuation and expansion of the insights to be found in the writings of these two theorists. Her approach to accumulation reflects a combination of the two in which Kalecki's influence predominates (Asimakopulos, 1988). Robinson believed that this also held for 'post-Keynesian' economics. 'Kalecki's version of the General Theory, rather than Keynes', has been incorporated in the post-Keynesian tradition' (Robinson, 1975b, p. xiv).

The focus in this introductory chapter is on the similarities and differences in the theories of Kalecki, Keynes and Robinson on investment, distribution and employment. This examination also serves as a commentary on the subsequent eight chapters that are concerned with these theories.

Investment, profits and employment

Kalecki's 1933 essay on the business cycle (the title in Polish is 'Próba teorii koniunktury') contains his basic vision of the macroeconomic operation of a capitalist economy. The key to the business cycle is the investment process – investment decisions that are followed by investment expenditures and then by the delivery of capital goods. Current investment depends on investment decisions made in the past, while current investment (and capitalists' consumption) expenditures determine current profits, which have an important influence on current investment decisions and thus on future investment. Changes in productive capacity that lag behind investment expenditures also affect investment decisions, and they play an important role in determining the turning points of the cycle. In the introduction to a selection of his essays that he considered to be his 'main contributions to the theory of dynamics of the capitalist economy' (Kalecki, 1971b, p. vii), Kalecki wrote:

It is interesting to notice that the theory of effective demand, already clearly formulated in the first papers, remains unchanged in all the relevant writings, as do my views on the distribution of national income. However, there is a continuous search for new solutions in the theory of investment decisions, where even the last paper represents – for better or worse – a novel approach. (Kalecki, 1971b, p. viii)

But this search for new solutions always started with the double-sided relation between investment and profits that first appeared in that 1933 essay.

A full appreciation of Kalecki's writings, with due regard to the time when various theoretical elements first appeared, is difficult to achieve for those who do not read Polish, because the articles available in English sometimes contain portions written at different dates. A full translation of the 1933 essay has yet to be published. What we have are translations of parts of it, but mixed in with those parts is some material on the money market and prices that was written after 1933. Kalecki presented a paper at the European Meeting of the Econometric Society held in Leyden in October 1933 which was based on the 1933 essay. An amended version of this paper was published in the July 1935 *Econometrica* (Kalecki, 1935b), and it had been preceded by another article in the *Revue d'Economie Politique* (Kalecki, 1935a) that also drew from the 1933 essay but omitted mathematical detail. The latter gave more attention to the changes in prices that could accompany cyclical fluctuations, and to the conditions in the money market that allowed an expansion in economic activity to take place. In the Foreword to the first publication in English of his early writings on the business cycle, Kalecki noted that the first chapter in that book (it is also the first chapter in Kalecki (1971b)), entitled 'Outline of a theory of the business cycle', 'is the first (and most essential) part of my booklet *An Essay on the Theory of Business Cycle* which was published in 1933. I supplemented this study by a short passage concerning the problem of the money market taken from . . . [Kalecki, 1935a]. Apart from this nothing of importance has been added either to this or to other items' (Kalecki, 1966, p. 1).[3]

The 1933 essay begins with the examination of the determinants of profits in a closed economy with negligible government economic activity, in which only two social classes, workers and capitalists, are distinguished. The national income identity between total income (the sum of gross profits and wages) and total expenditure (capitalists' gross investment and consumption expenditures, plus workers' consumption expenditures) is used to derive an equality between gross profits and total capitalists' expenditures, when it is assumed that workers' consumption is equal to total wages. This identity's transformation into a short-period equilibrium result is completed with Kalecki's assumption that capitalists' consumption in each unit of time is in the desired relation to their current income, as shown by their consumption function, which consists of two parts, one that is constant and one that is proportionate to current profits. Equilibrium profits are thus proportional to the sum of the constant part of capitalists' consumption and investment expenditures. The value for this factor of proportionality is equal to one over the marginal propensity to save out of gross profits.

Kalecki's interest in this essay is on the business cycle, the changes in activity over a sequence of time periods, rather than in a detailed examination of employment and output in his unit period of time. The time lags in the investment process play a critical role in this explanation, with current investment feeding current profits that in turn positively affect future investment, through their influence on the expected profitability of investment, while the increase in productive capacity that lags behind investment activity has a negative effect on investment decisions. It is implicitly assumed that the unit period of time – whose length is not specified – is characterized by short-period equilibrium, and that the multiplier effects of changes in investment expenditures are all completed within this period.[4] There is no employment constraint on output and a reserve of unemployed is taken for granted, an assumption that is made explicit in Kalecki (1935a, p. 296n.; 1935b, p. 343n.).

The fluctuations in aggregate production over the cycle are inferred from the changes in gross profits, with the latter 'expressed as the product of the volume of the aggregate production and of the profit per unit of output' (Kalecki, 1971b, p. 11). One of the reasons why the latter is assumed to change in the same direction as aggregate production is 'the fact that a part of wages are overheads' (p. 11n.). In addition, prices are assumed generally to increase with output (p. 13). This presumption about changes in prices is found in the material on the money market that originally appeared in Kalecki (1935a). The latter examined the relationship, given changes in profits, between the nature of the market structure, the degree of utilization of productive capacity, and profit per unit of output. In competitive markets (the only case that is considered in the amended version of the 1933 essay in Kalecki (1971b)), prices move in the same direction as changes in profits. The consequent changes in profit per unit of output serve to moderate the changes in output required to obtain the given change in total profits, while the relatively rigid prices under cartel or oligopolistic arrangements require more extensive changes in output. Kalecki, in his later writings, tied down these differences in the degree of responsiveness of prices to conditions of supply for manufactured and primary goods.

> Short-term price changes may be classified into two broad groups: those determined mainly by changes in cost of production and those determined mainly by changes in demand. Generally speaking, changes in the prices of finished goods are 'cost-determined' while changes in the prices of raw materials inclusive of primary foodstuffs are 'demand-determined'. The prices of finished goods are affected, of course, by any 'demand determined' changes in the prices of raw materials but it is through the channel of *costs* that this influence is transmitted.
>
> It is clear that these two types of price formation arise out of different conditions of supply.. The production of finished goods is elastic as a result of existing reserves of productive capacity. When demand increases it is met mainly by an increase in the volume of production while prices tend to remain stable. The price changes which do occur result mainly from changes in costs of production.
>
> The situation with respect to raw materials is different. . . . With supply inelastic in short periods, an increase in demand causes a diminution of stocks and a consequent increase in price. (Kalecki, 1954, p. 11)

My 1975 income distribution paper, reprinted in chapter 2, concentrates on a particular short-period situation and tries to draw together the two elements in Kalecki's theory: the role of capitalists' expenditures in determining the level of profits; and the mark-ups over unit prime costs that manufacturing firms can establish because of the degree of monopoly protecting their markets.[5] It deals only with a closed economy, and in the main text it is assumed that the workers' propensity to save is zero. This leads to Kalecki's conclusion, as paraphrased by Kaldor (1955–6, p. 96), 'capitalists earn what they spend and workers spend what they earn'. The last part of this statement is a necessary condition for the first part, because if workers save, capitalists would earn less than they spend. The theory of income distribution presented in chapter 2 is *not*, however, dependent on the assumption of zero saving by workers. What is crucial to that theory is a greater propensity to save out of profits than out of wages. If the propensity to save of workers is zero then, in this model of a closed economy with no government economic activity, both profits and the profit share in total income are directly related to the level of investment expenditures. (The latter holds even though the ratio of price to unit prime cost is unchanged, because it is assumed that there is overhead labour.) The level of profits, in this special case, is independent of the value for the mark-up, but it is shown in the appendix of chapter 2 that this conclusion has to be discarded if the propensity to save out of wages is positive. The introduction of government economic activity and international trade into the model would also have this effect. A Kaleckian theory of distribution cannot thus, in general, be split into two separate parts, with the level of capitalists' expenditures determining the level of profits and mark-ups having an influence only on the profit share. Robinson's statement that in Kalecki's analysis of profits 'we find the very striking proposition that firms, considered as a whole, cannot increase their profits merely by raising prices' (Robinson, 1980b, p. 192), is thus based on the most restricted version of Kalecki's theory.

The incidence of taxation

Kalecki used his theory of distribution to examine the economic incidence of taxation in a paper that Keynes accepted for publication in the June 1937 issue of the *Economic Journal*. The terminology used in this paper reflects Kalecki's exposure to *The General Theory* – the 'analysis is confined to the short period' (Kalecki, 1971b, p. 36), with values measured in wage units – but the analysis stems from his earlier work. The one important element of the 1933 essay that is changed is the introduction of government expenditure and taxation, but it is assumed that the government budget is always balanced. The time lag between investment decisions and investment expenditures still has an important role, even though attention is concentrated on an individual short period rather than on cyclical movements over a sequence of such periods. It allows Kalecki to assume that the investment expenditures in a period are predetermined by investment decisions made in earlier periods, and they are thus unaffected by the imposition of tax changes at the beginning of the period. Capitalists' consumption expenditures in the period respond only to realized changes in their current after-tax incomes, and they are thus unaffected by the announcement of tax changes.

Kalecki considers the effects of changes in three types of taxes (with receipts in all cases being used to increase payments to the unemployed): (a) a tax on wage goods; (b) a tax on capitalists' incomes; and (c) a tax on the value of all assets (i.e. a tax 'on every type of owned capital' (1971b, p. 41)).

An increase in the tax on wage goods would have no effect on gross profits (pre- or after-tax) under these circumstances. The total amount of money spent on wage goods increases by the increase in payments to the unemployed, since the recipients use it to purchase goods. But the short-period supply curve of wage goods is also shifted up by the amount of the increase in the unit tax on wage goods, so that the net effect of the equal shifts in the demand and supply curves is to increase the price paid by consumers by the amount of the tax. Purchasing power has been shifted from the employed to the unemployed, and the former thus bear the full burden of the tax.

An increase in the tax on capitalists' incomes would, in contrast, result in an increase in output and employment in the new short-period equilibrium, because the positive effect of the tax-fed increase in demand for wage goods is not offset by a shift in their supply curve. Even though capitalists' tax payments are higher in this short-period equilibrium, their pre-tax incomes are also higher by the same amount due to the increase in output and the higher price that accompanies it.[6] Kalecki's reference to the increase in prices that results from the increase in demand makes clear that he is assuming competitive conditions in this paper. The economic incidence of the tax on capitalists' incomes falls, in part, on employed workers whose real incomes are lower because of these higher prices, with the remainder being absorbed by the increase in output.

To complete this analysis Kalecki considers the possible effects of these changes on the expected profitability of investment. He uses a numerical example for this purpose, and he eliminates possible monetary constraints by assuming that the supply of money for transactions purposes is perfectly elastic at the ruling rate of interest. An increase in the tax rate from 15 to 25 per cent is stipulated, and it is implicitly assumed that the net interest rate received by rentiers is the minimum amount they need in order to continue lending to firms for investment at the same levels. With an initial interest rate of 3 per cent, the net rate (with a 15 per cent tax) is 2.55 per cent. In order to achieve this required net rate when the tax is 25 per cent, the gross rate paid by entrepreneurs must be 3.4 per cent. Kalecki assumes that the prospective gross rate of profits on investment is directly related to current gross profits. The gross profits in the post-tax increase equilibrium must be larger than the gross profits that would have been obtained in the absence of this increase, in the ratio of 0.85 to 0.75 (or 1.133), in order to ensure that after-tax profits at a 25 per cent tax rate are the same as those at a 15 per cent rate. But since gross profits have increased sufficiently, as we have seen, to leave after-tax profits unchanged they must stand in a ratio of 1.133 to the pre-tax increase in gross profits. If 9 per cent would be the prospective gross rate of return on investment in the absence of the tax increase, then 10.197 per cent (= 9 × 1.133) would be the new prospective rate under these assumptions. The prospective *net* rate of return is the same in both cases: (9−3) × 0.85 = (10.197 − 3.4) × 0.75 = 5.1. Kalecki thus concludes that this increase in the tax on capitalists' incomes will not have an adverse effect on the inducement to invest.[7]

Kalecki derives even more dramatic effects from a tax on capital whose proceeds are turned over to the unemployed. The expenditure of these tax receipts results, in the new short-period equilibrium, in an increase in gross profits by the amount of the tax, with output, employment and prices being higher. After-tax profits also increase in this case because the tax is on capital, rather than on the income from capital. Given the assumptions of Kalecki's analysis, the inducement to invest has been enhanced. In spite of these favourable outcomes, Kalecki does not expect that governments are likely to resort to capital taxation as a way of stimulating business activity 'for it may seem to undermine the principle of private property . . .' (1971b, p. 42). But this consideration also raises questions about the validity of the basic assumptions underlying Kalecki's analysis of the incidence of taxation. If the principle of private property appears to be undermined by a tax, then capitalists' expenditures are unlikely to be unaffected by the announcement of such a tax. If these expenditures are decreased, then the beneficial effects of the financing of increased payments to the unemployed through a tax on capital would be diminished, and they might even become negative.

It is interesting to note that Keynes, after accepting Kalecki's article for publication, and having made suggestions for clarifying the assumptions on which the analysis is based, added 'As a private critic . . .' (Keynes, 1983, p. 797) that he (Keynes) regarded the assumption that there would be no effects on investment and capitalists' consumption expenditures 'as unplausible'. These effects, if they were present, would alter the conclusions of Kalecki's analysis, but his analytic framework for the examination of the incidence of taxation would be unaffected. Once the extent to which the tax changes have altered capitalists' expenditures in the short period is specified, Kalecki's approach can be used to determine the effects of the postulated tax changes. Chapter 3, below, on the short-period incidence of taxation, jointly written with John Burbidge puts particular emphasis on the framework of the analysis. Within that framework, different market structures are examined, and a variety of combinations of tax and expenditure changes are stipulated. The short-period equilibrium comparisons – the 'strong' effects – are presented in the tables to indicate one set of possible outcomes. But it is recognized that the values for the parameters, other than for the tax and expenditure changes stipulated, might not remain constant over the period, and a variety of outcomes is possible depending on the changes in the values of these other parameters. Some of these possibilities are examined in that chapter in what are called 'extensions' of the competitive and non-competitive versions of the model. There is also a comparison with the results obtained for the short-period incidence of taxation from neoclassical theory that points up the basic role of the theory of distribution in judgements about the incidence of taxation. It is possible to duplicate the neoclassical conclusions – e.g. that the short-period incidence of a tax on profits is the same as the legal incidence – by assuming suitable changes in the values for some of the other parameters. These are, of course, only some of the many possibilities allowed for by our model. The incidence of taxation in a particular case depends on the circumstances of that case, but the framework provided is sufficiently general to deal with a wide variety of particular cases.

The determinants of profits

Kalecki's approach to the determinants of profits can be used to explain the level of profits obtained in actual capitalist economies in any short period of time. These economies are 'open' to international trade, and government budgets need not be balanced in any period. The profits equation must thus allow for the effects of these items (as well as for possible saving by workers). It can be derived, as is done in chapter 4, by rearranging the items appearing in the national income identity. The version used there shows gross retained earnings of firms to be equal to the sum of gross investment, the government deficit, the international surplus and the negative of personal saving.[8]

This profits equation, even though it is derived from an identity, provides a causal explanation of profits when the unit interval of time for the data is brief. In such a case, the time lag between investment decisions and the resulting investment ensures that current investment is independent of current profits. If the current values for the other terms on the right-hand side of the profits equation are also independent of current profits, the necessary equality between the two sides of the equation can be considered to result from profits taking the required value. This causal interpretation does not deny the importance of profits as determinants of investment decisions. They influence expectations of the profitability of investment, and provide some of the finance for investment activity. It is only the time lag between investment decisions and investment activity, and the use of an interval for the data that is shorter than this lag, that allows a causal interpretation of the profits equation.[9] In using this equation to explain profits, and changes in profits, it is necessary to recognize the interdependence of the items on the right-hand side of the equation. For example, an increase in gross investment by $100 million would appear to increase profits by an equal amount, but this increase would also tend to decrease the value for the government deficit and the international surplus, while increasing personal saving, so that its net effect on profits would be less than its own value.

Kalecki sees his theoretical framework as one that would make it possible to arrange and interpret the statistics available, and it is in this spirit that the profits equation is used in chapter 4 to examine the changes in profits and its determinants for the United States economy in recent years. The unit time period of this empirical examination is a quarter of a year, an interval short enough to allow for the causal interpretation given to the profits equation. This examination of the short-period determinants of profits should be seen as only the first step in the analysis of the determination of profits, because a full analysis must allow for the complex ties between profits and investment over time that are suggested by the double-sided relationship between profits and investment.

Keynes and the theory of effective demand

Keynes had a strong intuitive grasp of the functioning of capitalist economies in the world around him, an understanding of the factors that result in cyclical fluctuations in output and employment and that are reflected in average employment levels over time that could be substantially below levels that could be characterized as full employment. This sense of the real world permeates all his economic writings, and gives them strength and vitality. Keynes was not, however, a meticulous theorist, and the theoretical structures he built to embody his vision of the operation of capitalist economies often contained minor inconsistencies. These inconsistencies in *The General Theory* do not affect the main thrust of his analysis, or his major policy conclusions, but they have caused problems for those trying to understand and to explain the details of the theory presented in that book. Chapter 5, below, 'Keynes's Theory of Effective Demand Revisited', contains a restatement of Keynes's theory of effective demand that consistently observes the Marshallian microfoundations of that theory – a restatement that has been found useful for teaching purposes.

The formal definition of the aggregate demand function provided by Keynes (the relationship between D and N, where D represents 'the proceeds which entrepreneurs expect to receive from the employment of N men' (Keynes, 1936, p. 25)) is inconsistent with the competitive microfoundations of his model. The proceeds that competitive firms expect to receive depend on expected prices for their products, since they produce those rates of output that equate their marginal costs to these prices – prices that are independent of their individual rates of output and employment. As Keynes subsequently noted, output and employment decisions are made on the basis of short-term expectations that are 'concerned with the price a manufacturer can expect to get for his "finished' output at the time when he commits himself to starting the process which will produce it' (1936, p. 46). The relationship between proceeds and employment that is found in Keynes's definition is one that could be observed by an economic analyst as an *ex post* relationship, in a situation of short-period equilibrium. It is not an 'expected' relationship in the minds of competitive entrepreneurs. Fortunately for Keynes's analysis, it is only used as an *ex post* equilibrium relationship.

Hawtrey's name should be added to those mentioned in chapter 5 as having noticed that inconsistency in Keynes's definition of the aggregate demand function. He drew Keynes's attention to it when he saw the page proofs of *The General Theory* by writing: 'Each employer's (hypothetical) expectation is presumably confined to his own product, and I do not see how you are going to aggregate these particular expectations into a total of consumption and a total of investment . . .' (Keynes, 1973a, p. 597). Keynes's defence, 'The demand which determines the decision as to how much plant to employ must necessarily concern itself with expectations' (p. 602), misses the point, because it is the expectation of individual product prices that is relevant, and not the expectations found in his definition of the aggregate demand function.

There is no problem with the microfoundations of Keynes's aggregate supply function. It has a firm basis in Marshall's short-period industry supply curves. Some of the possible ways of moving conceptually from industry short-period supply curves to the aggregate supply function are presented in chapter 5. It is argued there that 'effective demand', if it is taken to represent what determines employment in a given period, must be the point on the aggregate supply function that corresponds to the firms' expectations of proceeds. Aggregate demand enters into the picture in so far as it affects these expectations through the realized proceeds that are a function of the level of employment. Expected proceeds comprise the independent variable in the aggregate supply function, with employment being the dependent variable, while employment is the independent variable and realized proceeds make up the dependent variable in the aggregate demand function. This interpretation of effective demand, and the role of these functions, is consistent with statements found in Keynes's rough notes for his 1937 lectures. 'The *expected* results are not on a par with the *realised* results in a theory of employment. The *realised* results are only relevant in so far as they influence the ensuing expectations in the next production period' (Keynes 1973b, p. 179).

The time period of the analysis

Keynes's analysis in *The General Theory* takes place in Marshall's short period – 'a few months or a year' (Marshall, 1920, p. 379) – during which the changes in productive capacity that occur continuously in a dynamic economy can be legitimately ignored, because on average over this period they are small relative to the initial productive capacity. Keynes's analysis is thus set, subject to the necessary abstractions of any theory, in an actual period of time, a 'present' that separates a 'past' that has provided the equipment for current production from a 'future' many of whose features cannot be known with any substantial degree of certainty. It concentrates on situations of short-period equilibrium. Keynes stated that 'the essence of the General Theory of Employment' has to do with 'the volume of employment in equilibrium'. This volume 'depends on (i) the aggregate supply function . . . (ii) the propensity to consume . . . and (iii) the volume of investment' (Keynes, 1936, p. 29). These short-period equilibrium positions were seen as strong poles of attraction for actual values, and thus the analysis could be appropriately focused on them. 'The main point is to distinguish the forces determining the position of equilibrium from the technique of trial and error by means of which the entrepreneur discovers where the position is' (Keynes, 1973b, p. 182). Keynes did not always avoid the dangers of dealing almost exclusively with equilibrium values. Insufficient attention was paid to the time required to move from one set of short-period equilibrium values to another when the values of a parameter changed, even when the passage of time, as we shall see below, was relevant to his argument.

Keynes's short period, because it is a theoretical representation of an actual interval in historical time, provides an appropriate setting for dynamic analysis. But Keynes's formal analysis in *The General Theory* did not go beyond the short period, even though he included notes on the trade cycle that made use of concepts developed there to explain the determination of short-period equilibrium. It is for this reason that a sharp contrast is drawn in chapter 6 below between the perspective of Sraffa's model in his *Production of Commodities by Means of Commodities* that deals with prices of production that would hold in situations of long-period equilibrium and that of Keynes in *The General Theory*. The attempts by Eatwell (1979) and Milgate (1982) to interpret Keynes's theory of output and employment as concerned with the 'long-period level of output' are also critically examined in that chapter. The conclusion of this examination is that there is no long-period level of output that can be said to act as a 'centre of gravitation' for actual values, in Keynes's vision of the operations of capitalist economies.

Kalecki and Keynes: similarities and differences

Keynes found that the composition of *The General Theory* had been 'a long struggle of escape . . . from habitual modes of thoughts and expression' (Keynes, 1936, p. viii), because in that book equilibrium is no longer associated with a situation of full employment. The latter, which he saw as the position assumed by 'classical theory', had become only 'a limiting point of the possible positions of equilibrium' (p. 3). In his earlier *Treatise on Money* there had been discussion of cyclical fluctuations in output, but it had been implicitly assumed that in the absence of such fluctuations the economy would be characterized by full employment, a presumption that was found to have no theoretical justification in *The General Theory*. As noted above, the formal analysis in the latter was concerned only with the factors determining the equilibrium level of employment in a particular short period. This equilibrium level – quite apart from cyclical fluctuations whose existence was no less real for Keynes at the time of writing his later book than it was when he wrote the *Treatise* – was no longer necessarily associated with full employment. The term 'equilibrium' was used in this context to signify a position of 'rest' for employment, given the values for the other parameters (cf. Asimakopulos, 1973). But firms, unlike workers, could be said to be in equilibrium according to an alternative definition of equilibrium – a 'chosen' position – because they are producing at points on their short-period supply curves. Both consumption and investment expenditures can be said to be in 'equilibrium' according to this second definition, in a situation of short-period equilibrium. The former is given by the economy's consumption function and the level of income, while it is assumed that the rate of investment is 'pushed to the point on the investment demand-schedule where the marginal efficiency of capital in general is equal to the market rate of interest' (Keynes, 1936, pp. 136–7). The position of the investment demand schedule depends on long-term expectations that Keynes treats as independent of current conditions in his presentation of the marginal efficiency of capital. Keynes's analysis shows that there is no reason to expect that the rate of investment would take the value required to achieve full employment of labour, given the economy's consumption function. The rate of interest is determined in his model by monetary factors, and it is not free to adjust in such a way as to equate saving and investment at full-employment levels of output. It is the variation in the level of output, given the rate of investment, that brings about the appropriate rate of desired saving.

Kalecki's formal analysis, given his focus on the business cycle, covers a much longer interval of time than Keynes's short period. In the former's major pre-1936 writings, the examination of the characteristics of particular short-period situations were subordinated to a consideration of the forces that produce cycles. Kalecki's 'central message' concerns the mechanism of the cycle, and this is the reason for my agreement in chapter 8 with Patinkin's (1982) judgement that Kalecki cannot be said to have anticipated *The General Theory*. This is not to deny the important similarities between Kalecki's analysis and that of Keynes. In both it is investment that is the causal determinant of saving in short-period equilibrium, through its effects on the level of output (and, for Kalecki, on the distribution of income as well).

Kalecki was uncertain, especially during his first years in England, whether and how to make claims for priority in connection with important elements of *The General Theory*. In his review of this book that appeared in Polish in 1936, three footnote references were made to similar propositions contained in his 1933 essay. They refer to the key role of investment in determining the total level of output, to its causal determination of saving, and to the independence of the level of output from nominal wages (Targetti and Kinda-Hass, 1982, pp. 250–1). Some of the material from this review appeared in Kalecki (1937a), but no reference was made there to any of his prior writings. This self-effacement was carried into his 1939 book, where he wrote appreciatively of Rosa Luxemburg's work on the importance of investment in the realization of profits: '. . . the necessity of covering the "gap of saving" by home investment or exports was outlined by her perhaps more clearly than anywhere else before the publication of Mr. Keynes's *General Theory*' (Kalecki, 1939, p. 46). It was in 1942 that the first English reference to priority was made. 'The theory of profits presented here is closely allied to Mr. Keynes' theory of saving and investment. It has been, however, developed independently of Mr. Keynes in . . . [Kalecki (1935a; 1935b)]' (Kalecki, 1942, p. 260n.).[10] It was only in the 'Introduction' to Kalecki (1971b), which appeared posthumously, that Kalecki claimed to have published 'in Polish before Keynes' *General Theory* appeared . . . its essentials' (p. vii).[11]

A major difference between Kalecki and Keynes, as our presentation of their theories makes clear, is in the nature of the investment process. Kalecki criticized Keynes's approach in his 1936 review, and in Kalecki (1937a), because it ignores the time lag between investment decisions and investment, and attempts to derive an 'equilibrium' rate of investment in a short period that is inconsistent with the changes taking place in that period. Not only would the prices of investment goods rise when investment increased, but so too would the prices of other goods. The latter would have effects on the expectations of future profitability that Keynes arbitrarily excludes from his analysis. Keynes's response to this criticism was to exaggerate its nature and then to dismiss this exaggeration! '. . . you seem to be assuming not merely that the current rise of prices will have a disproportionate effect on expectations as to future prices, but that future prices will be expected to rise in exactly the same proportion. Surely this is an extravagant over-emphasis of the effect of the immediate situation on long-term expectations?' (Keynes, 1983, p. 793). Kalecki's reply (Keynes, 1983, p. 795) makes clear that his criticism uses only the direction of change in expectations and not its size, and that even if an 'equilibrium', with the value of investment decisions equal to investment, is reached, this convergence would only occur over a sequence of short periods. Keynes took this convergence – he considered it 'a version of Achilles and the tortoise' (p. 798) – as a justification of his approach, and ignored its transient nature in a cyclical process.

Keynes's comments in this correspondence on Kalecki's treatment of the determination of investment decisions reinforce those he had made in earlier writings on the limitations of mathematics in economic analysis. He was critical of 'the precision of your conclusion' (p. 798), rather than of the factors introduced by Kalecki in arriving at that conclusion. Kalecki kept trying to arrive at mathematical equations whose coefficients allow the tracing out of business cycles, while Keynes saw the 'nature of economic thinking' as being much more limited, as providing 'an organised and orderly method of thinking out particular problems' (Keynes, 1936, p. 297).

Finance, investment and saving

The independence of the current rate of investment from current saving that is an essential element in the theories of Kalecki and Keynes requires that entrepreneurs have access to increased means of command over resources that enable them to increase investment. Both economists pointed to credit provided by the banking system as the means that enabled firms to increase investment.[12] Keynes's treatment of these questions in his *Economic Journal* articles on finance were part of his attempt to maintain the distinction between his liquidity preference theory of interest and the loanable funds approach that Ohlin (1937b) and Robertson (1938) were proposing. His desire to keep the rate of interest from having any role in equating investment and desired saving led him, at times (as noted in chapter 7), to mistake the definitional equality between investment and saving for the equilibrium equality that is not instantaneous and holds only in short-period equilibrium. It is the latter that is required if finance is to be, as far as the banks are concerned, a 'revolving fund' (Keynes, 1973b, p. 219). Investing firms, if they tap this increase in desired saving by selling long-term securities, can repay their bank advances (cf. Kalecki, 1939, pp. 107–10).

The criticisms in chapter 7 of aspects of the presentations by Kalecki and Keynes of possible interrelations between finance, investment and saving should not obscure the very large measure of my agreement with their theories. Actual investment expenditures will result in actual saving of equal amounts at each point in time and, in many circumstances, investment decisions are not constrained by the saving propensity. But investment decisions are based on, in addition to expectations about the gross profitability of investment, considerations of the terms at which finance is available. Long-term interest rates are relevant in this connection for investment in plant and equipment, and only if the term structure of interest rates is expected to be unchanged is it sufficient to concentrate *solely* on the banks, and their short-term loans, as holding 'the key position in the transition from a lower to a higher scale of activity' (Keynes, 1973b, p. 222).[13] Kaldor (1939, p. 51) had drawn attention to the possibility that an open economy could run into a saving obstacle to a continuing increase in investment, because of an adverse change in the term structure that could serve to choke off investment even though short-term loans are available from banks. It is pointed out in chapter 7 that such a phenomenon could also occur where government deficits are large relative to personal saving. Keynes, with his assumption that long-term expectations are generally independent of events in his short period, did not allow for the possibility that concern over the future implications of current conditions could adversely affect the long-term rate of interest and thus investment decisions.

Joan Robinson and economic theory

The examination in chapter 9 of Robinson's writings on economic theory shows the importance she attached to explaining and extending the theories of Kalecki and Keynes. It is a reflection of the strong attraction for her of Kalecki's approach that she adopts it in her 'generalisation of the *General Theory* . . . an extension of Keynes's short-period analysis to long-run development' (Robinson, 1956, p. vi). This work required her to deal with the problem of how to treat capital in a process of growth over time. Her consideration of it led to pointed criticisms of the use of capital in aggregate production functions (Robinson, 1960a, pp. 114–31). They were the opening salvos in what came to be called the 'Cambridge Controversies in the Theory of Capital' (Harcourt, 1972).

Robinson became increasingly concerned with the treatment of time in economic analysis, and with what she saw as the incompatibility of analyses that try to deal with historical time and those that make use of the concept of equilibrium. Even short-period equilibrium and the short period itself used in its Marshallian sense were considered inappropriate (Robinson, 1978b, p. 13). But it is by no means clear that this taking away of the setting for Keynes's theory would leave a sufficient analytical framework for theoretical consideration of the factors determining the level of employment at a point in time, and for their changes over time. Economic theory that tries to be 'realistic' must observe the features of historical time that Robinson rightly emphasized, but some theoretical abstractions – and the short period may be one of them – cannot be avoided.

Notes

1 The year for this letter is incorrectly shown as 1937, instead of 1936, in Patinkin (1982), but this error is corrected in the 1984 paperback edition of that book.
2 The reference to 'oil and vinegar' in this quotation can be traced to Robinson's 1971 review of Kalecki's *Selected Essays in the Dynamics of a Capitalist Economy*, in which she had written: 'After reading the *General Theory*, Kalecki came to Cambridge and started arguing with the young Keynesians. (Keynes himself was rather aloof. Temperamentally, oil and vinegar would not mix)' (Robinson, 1973, p. 87).
3 Some of this material on the money market and comments on price changes appears to have been added to the paper presented in Leyden

before it was published in *Econometrica*. Osiatyński, the editor of Kalecki's complete works, has pointed out in correspondence that the 1933 essay contained a section examining price changes during cyclical fluctuations that was not included in the English translation of a short version of that essay.

4 In Kalecki (1935b, pp. 337–8), a value for the average gestation period of investment, 0.6 years, is obtained from data for Germany in order to estimate the duration of the cycle derived from his theory. Kalecki's presentation makes clear that he expects the unit period of time to be less than this gestation period. In his discussion of the money market it is implicitly assumed that the full multiplier effects on profits of an increase in investment are completed 'in the course of the same year . . .' (Kalecki, 1935b, p. 343).

5 In Asimakopulos (1975), the equation for the mark-up in Kalecki (1971a) was treated as a new formulation, but the text in chapter 2, below, accepts the view of Basile and Salvadori (1984–5) that it is simply a rearrangement of the pricing equation in Kalecki (1954).

6 Kalecki mistakenly refers to this short-period equilibrium result as 'the immediate result' (Kalecki, 1971b, p. 39). The time required for the multiplier process to be completed is forgotten in this statement.

7 There are offsetting errors in Kalecki's numerical examination of this case (1971b, p. 40) that permit him to arrive at this correct conclusion.

8 Kalecki only allowed for the possibility of non-zero values for the government deficit and the international surplus in Kalecki (1954, pp. 48–9). He considered the profits equation in Kalecki (1942), as he wrote to Keynes, to be 'definitely not applicable to a war economy' (Keynes, 1983, p. 841), because he retained the postulate of a balanced government budget.

9 In Kalecki (1939, p. 126) it is estimated from 'available statistics' that the average time lag of investment activity behind investment decisions is 3–6 months. The investment activity in a particular quarter of a year can thus be considered to be predetermined, and thus independent of current profits.

10 This statement was repeated in Kalecki (1943, p. 50) when this material on profits reappeared, but the reference to Keynes was dropped in Kalecki (1954, p. 45).

11 Osiatyński draws attention to an additional paper, published in 1934, where Kalecki introduced 'a notion of "quasi-equilibrium" which is strikingly similar to Keynes's "unemployment equilibrium" concept' (Osiatyński, 1987, p. 1).

12 Reference is made in chapter 7 to Keynes's explicit mention, in the *Treatise on Money*, of the important role of credit expansion in making possible an increase in investment. Osiatyński has brought to my

attention a 1932 article, 'Koniunktura a inflacja' (whose title he translates as 'Business cycles and inflation'), in which Kalecki emphasizes the central role of the banking system in financing investment.

13 The one change in chapter 7 from the original version is due to Graziani (1984) who pointed out that, contrary to the assertion in Asimakopulos (1983b, p. 226), Keynes was referring to the long-term rate of interest in Keynes (1973b, p. 217). But with Keynes's assumption of an unchanged term structure, the long-term interest rate effectively disappears from the analysis as a potentially independent variable (cf. Asimakopulos, 1985).

2

A Kaleckian Theory of Income Distribution

Michal Kalecki's writings contain a theory of distribution that combines microeconomic and macroeconomic aspects of the economy. Income shares are influenced both by the mark-ups firms are able to establish in oligopolistic markets and by the level of effective demand. A higher level of effective demand Would lead to a higher share of profits even with the mark-up unchanged, if there is overhead labour in the model. This point was made in a paper Kalecki published (in Polish) in 1933.[1] Discussions of Kalecki's theory of distribution have centred on his 'degree of monopoly' and have ignored the role of overhead labour in providing a means by which changes in effective demand can influence income shares even when mark-ups are constant.[2] Kalecki also tended to abstract from overhead labour in his later writings.[3]

The publication of Kalecki's *Selected Essays on the Dynamics of the Capitalist Economy* (1971b), which he characterized as including 'what I consider my main contributions to the theory of dynamics of the capitalist economy' (p. vii), provides a convenient source from which to construct a Kaleckian theory of distribution. One of the important differences between Kaldor's 'Keynesian' theory of distribution and Kalecki's is that the former is restricted to full employment situations, while the latter is not. Kaldor (1955–6,

I am grateful to J. B. Burbidge, P. Davenport, H. Flakierski, J. Henry and S. Ingerman for comments on an earlier draft of this chapter. They are not, of course, responsible for any errors or for this interpretation of Kalecki's writings. The first drafts of this chapter were written while I was a visiting professor at Monash University.

p. 94) makes a distinction between 'short-run theory' and 'long-run theory' and wants to use the multiplier principle to explain variations in output and employment in the former but as a distribution theory in the latter. Kalecki denies that such a distinction between short- and long-run theory is possible. 'The long-run trend is but a slowly changing component of a chain of short-period situations: it has no independent entity' (Kalecki, 1971b, p. 165). The building blocks for this Kaleckian theory of distribution will thus be the short-period relations.

Kalecki's presentation of the degree of monopoly to explain the determination of mark-ups has been criticized as no more than a tautology, simply *defining* the ratio of price to unit prime costs as the degree of monopoly.[4] There are many places where Kalecki's language seems to invite this interpretation, but 'no problem of *tautology* is involved' (Kalecki, 1971b, p. 168) if the ratio of price to prime costs in a given situation is taken as a reflection of the degree of monopoly rather than its definition.

This paper draws together the various elements of Kalecki's analysis of distribution. In the process some of his formulations, particularly the price equations, are amended. It is emphasized that what a higher degree of monopoly makes possible, and protects, is the higher profitability of firms in the industry. This is not, in general, as Kalecki's use of the term implies, the same as the ratio of price to prime costs. Over time, and in comparison with other industries, a higher degree of monopoly would enable the main firms in the industry to obtain higher rates of profits. It is thus the realized rate of return on investment which is a reflection of the degree of monopoly.[5] The approach presented here assumes that estimates of these rates of return, used for purposes of planning, are included in the mark-ups applied to unit prime costs in order to arrive at prices. Because of the amendments to Kalecki's presentation the model presented here is better described as a 'Kaleckian theory' rather than 'Kalecki's theory'. A test of its Kaleckian nature is provided by using the theory to answer the questions he posed in his posthumously published paper, 'Class struggle and the distribution of national income' (Kalecki, 1971a).

Kalecki's pricing equations

Kalecki distinguished between two types of short-term price changes, 'cost-determined' and 'demand-determined'. 'Generally speaking, changes in the prices of finished goods are "cost determined" while changes in the prices of raw materials inclusive of primary foodstuffs are "demand determined"' (Kalecki, 1971b, p. 43). Supply conditions are given as the reason for this difference.

The production of finished goods is elastic as a result of existing reserves of productive capacity. When demand increases it is met mainly by an increase in the volume of production while prices tend to remain stable. The price changes which do occur result mainly from changes in costs of production. . . . The situation with respect to raw materials is different . . . With supply inelastic in short periods, an increase in demand causes a diminution of stocks and a consequent increase in price . . . A primary rise in demand which causes an increase in prices is frequently accompanied by secondary speculative demand. This makes it even more difficult in the short run for production to catch up with demand. (pp. 43–4)

Kalecki's analysis of prices and his theory of distribution are concerned with finished goods. For raw materials he simply states: 'the relative share of wages in the value added depends mainly on the ratio of prices of the raw materials *produced* to their unit wage costs' (p. 64). He does not go on to consider the factors tending to change unit wage costs in these industries, but it is consistent with statements made in other connections (e.g. pp. 56, 73) to infer that they include the degree of organization of workers and the power of trade unions.

Unit prime costs (composed of wages and raw material costs) in plants in manufacturing industries are assumed to be constant for a substantial range of output, and then to increase sharply when normal productive capacity is reached. They can thus be represented by reverse-L-shaped curves. Firms in these industries typically sell in oligopolistic markets and, at the prices they set, their plants generally operate at less than normal capacity. Unit prime costs are thus assumed to be constant in the range of output

Kalecki considers. In setting prices firms are faced with conditions of uncertainty, with respect to both the immediate and longer-term consequences of their decisions. The options open to them are influenced by the decisions of other firms, which in turn are not independent of their own, and the prices they set now may affect their prospects in future periods. There is no simple demand curve, even for a price leader, that can form the basis for the maximization of profits by bringing marginal revenue and marginal costs to equality. Even though firms in Kalecki's model are constantly striving for profits, in view of the general atmosphere of uncertainty facing them 'it will not be assumed that the firm attempts to maximize its profits in any precise sort of manner' (p. 44).[6]

Kalecki's approach to the pricing of manufactured goods is an important element in the Kaleckian theory of distribution developed here, but his particular formulations of the price equation are discarded. He assumed that a firm arrives at a price for one of its products by marking up its unit prime costs in order to cover overheads and achieve profits. These mark-ups reflect, in his view, the 'semi-monopolistic influences . . . resulting from imperfect competition or oligopoly' (p. 160). The more imperfect are the market conditions faced by the firm, the stronger is its position *vis-à-vis* other firms in the industry and potential entrants in terms of costs, product differentiation etc., and, other things given, the higher is the firm's mark-up. Two pricing equations appear in Kalecki (1971b), both trying to relate a firm's price to its prime costs and average price in the industry. The earlier formulation (first published in its final version in his *Theory of Economic Dynamics*, 1954) is

$$p = mu + n\bar{p}, \qquad (2.1)$$

where p is the firm's price, u is unit prime cost, m and n are positive coefficients and $\bar{p}$ is the weighted average price of all firms. The mark-up on prime costs $(p - u)/u$ as determined by this equation is

$$\frac{p-u}{u} = (m-1) + \frac{n\bar{p}}{u} \qquad (2.2)$$

The values of the two parameters m and n 'reflect what may be called the degree of monopoly of the firm's position' (Kalecki,

1971b, p. 45). Kalecki combines them into a single measure $m/(1 - n)$. He argues that different firms in the industry would have different values for these parameters and thus set different prices.

Kalecki's attempt to allow for both the interdependence of the firms' pricing decisions and for the special features of the position of a particular firm is commendable, but the explanatory power of his equation is very limited. At times Kalecki writes as though firms actually arrived at prices on the basis of this equation. 'The influence of the emergence of firms representing a substantial share of the output of an industry can be readily understood in the light of the above considerations. Such a firm knows that its price p influences appreciably the average price $\bar{p}$ and that, moreover, the other firms will be pushed in the same direction because their price formation depends on the average price $\bar{p}$. Thus, the firm can fix its price at a level higher than would otherwise be the case' (p. 50). This is much too simplified a representation, even at this level of abstraction, of the forces determining the prices charged by firms in these market structures. It is true that a firm is more likely to raise its price in a given situation if other firms would follow its action, but this following of a price rise is not the mechanical result of the initial change in average price. In the absence of price agreements it could be due to a similar view of the profit potential of a higher price, or to the fear of starting a price war, or to some combination of these factors.

There are also technical problems with Kalecki's pricing equation. He deduces that $n < 1$ from the observation that 'where the price p of the firm is considered equal to the average price $\bar{p}$ we have $p = mu + np$, from which it follows that n must be less than one' (p. 45). But this conclusion does not necessarily follow. In situations where price is set by a price leader and followed by others, n would be equal to one for the price followers and thus m would be equal to zero.[7] The ratio of proceeds to prime costs for a price follower would thus be equal to the ratio of the prevailing industry price to its unit prime costs. For the price leader, on the other hand, n would be equal to zero and the value of m would depend on many (interdependent) factors, such as its view of an appropriate rate of return on its capital over time, pressures from other firms in the industry and from potential entrants, the rate of profits tax etc.

Kalecki rearranged his equation for the mark-up in a paper that was published posthumously in 1971.[8] He wrote $(p-u)/u = f(\bar{p}/p)$, which becomes

$$p = u\,[1 + f(\bar{p}/p)] \qquad (2.3)$$

Basile and Salvadori (1984–5) have argued convincingly that, contrary to the position taken in Asimakopulos (1975, p. 318), the function $f(.)$ is not defined implicitly by equation (2.3). This function simply shows that the firm's price is related to the average industry price, and it is thus consistent with equation (2.1). If both sides of the latter equation are divided by p and rearranged, we find that

$$1 = mu/p + n\bar{p}/p \qquad (2.4)$$

It can be deduced from equation (2.4) that, in a given situation with specified values for m, n and u, $\bar{p}/p$ is directly related to the price. Kalecki thus wrote that 'f is an increasing function: the lower is p in relation to $\bar{p}$, the higher will be fixed the mark-up' (Kalecki, 1971b, p. 160).[9] In spite of a more general appearance, this is no more than a restatement of the partial dependence of a firm's price on the average of the prices set by its competitors.

Kalecki tried to distinguish between this theory and that of the 'full-cost pricing' theory (see Hall and Hitch, 1939), on two grounds. His 'emphasis on the influence of prices of other firms' and the belief that 'the degree of monopoly *may*, but need not necessarily, increase as a result of a rise in overheads in relation to prime costs' (Kalecki, 1971b, p. 51) were held to form the basis for this distinction. The former claim can be dismissed because of his failure, noted above, to incorporate this influence in any way that, on examination, is different from the general interdependence of firms' pricing policies common to all fully specified mark-up theories. The latter claim would only hold if his degree of monopoly was interpreted as measuring the ratio of proceeds to prime costs, rather than as indicating the imperfections in competition that permitted firms to achieve high *rates* of profits over time. Kalecki's writings on this point are confusing; there is a tendency to identify the degree of monopoly with the ratio of proceeds to prime costs, not only in the short run with given productive capacity and overheads when it is synonymous, under certain conditions,[10] with higher profitability, but also over long periods of time. In his examination of data on the ratio of proceeds to prime costs in manufacturing industries over historical periods he all but identifies the degree of monopoly with this ratio. He does qualify his comments, however, noting that 'the interpretation of the movement of the ratio of proceeds to prime cost in terms of changes in the degree of monopoly is really the task of the economic historian who can contribute to such a study a more thorough knowledge of changing industrial conditions' (p. 56). Whatever the judgement reached on Kalecki's use of the term 'degree of monopoly', a Kaleckian theory of distribution can be developed on the assumption that it acts to protect the rate of profits of established firms in the industry.

The determination of the mark-up

The theory of distribution presented here is based on the assumptions that prices in manufacturing industries are generally arrived at by marking up unit prime costs and that these mark-ups are relatively stable in the face of short-term fluctuations in demand and output, at least within some substantial range of output.[11] These mark-ups are designed to cover, over time, both overhead costs and profits. Their values would thus be dependent on the standard rates of utilization of productive capacity used to calculate standard costs[12] as well as on some expected rate of return. The rates of return built into the mark-ups are affected by what is considered to be a 'normal' return to industrial investment in the particular economy examined. In addition, those areas of industry with some degree of monopoly arising from seller concentration and barriers to entry can earn, on the average, more than these normal rates of profits.[13] Provision for such returns become formalized in their mark-ups in the guise of some target rate of return.[14]

The 'normal' rate of return for a given time and economy is, in Kalecki's approach, 'rooted in past economic, social and technological developments'.[15] It very much depends on the profits that firms have been able to earn in the past and on the profit share in total income. Profits are determined in this model, as we shall see, by the investment that firms have been able to achieve in conjunction with conditions of thriftiness. Both investment and the profit share may be affected by bargaining with trade unions (the 'class struggle'). Rising money wage rates may provoke monetary restraints which hamper investment and may lead to some erosion of mark-ups and the share of profits.

There is another feature of Kalecki's analysis that indicates a relationship between the growth possibilities for a firm and the rate-of-return portion of its mark-up. Kalecki's analysis is based on what he considered to be the characteristic features of the capitalist mode of production. The means of production are owned by capitalists who, in a closed system with government activity excluded, do all the saving. The saving of workers in a capitalist economy would be small in comparison with that of capitalists and is ignored in his writings. Kalecki distinguished between two types of capital, entrepreneurial capital and rentier capital.[16] The former is capital owned by the firm while the latter is the capital it tries to borrow. He wrote that 'the access of a firm to the capital market, or in other words the amount of rentier capital it may hope to obtain, is determined to a large extent by the amount of its entrepreneurial capital', and 'the expansion of the firm depends on its accumulation of capital out of current profits' (Kalecki, 1971b, pp. 105, 106). A firm's ability to grow thus depends on the profits it can generate to finance its investment plans both directly (retained earnings) and indirectly through borrowing related to its internal funds. Given the general profitability of the economy, a firm's profit expectations are dependent on the degree of monopoly it enjoys and are indicated by its target rate of return. Where growth is an important goal for a firm, its target rate of return can serve as an indicator of its growth possibilities, i.e. the rate at which it can increase the value of the capital assets under its control.[17]

Macroeconomics and the level of abstraction

The theory of distribution developed here is a macro theory, concerned with aggregates, total investment, total consumption and total output. It is thus very far removed from the action of individual decision-making units that decide on their own level of investment, consumption, prices, output and so on, even though it tries to justify the aggregate relations it uses on the basis of their consistency with particular types of individual behaviour. Macroeconomic analysis thus proceeds at a very high level of abstraction and such variables as the difference in prices charged by firms in the same industry because of product differentiation, which Kalecki emphasized in setting up his price equations, are generally ignored. Product differentiation can still have a role in this model by its influence on the mark-ups that firms use to arrive at prices. Consolidation does not stop at this point; industries themselves are combined in very broad aggregates, such as 'investment goods' and 'consumption goods'. Again, some of the aspects of the underlying reality, the large number of industries comprising one of these sectors, can be introduced indirectly by indicating the effects on the aggregate in question of some of the diversity they tend to obscure. For example, in explaining the possible power of strong trade unions to erode mark-ups, Kalecki argues that an industry facing much higher wage rates and attempting to maintain mark-ups would find 'its product more and more expensive and thus less competitive with products of other industries . . . trade union power restrains the mark-up.'[18]

   In this paper the degree of aggregation will be carried one step further, and no distinction will be made between investment goods and consumption goods production sectors. The effects on our results of introducing two production sectors along these lines will be noted. The raw materials producing sector will also disappear from view;[19] it is not an integral part of Kalecki's theory of distribution, which is largely concerned with manufacturing industries. Firms will therefore be assumed to be fully integrated, producing all the materials required for their final output, and prime costs will thus be made up only of labour costs.

   Output will be assumed to consist of a multipurpose good which can be consumed or invested as capital equipment or as inventories. As soon as it is set aside for formation into capital equipment its characteristics are assumed to change. It is formed into capital equipment, with no further expenditure of labour, by accumulating this good over time.[20]

   One final element of abstraction concerns the shares of the different plants in total output. These shares will be taken as given in any short period and will not be explained by the analysis.[21] They will be represented by the relative amounts of direct labour employed by each plant. These direct-labour employment ratios will be the same for all comparisons made with respect to any particular short period.

The model

The following notations will be used:

w money wage rate,
a average output per unit of direct labour,
L_1 level of employment of direct labour,
$\bar{L}_1$ maximum possible employment of direct labour with existing plant,
L_0 level of employment of overhead labour,
L level of total employment,
p price of the output,
μ mark-up over unit prime costs,
Y value of gross output
W the total wage bill,
Π value of total gross profits,
C value of total consumption,
A constant element in capitalists' consumption in real terms,
λ small fraction expressing dependence of a portion of capitalists' consumption on current profits,
S value of gross saving,
I value of gross investment, and
$\bar{I}$ gross investment in real terms.

The unit prime costs of the ith plant, in the range of employment where they are constant ($L_{1i} \leq \bar{L}_{1i}$), are equal to w/a_i. Average output a per unit of direct labour in the economy is equal to $\sum_{i=1}^{n} a_i L_{1i}/L_1$, where n is the total number of plants utilized. Our assumption about output shares means that L_{1i}/L_1 is assumed to be unchanged in all the short-period comparisons. Average unit prime or direct costs can thus be represented by w/a. It is assumed that the price is arrived at by a price leader setting a mark-up over unit prime costs and that other firms follow this price. The ratio of this price to average unit prime costs is stable in the face of short-term fluctuations in demand and output.

The mark-up μ over this average unit prime cost is equal to $p/(w/a)-1$, so that we can write

$$p = (1 + \mu)(w/a) \qquad (2.5)$$

There are thus three elements in the determination of the price level in this model: the mark-up, the money wage rate, and the average output per unit of direct labour. The latter is given by present-day operating knowledge and the technical features of the plant and equipment inherited from investment in earlier time periods and utilized in the present. Money wage rates are set as a result of bargaining between employers and trade unions. This wage level is not explained by the model, it is taken as given, and the effects of different values for it will be considered.

There is a banking system in this model, even though it does not appear explicitly. It provides the money supply, holds deposits of households and lends working capital to firms. Banks' interest income represents a share of total profits and is assumed to be remitted to their shareholders. When different levels of output and prices are considered the supply of money by the banks is assumed to be 'elastic at the ruling rate of interest'.[22] Firms can generally obtain finance for their planned investment. Credit restraints, and the inability to achieve planned rates of investment, only arise in inflationary situations.

The remaining features of this model can be quickly sketched in. The value of output produced in the particular short period (e.g. three months or a year) examined is

$$Y = p \, a \, L_1, L_1 \leq \bar{L}_1 \qquad (2.6)$$

It will be assumed that Keynes's short-term expectations, which determine the degree of utilization of existing plant, are always borne out by events because they can be quickly adjusted to conform to actual conditions. Thus the value for the amount produced in the particular short period turns out to be equal to the value of the amounts demanded for consumption and investment, at the set price. The value of total gross output produced is divided on income account into two categories, wages and gross profits:

$$Y = W + \Pi, \qquad (2.7)$$

$$W = wL \qquad (2.8)$$

Total employment L is made up of two categories, total direct labour L_1 which appears in equation (2.6) and total overhead or indirect labour L_0. In order to operate a plant at any non-zero degree of utilization, a certain number of workers are required (for the ith plant this number would be represented by L_{0i} and, for all plants, $L_0 = \Sigma_{i=1}^{n} L_{0i}$). This number, unlike that of direct labour employed, is independent of the degree of utilization of the plant (as long as it is utilized). Therefore, our assumption of constant output per unit of direct labour in the output range considered means that labour productivity, output per unit of *total* labour employed, is an increasing function of total output in this range:

$$L = L_0 + L_1, \tag{2.9}$$

where L is less than or equal to the total labour force.

The one time lag that appears in all of Kalecki's writings on effective demand and distribution is that between investment decisions and investment (see Kalecki, 1971b, pp. 2, 166), and it appears in this model. On the other hand he occasionally abstracts from the lag in consumer expenditure,[23] and it will be ignored here. The effect of the latter assumption is to allow the multiplier to take its full value in the short period in which investment is increased. Kalecki abstracts from 'workers' savings, which are definitely unimportant' (p. 166), while capitalists' consumption contains an important element that is 'a slowly changing magnitude dependent on past economic and social developments' (p. 167) as well as another element that is proportionate to profits. The equation for the value of total consumption expenditures will be written here as

$$C = W + \lambda\Pi + pA \tag{2.10}$$

Gross saving is thus equal to

$$S = (1 - \lambda)\Pi - pA \tag{2.11}$$

Investment in real terms in the short period is exogenous, determined by investment decisions made in an earlier period subject to two possible constraints. One is that planned investment plus the associated consumption do not exceed the normal productive capacity of the available plants or require more labour than can be provided by the labour force, and the other is that the 'inflation barrier' is not reached. This constraint would operate if pressures in the labour market led to rapidly rising wages and prices, to which the monetary authorities respond by imposing severe credit restrictions that would prevent firms from achieving their planned investment

$$I = p\bar{I} \tag{2.12}$$

Finally, we have the necessary equality between saving and investment:

$$I = S \tag{2.13}$$

Gross saving, as given by equation (2.11), is desired saving, while gross investment in equation (2.12) is intended investment, and thus equation (2.13) indicates not only the necessary *ex post* equality between saving and investment but a position of short-period equilibrium as well.

There are nine unknowns (p, Y, L_1, W, Π, L, C, S, I) in this model. We take as given the values for w, a, μ, L_0, λ, A and $\bar{I}$. Solving, for the variables of interest, we find that profits for the period can be derived by combining the last three equations and rewriting:

$$\Pi = \frac{(1 + \mu)w(\bar{I} + A)}{a(1 - \lambda)} \tag{2.14}$$

Equation (2.14) rearranges an equation ($\Pi = p\bar{I} + \lambda\Pi + pA$) that expresses Kalecki's conclusion with respect to the determination of profits. Profits are determined by the value of capitalists' expenditure – their gross investment and consumption.[24] This conclusion reappears in all his writings on distribution.[25] Profits in real terms are not a function of the mark-up. This can be readily deduced from equation (2.14) by dividing both sides by p.

To obtain the total wage bill and to derive income shares it is necessary to solve for total output, that is, the total amount of direct labour employed. By combining equations (2.5)–(2.9), and making use of (2.14), we obtain

$$L_1 = \frac{1}{\mu}\left[L_0 + (1 + \mu)\,\frac{\bar{I} + A}{a(1 - \lambda)}\right] \tag{2.15}$$

A more revealing form of this expression for the amount of direct labour employed is obtained by substituting, from equation (2.5), p/w for $(1 + \mu)/a$. It becomes

$$L_1 = \frac{1}{\mu}\left[L_0 + \frac{p(\bar{I} + A)}{w(1 - \lambda)}\right] \qquad (2.16)$$

The amount of direct labour employed is thus seen to be equal to the product of the reciprocal of the mark-up and the sum of indirect labour employed in the plants utilized, and investment and capitalists' consumption expenditures expressed in wage units. The gross profit share in value of gross output can thus be written as

$$\frac{\Pi}{Y} = \frac{\mu(\bar{I} + A)}{a(1 - \lambda)L_0 + (1 + \mu)(\bar{I} + A)} \qquad (2.17)$$

The profit share in total output is a function of the mark-up even though the level of profits in real terms is not. (The assumption of no workers' saving and a closed economy with no government expenditures or taxation are essential for the latter conclusion.) This level is determined solely by capitalists' expenditure in real terms. The degree of utilization of capacity, as reflected in the amount of direct labour employed, is also a function of the mark-up. A higher mark-up, other things given, would lower the degree of plant utilization and increase the profit share. Higher capitalists' expenditure, whether on investment or consumption, because of the presence of overhead labour not only increases profits but also increases the profit share in total output.[26] This share is not determined solely by the mark-up; it varies with short-term fluctuations in the level of output. Its increase is consistent with a constant real wage rate.

This Kaleckian theory of distribution combines two of Kalecki's important contributions: his recognition of the role of the degree of monopoly in the setting of mark-ups, and his demonstration of the role of capitalists' expenditures in determining profits and the level of employment. Concentration on the degree of monopoly aspect of Kalecki's theory of distribution (e.g. as in Kaldor (1955–6)) does not do full justice to his writings in this area. The reintroduction of overhead labour into Kalecki's model means that labour productivity, output per unit of *total* labour employed, would vary directly with demand. Consequently, an increased demand for labour due to higher capitalist expenditure leads to a higher profit share as well as to higher output, even though the mark-up is constant.[27] The model predicts that real wage rates are more stable than output per worker in the course of short-term fluctuations in output.[28]

Unlike Kaldor's version of the 'Cambridge' theory of distribution this one is not tied to the assumption of full employment of labour; higher investment brings about a higher profit share even though the mark-up is constant and employment is also increased.[29] Kaldor's results can be readily obtained from this model by assuming that labour is fully employed and then deducing the effects on the mark-up and on income shares of a higher level of investment. With both labour and productive capacity available to increase output the employment multiplier as derived from equation (2.15) is equal to $(1 + \mu)/\mu a(1 - \lambda)$; the corresponding income multiplier is equal to $(1 + \mu)/\mu(1 - \lambda)$. There is no conflict in the two 'uses' of investment in this model. It determines, given the propensities to save, both the level of employment and the distribution of income.[30]

Class struggle and the distribution of national income

The 'Kaleckian' nature of the model developed here[31] can be illustrated by deriving the results Kalecki obtained in his posthumously published article, 'Class struggle and distribution of national income'.

Kalecki argued that, in a closed system, *if* 'wage rates in all industries increase in the same proportion, $1 + \alpha$ times . . . all prices will also increase $1 + \alpha$ times *provided that functions* f *in industries to which they are relevant are unchanged* . . . It follows that if these conditions were fulfilled we should arrive at the . . . conclusion . . . that a general increase in money wages in a closed economy does not change the distribution of national income' (Kalecki, 1971, p. 161). (The 'functions f' are the mark-ups.) Investment and rentiers' expenditures are assumed to be unaffected in real terms as a result of the higher money wage rates. His conclusions can be easily deduced from equation (2.17) above. The profit share in total income is constant, no matter what the value of w, as long as μ, λ, and $\bar{I} + A$ have unchanged values.[32]

Kalecki's analysis does not end with this mechanical result. He believed that in certain circumstances mark-ups depend on trade union activity. This occurs because wage rates are not raised simultaneously in all industries and bargaining tends to proceed industry by industry. 'High mark-ups in existence will encourage strong trade unions to bargain for higher wages since they know that firms can "afford" to pay them' (p. 161). Kalecki believed that competitive pressures in their markets from those in other industries will lead them to lower mark-ups and thus raise prices by less than the increases in unit prime costs.[33]

Kalecki distinguished between two types of wage increases. 'Normal' wage increases that usually leave the mark-ups unchanged and which serve to prevent the increases that would otherwise occur 'because of the rise in productivity of labour' (p. 162). Spectacular wage rises that are due to increases in bargaining capacity are assumed to depress the mark-ups somewhat, so that, as can be seen from equation (2.17), redistribution of national income from profits to wages occurs. In the process, with the volume of investment and capitalists' consumption expenditures unchanged in real terms, total employment and output will be higher, as can be easily deduced from equation (2.15). Although Kalecki's model in his 'Class struggle' paper distinguishes between three departments of production – department I producing investment goods, II producing consumption goods for capitalists and III wage goods – all his results can be obtained with our one-sector model. We can conclude, as does Kalecki, 'It follows from the above that a wage rise showing an increase in the trade union power leads – contrary to the precepts of classical economics – to an increase in employment. And conversely, a fall in wages showing a weakening in their bargaining power lead to a decline in employment. The weakness of trade unions in a depression manifested in permitting wage cuts contributes to deepening of unemployment rather than to relieving it' (p. 163).

It is important to note, with Kalecki, that the 'redistribution of income from profits to wages is feasible only if excess capacity is in existence. Otherwise, it is impossible to increase wages in relation to prices of wage goods because prices are determined by demand' (p. 164). When it is no longer possible to increase output in the short period because of the absence of unemployed labour or unused productive capacity, the class struggle would be reflected, not in the mark-ups, since they would largely be determined by demand in the face of inelastic supplies,[34] but in the shares of total output accounted for by capitalists' expenditure.

A stronger bargaining position of workers would be reflected in a diminution of capitalists' expenditure in real terms and thus in a higher share for workers in total income.

The key elements in the struggle over income shares in a Kaleckian theory of distribution, given the propensities to save, are thus the mark-ups and capitalists' expenditures in real terms. Trade unions will succeed in increasing workers' share in total output if, in successfully bargaining for higher money wage rates, they can lower mark-ups and/or capitalists' expenditures. This may present trade unions with a dilemma in so far as investment expenditures would be cut if money wage rates were sharply increased, say, as a result of credit restrictions imposed to try to curb the resulting inflationary pressures, even if employment is maintained. The improvement in the workers' share and level of income in the present may be at the expense of future income that will be affected by the lower rate of current investment.

Appendix

A positive propensity to save out of wages

Some of the assumptions made in setting up the model in the text were introduced for simplicity in presentation. They can be relaxed without affecting the general nature of the conclusions. With respect to saving, the critical assumption is not the absence of workers' saving but the difference in the propensities to save out of the two categories of income, profits and wages. This can be illustrated by considering a situation in which the propensities to save out of wages and out of distributed profits (rentiers' incomes) are the same. The propensity to save out of profits would still be greater than the propensity to save out of wages, because of the retention by firms of parts of profits.

Let s be the common propensity to save of individuals and β the proportion of profits distributed. The equation for total (desired) gross saving is now

$$S = \Pi(1 - \beta) + s\beta\Pi + sW, \qquad (2.1a)$$

and this replaces equation (2.11). All the other equations describing the model are unchanged. By substituting the equations $S = I$ and $I = p\bar{I}$ in the above equation for S, and rearranging, we have

$$\Pi = p\bar{I} + (1 - s)\,\beta\Pi - sW \qquad (2.2a)$$

The level of profits no longer depends solely on capitalists' expenditure because workers no longer spend what they earn. It is equal to capitalists' expenditure plus workers' consumption out of their share of distributed profits minus workers' saving out of wage incomes, as can be seen from equation (2.2a). In order to express the level of profits as a function of the exogenous variables it is necessary to obtain from the full model an expression for L_1 in terms of the exogenous variables. Solving for L_1 from equations (2.5)–(2.9) and (2.2a), we obtain

$$L_1 = \frac{(1 + \mu)\bar{I} + aL_0(1 - \beta + s\beta - s)}{a[\mu(1 - \beta + s\beta) + s]} \qquad (2.3a)$$

When this expression is substituted for L_1 in equation (2.2a), since $W = wL_0 + wL_1$, we obtain

$$\Pi = \frac{(1 + \mu)w(\mu\bar{I} - saL_0)}{a[\mu(1 - \beta + s\beta) + s]} \qquad (2.4a)$$

Finally, in order to obtain the profit share in total income, expression (2.4a) is divided by the equation for Y ($= (1 + \mu)wL_1$) with equation (2.3a) substituted for L_1. It is equal to

$$\frac{\Pi}{Y} = \frac{\mu\bar{I} - saL_0}{(1 + \mu)\bar{I} + aL_0(1 - \beta + sB - s)} \qquad (2.5a)$$

It can be seen from equation (2.4a) that, as in the main model, the level of profits in the short period is positively related to the level of investment. By differentiating this equation with respect to s and β it can be readily deduced that the level of profits is inversely related to the propensity to save of individuals and directly related to the proportion of profits distributed. With workers' saving, however, the level of profits as well as the profit share is affected by the value for the mark-up.

A higher value for investment in terms of wage units increases the profit share, even with the mark-up constant as in the basic model, because of the presence of overhead labour.

Saving not in the desired relation to income

All the results derived in this paper have been based on a necessary assumption for short-period equilibrium, that saving is in the desired relation to income. When this condition is not satisfied, the equation for actual saving, for the saving propensities used in this Appendix, would then be written as

$$S = \Pi(1 - \beta) + s\beta\Pi + sW + S^*, \qquad (2.1b)$$

where $S^* \neq 0$. The equation for profits then becomes

$$\Pi[1 - \beta + s\beta] = p\bar{I} - S^* - sW \qquad (2.2b)$$

All the other expressions can be readily derived. Disequilibrium saving S^* is seen to modify the effects of the planned level of investment in these expressions. For example, if S^* is positive the employment in the short period examined resulting from any given values for $\bar{I}$ and the propensities to save is lower, and both profits and profits share are lower. By specifying the factors determining S^*, e.g. the time lag between changes in income and changes in consumption, S^* can be 'explained'. Introduction of S^* into the analysis does not change the nature of the conclusions.

Notes

1 The paper's title in the English translation printed in Kalecki (1971b) is 'Outline of a theory of the business cycle'. The assumption appears in a footnote: 'We assume here that aggregate production and profit per unit of output rise or fall together, which is actually the case. This results at least to some extent from the fact that a part of wages are overheads' (p. 11n.).

2 An important exception has been Professor Joan Robinson (1969c), who made use of overhead, or indirect, labour in her reformulation of Kalecki's pricing equation.

3 See for example, chapter 15, 'Trends and business cycles', in Kalecki (1971b), which was first published in 1968.

4 This criticism is made by, among others, Kaldor (1955–6) and Nuti (1970).

5 Riach (1971) has argued that Kalecki's 'degree of monopoly' should be reformulated in this way. In the same spirit Joan Robinson's reformulation of Kalecki's pricing equation (Robinson, 1969c) makes use of an expected rate of return on investment.

6 Kalecki's final version of his theory thus does not make use of the elasticity of the individual firm's demand curve.

7 This conclusion also holds when there is product differentiation. The price equation for a price follower would still have m equal to zero, with $p_f = p_l + d$ or $p_f = (1 + d)p_l$, where p_f and p_l represent the

prices of the follower and the leader and d is the recognized price differential, expressed either in absolute terms or as a ratio, whichever is appropriate.

8 The paper, 'Class struggle and distribution of national income', (Kalecki, 1971a) first appeared in *Kyklos* in 1971. It is reprinted (with some typographical errors) in Kalecki (1971b).

9 There is a misprint in the text of Kalecki (1971b): the bar has been omitted from the second $\bar{p}$.

10 A higher price, relative to prime costs, will result in higher profits in the short period as long as it is not accompanied by sales that are sufficiently lower to outweigh its beneficial effects on profits. More formally, we can state that a higher mark-up will lead to higher profits in the short period if the value for the elasticity of employment of direct labour with respect to the mark-up is numerically less than one.

11 For empirical support for the hypothesis of mark-up pricing in manufacturing industries, see Nordhaus and Godley (1972).

12 Standard output is less than normal productive capacity output. Lanzillotti found that for the firms in his sample 'the standards premised on an assumed rate of production, typically about 70 per cent to 80 per cent of capacity' (Lanzillotti, 1958, p. 923, n.5). Firms in Kalecki's model are assumed to plan on having some excess capacity – they provide for more than their expected rates of output. This feature is also prominent in Kaldor's models (see, for example, Kaldor (1970, p. 4) and Kaldor and Mirrlees (1962, para. 3)). What firms take as standard rates of output, and thus mark-ups, would change over time with changes in the experienced rates of utilization of plant.

13 Some empirical findings on the positive relationship between rates of return on one hand, and seller concentration and barriers to entry on the other, are to be found in Bain (1956) and Mann (1966).

14 For some indication of the importance of target rate-of-return pricing, see Lanzillotti (1958) and Kaplan, Dirlam and Lanzillotti (1958).

15 Kalecki, 1971b, p. 183. These terms are used by Kalecki in referring to his approach to the rate of growth of an economy at a given time. They are also appropriate in describing a Kaleckian theory of pricing since it is an important element in a theory of growth. In a particular short period various factors, such as views on what constitutes a normal rate of return, as well as available productive capacity are taken as given. However, over a sequence of short periods, i.e. over time, these views may be altered by experience. A Kaleckian model provides a framework for analysing a particular economy, but for the analysis to be completed the institutional features and history of that economy are required.

16 See in particular the chapter on 'Entrepreneurial capital and investment' in Kalecki (1971b, pp. 105–9). The first version of this chapter was published in 1937.

17 An alternative explanation for the determination of the mark-up in oligopoly is contained in an interesting paper by Eichner (1973). He explains changes in the mark-up as responses to the demand for additional investment funds. There is a cost of generating more funds for investment from the higher immediate profits that result from a higher mark-up because of the substitution over time by consumers of other products, the entry of other firms into the industry, and possible government intervention. Eichner expresses this implicit cost of the additional investment funds generated in this way as an 'interest' payment. This enables him to 'derive a supply curve for additional internal funds . . . indicating how the implicit interest rate . . . on these funds varies as the amount of additional funds obtained per planning period . . . varies' (Eichner, 1973, p. 1193). A supply curve for external funds is added to this function to obtain the total supply function for additional investment funds for the firm. The changes in the firm's investment and mark-up are then determined by bringing in its demand curve for additional investment funds, which is 'simply the familiar marginal efficiency of investment curve' (p. 1190).

The results obtained from Eichner's approach and that presented here would often be similar even though they give opposite signs for the direction of causation between the rates of return and growth. In this model a higher mark-up, due to a greater degree of monopoly, would permit a firm that is fully committing its resources to expansion to grow at a faster rate. In Eichner's model the desire for a higher growth rate, given the degree of monopoly, would lead to a higher mark-up. It would often be difficult to disentangle these two elements from data on growth and profit rates. Another difference is that Eichner's approach is not designed to explain 'the absolute price level but rather the change in the margin above costs from one pricing period to the next' (p. 1195). The use of a marginal efficiency of investment schedule in a Keynes- or Kalecki-type model has been criticized in Asimakopulos (1971). See also Shackle (1967, especially chapter 11) and Robinson (1962; 1964).

18 Kalecki, 1971b, p. 161. He comments in a footnote: 'Despite the fact that for the sake of simplicity, we assumed that all wage rates are raised simultaneously in the same proportion, we consider realisticaly that bargaining is proceeding by industries'.

19 It should not be necessary to emphasize that this and the exclusion of international trade and governmental activities are important omissions. The present model can best be viewed as a 'basic' one, to

which these other features should be added. Some aspects of government activity, within the context of this type of model, are examined in Asimakopulos and Burbidge (1974).

20 This device of multipurpose output was used in Asimakopulos (1969; 1970) and again in Asimakopulos and Burbidge (1974).

21 The different plants are thus assumed to be operated in parallel fashion, even though they may contain equipment of different 'vintages' that give rise to differences in labour productivity. This results in a perfectly elastic supply curve for output at the established price, without the need to assume that the marginal costs are constant and equal for each plant (cf. Davidson, 1960, p. 53). That plants of differing efficiency share in total output through imperfections in competition that offer protection for the market shares of firms owning these plants can be inferred from the data discussed by Kaldor (1970). He noted that 'the share of gross profit in value added shows a very high variation as between different "establishments"' (p. 2). He also noted that 'the share of profits in relation to the value added shows the same kind of scatter among "firms" as it does among "establishments" . . . It is perfectly possible, therefore, that the "marginal equipment" of the least efficient firm is one that is considerably older than the "marginal" equipment of a high profit firm' (p. 3).

22 This assumption is implicit in many of Kalecki's papers (e.g. Kalecki, 1971b, pp. 13, 159n.).

23 In making this assumption he noted that 'this . . . is realistic with regard to workers' consumption, but not so with regard to that of capitalists. However, as long as the time-lag between investment decisions and investment is emphasized, disregarding that between profits and capitalists' consumption does not distort the analysis' (Kalecki, 1971b, p. 166).

24 This sole dependence of profits on the expenditure of capitalists disappears if saving by workers is significant. In that case total profits would be equal to the sum of investment, capitalists' consumption expenditure and workers' consumption expenditure out of their share of profits less workers' saving out of their wage incomes. Capitalists would no longer 'earn what they spend' because workers do not 'spend what they earn'. The introduction of workers' saving would not disturb the main features of a Kaleckian theory of distribution. This point is illustrated in the Appendix.

25 In his paper, first published in 1933, he wrote: 'Thus capitalists, as a whole, determine their own profits by the extent of their investment and personal consumption. In a way they are "masters of their fate"; but how they "master" it is determined by objective factors, so that fluctuations of profits appear after all to be unavoidable. Capitalists'

consumption is a function of the gross accumulation. The gross accumulation which is equal to the production of investment goods is determined by investment orders which in turn were undertaken in a past period on the basis of the profitability in that period, i.e. on the basis of the gross accumulation and the volume of capital equipment in that period' (Kalecki, 1971b, p. 13). The factors underlying investment decisions, alluded to above, will not be examined here since their consideration would turn this chapter into a full-fledged investigation of the theory of economic growth.

26 This is the one conclusion from this model that might have to be modified if separate investment and consumption goods producing sectors are introduced. Higher values for investment or capitalists' consumption expenditures might alter the ratio of investment to consumption expenditures in the model, thus changing the weights to be used in arriving at the overall ratio of profit to output. If the mark-ups differ in the two sectors, it is possible that the overall ratio of profit to output will fall, even if this ratio increases in each sector.

27 This Kaleckian theory of distribution belongs, of course, to the genus, 'Cambridge' theory. As Kaldor (1970, p. 5) has phrased it: 'According to the "Cambridge" theory, the labour market does *not* behave in accordance with the postulates of neo-classical theory: with a rise in the demand for labour, there is a rise in the share of profit, and a fall in the share of wages, and not the other way round. (This of course is not inconsistent with a rise in *absolute* wages – in wages per man – if output-per-head also rises with rising employment.) This is because a high demand for labour is associated with a high rate of investment and a high rate of profit on capital. Empirically, the evidence here supports Cambridge, and not the implications of neo-classical theory: the share of profit and the level of employment are *positively* correlated, not negatively' (Kaldor, 1970, p. 5).

28 This consequence of our model is in agreement with empirical observations of the behaviour of real wage rates and labour productivity over the cycle. See Kuh (1960) and Neild (1963).

29 This Kaleckian model is thus, in Rothschild's phrase, 'fully in the Keynesian spirit' (Rothschild, 1971, p. 25). Kaldor's (1955–6) results can be readily obtained from this model by assuming that labour is fully employed and deducing the effects on income shares of a higher level of investment. The mark-up would in this case be positively related to the level of investment in terms of wage units, as shown in note 34 below.

30 Lydall, in criticizing Kaldor's theory of distribution, has argued that 'if the Keynesian theory of employment is to retain its validity we must assume y [the share of profits in national income] constant (or nearly so)' (Lydall, 1971, p. 92). This argument is refuted by our

Kaleckian–Keynesian model. It provides an explanation for the level of employment without requiring the profit share to be constant. Keynesian theory does not require the overall propensity to save in the economy to be constant. It may vary with changes in the distribution of income even though the propensities to save in the different classes in the economy are constant.

31 A similar model, which included government expenditure and taxation, was used to investigate the short-period incidence of taxation in Asimakopulos and Burbidge (1974). They duplicate and extend the results obtained by Kalecki in his 1937 article, 'A theory of commodity, income and capital taxation', reprinted in Kalecki (1971b, pp. 35–42).

32 If a higher money wage rate leads to a fall in the value of capitalists' expenditure in real terms, e.g. because a portion of their incomes is fixed in money terms and they cut their consumption expenditure in real terms in the face of higher prices, then the higher wage rates would depress the profit share. This increase in their share of total gross income is not all gain for workers, however, since the level of employment, as indicated by equation (2.15), would also be lower in such a case.

33 Profits in real terms would also be adversely affected during periods of rising wages and prices if firms based mark-ups and prices on historical costs. Nordhaus, who uses mark-up pricing in his investigation of profit shares, argues that 'most businessmen . . . base their actual calculations of prices, sales, and profits on historical cost' (Nordhaus, 1974, p. 187).

34 If situations in which maximum possible output is being produced are compared, equation (2.15) should be reversed to show the mark-up μ as a function of effective demand. Let L_{1m} denote the maximum amount of employment of direct labour possible, either because of full employment of labour or because of available productive capacity; we have

$$\mu = \frac{a(1-\lambda)L_0+(\bar{I}+A)}{a(1-\lambda)L_{1m}-(\bar{I}+A)},$$

and

$$\frac{\Pi}{Y} = \frac{\bar{I}+A}{a(1-\lambda)L_{1m}}$$

The mark-up is no longer exogenous and does not appear in the equation for the profit share. This share varies directly with the value of capitalists' expenditure in real terms and inversely with the maximum employment of direct labour.

3

The Short-Period Incidence of Taxation[1]

Co-authored with J. B. Burbidge

Recent work on the incidence of taxes has been largely carried out on the basis of neoclassical assumptions.[2] The models used are pre-Keynesian; real wage rates are determined in the labour markets, with full employment automatically achieved through price and wage flexibility. Investment is then determined by saving out of full-employment income.[3] It is concluded from these models, when competitive conditions are assumed, that in the short period the economic incidence of general taxes is the same as their legal incidence. We have obtained different results by examining the short-period incidence of taxation in a model that uses different assumptions and is based on the work of Kalecki and Keynes. By a short period we mean a period of time within which changes in productive capacity can be neglected.

General features of the model

Three groups are distinguished in this model of a closed economy: workers, rentiers and firms. Real incomes for workers and rentiers are measured in terms of the command of their disposable incomes over consumption goods and for firms in terms of the command of their after-tax profits over investment goods. Fixed investment in real terms, in the particular short period examined, is assumed to be given in most of the situations considered. It is determined by decisions taken by firms in earlier time periods and may vary from period to period. Our analysis concentrates on a particular short period and the basis for these investment decisions is not considered here.[4] We also make the less realistic assumption that investment in additional stocks and work in progress is based on a plan which was decided in a previous period and is not varied as a result of anything that happens in the one under consideration: we recognize, however, that there may be involuntary departures from that plan and treat these as indicating a disequilibrium situation. Saving is done by firms, who distribute only part of their profits, and rentiers who save part of their incomes – workers do no saving,[5] except accidentally in disequilibrium situations.

Our analysis is centred on situations of short-period equilibrium, where saving is in the desired relation to income and actual investment in real terms is equal to the predetermined, or intended, level of investment in real terms. The only time lag that appears in the main body of the chapter is that between investment decisions and the production of the relevant goods (including those added to stock etc.). Other time lags, e.g. the time required for saving to adjust to the desired relation to income when income is changed, and the possible effects of these time lags on our results are briefly considered in the sections of the chapter concerned with extensions of the basic model. Similarly, the effects on our results of differences between output and demand, and thus the unplanned build-up or run-down of stocks (i.e. differences between the predetermined intended level of investment and the actual level of investment), are considered in these extension sections.

The changes in tax rates considered here are all within the framework of an existing tax structure. They do not represent a radical departure from past practices and do not disrupt the normal operations of the economy. These tax changes are announced at the beginning of the short period being examined and take effect immediately. It is assumed that these announcements do not affect the level of investment including stockbuilding which firms planned to undertake in the current short period. The subsequent effects of the tax changes on investment decisions and investment depend on how they affect post-tax profits and activity in the economy. Our analysis ends with the consideration of the latter effects in the current short period.

Taxes on profits, rentiers' income, wage incomes and on output used for consumption appear in the model. The government's possession and use of the output purchased by its taxation revenue may have differential effects on the well-being of different groups, but the main concern of this chapter is with the incidence of the taxes on the command of the three private groups over goods in the market place, rather than with the government's use of its revenue.

The money wage rate is assumed to be the same in all the short-period equilibrium comparisons, i.e. to be unaffected by anything which happens in the period considered.[6] The real wage rate is then determined by this money wage rate and the market price of the wage good. We abstract from changes in monetary policy. When the government's budget is not balanced the central bank responds passively to cover the budget deficit or to absorb the surplus.

Many versions of the basic model were used to estimate the short-period incidence of changes in taxes since the results depend, in part, on the assumptions made with respect to the degree of price competition between firms, the possible variability in the level of employment, and the number of production sectors. Only the versions with a single production sector are presented here.[7]

Two features distinguish the basic model developed here from the neoclassical models used in incidence studies: (a) in our model, investment in real terms is treated as exogenously given for the particular short period being examined, as it is assumed to depend on past decisions, except when involuntary stock-building (or stock reduction) causes a departure from the planned level, and (b) the real wage rate is not determined in the labour market as part of a process that automatically establishes full employment. These differences affect the results obtained for the short-period incidence of taxation.

The model

The following notations will be used:

a average output per man,

β proportion of after-tax profits paid out to rentiers,

$\bar{C}$ total consumption in real terms,

$\bar{I}$ total planned gross private investment in real terms,

$\bar{G}$ total government expenditure (purchase of goods and services) in real terms,

$\bar{D}$ total depreciation in real terms,
O total output in real terms,
$\bar{U}$ difference between total output and total demand in real terms,
w money wage rate,
p factor-cost price of output,
p' market price of consumption good,
t_c tax rate on value of output used for consumption,
t_f tax rate on profits,
t_r tax rate on rentiers' incomes,
t_w tax rate on wage incomes,
Y gross national product at market prices,
S gross saving in money terms,
S^* difference between actual saving and the short-period equilibrium level of saving, in money terms,
Π profits in money terms, net of depreciation,
T total tax bill in money terms,
L total level of employment,
$\bar{L}$ total level of employment when all plant is utilized at normal productive capacity,
L_f total labour force,
λ average mark-up of price over unit prime costs, and
s_r propensity to save of rentiers.

Final output consists of a single multipurpose good which can be consumed, invested in fixed plant and equipment or as inventories, or used by the government.[8] This output is produced in plants in which labour is the only variable input and average prime costs are reverse-L-shaped.[9] The plants available for production in the current period are of different 'vintages' with different outputs per man and levels of capacity output. In the competitive version the profit-maximizing firms produce that output at which price is equal to marginal cost. A particular plant would thus be utilized at capacity levels if price is greater than the constant portion of the marginal (average variable) cost curve, and not utilized at all if price is less than this value. It will be assumed, in the main body of this chapter, that aggregate demand will be high enough to ensure that average variable costs can be covered on all existing plants.[10] Each plant is thus operated at normal productive capacity when competitive conditions are assumed, and total employment is thus fixed by the available plant. In the non-competitive versions the distribution of total employment among these plants is also assumed to be given even though there may be less than full utilization of capacity. With these assumptions, average output per man is a constant up to full utilization of capacity and total output can be expressed by

$$O = aL, L \le \bar{L}, L \le L_f \tag{3.1}$$

The factor-cost price of output can be represented as equalling average prime costs (taken over the whole industry) plus a mark-up on these costs:

$$p = (1 + \lambda)\frac{w}{a} \tag{3.2}$$

In the competitive versions of the model, λ is a variable determined by the price and the average unit labour cost. This market-determined price equates the total demand for the product to the total capacity output of the available plant. In the non-competitive versions price is set by price leaders adopting some fixed mark-up over their average prime costs when plant is operated at some standard or target rate of utilization. This standard rate is less than normal productive capacity. Other firms charge the same price. If the distribution of output over different plants is constant at all levels of plant utilization considered (and it is assumed here that it is constant) then the average realized mark-up is also constant. It is determined by the mark-up chosen by the price leaders, the technical characteristics of all the plants, and the output share of each plant.

The market price of the good when sold for private consumption can be obtained from its factor-cost price by adjusting for the tax on consumption:

$$p' = (1 + t_c)p \tag{3.3}$$

The total output produced in the short period is equal to the total quantity demanded plus unintended changes in inventories, and thus

$$O = \bar{C} + \bar{I} + \bar{G} + \bar{U} \tag{3.4}$$

This equality can also be expressed in money terms:

$$Y = p'\bar{C} + p\bar{I} + p\bar{G} + p\bar{U} \tag{3.5}$$

Gross national product at market prices can be expressed as the sum of factor incomes, indirect taxes and depreciation:

$$Y = wL + \Pi + t_c p\bar{C} + p\bar{D} \tag{3.6}$$

Taxation revenue is equal to[11]

$$T = t_w wL + t_f \Pi + t_r(1 - t_f)\beta\Pi + t_c p\bar{C} \tag{3.7}$$

In order to simplify the analysis the government's budget is assumed to be balanced in all but one of the versions of this model,[12] and thus (except in that case)

$$T = p\bar{G} \tag{3.8}$$

Desired saving is done by firms, who retain part of their after-tax profits, and rentiers who consume only part of their incomes. It is assumed, unless otherwise noted, that rentiers' incomes (before income tax) are a constant proportion of current profits (after profits tax) in the alternative short-period situations examined. The desired gross saving of firms is equal to depreciation plus an assumedly constant proportion (the retention ratio $1 - \beta$) of after-tax net profits, and the planned saving of rentiers is equal to some desired proportion (equal to their saving propensity s_r) of their after-tax incomes.[13] Total private gross saving in a particular short period would be equal to the sum of these components of short-period equilibrium private gross saving plus any disequilibrium amount of saving that occurs in that short period. Thus,

$$S = (1 - t_f)\Pi[(1 - \beta) + s_r(1 - t_r)\beta] + p\bar{D} + S^* \tag{3.9}$$

Gross private saving must be equal, by definition, to the value of actual gross private investment and the government deficit:

$$S = p\bar{I} + p\bar{G} - T + p\bar{U} \tag{3.10}$$

Gross private planned investment, depreciation and output per man, all in real terms, the money wage rate and the saving propensities (s_r and $1 - \beta$) are assumed to be exogenously given for the particular short period examined in all the basic versions of this model. The above set of ten equations contains 17 additional variables. They are O, L, p, λ, p', $\bar{C}$, $\bar{U}$, Y, Π, S, S^*, t_c, t_w, t_r, t_f, T and $\bar{G}$. Our analysis concentrates on situations of short-period equilibrium in which firms realize that their planned investment and saving is in the desired relation to income: we leave open the question by what mechanism and under what circumstances the economy is likely to be brought to short-period equilibrium in this sense. Thus both $\bar{U}$ and S^* are equal to zero. The competitive version of our model is then closed by taking L and four of the five government variables, which are t_f, t_w, t_r, t_c and $\bar{G}$, as exogenous; this implies that nothing which happens in the period can affect the level of the money wage, but that prices are completely flexible. However, we examine some of the consequences of relaxing various assumptions below.[14]

In the non-competitive without full employment version, λ and four of the government variables are exogenous, and in the non-competitive fixed employment version L is also exogenous and the balanced budget condition, equation (3.8), is dropped. Possible consequences of relaxing some of the above assumptions are examined below.

The effects on workers, rentiers and firms of substitutions among tax rates or of balanced changes in taxes and the level of government expenditure can be indicated by examining the resulting changes (differences) in after-tax profits, rentiers' consumption, after-tax real wage rates, the average mark-up and the level of employment. The following two equations are helpful in determining these changes.

From equations (3.8), (3.9) and (3.10) we obtain, for the short-period equilibrium situations where the government's budget is assumed to be balanced,[15]

$$(1 - t_f)\frac{\Pi}{p}[(1 - \beta) + s_r(1 - t_r)\beta] = \bar{I} - \bar{D} \qquad (3.11)$$

After-tax profits in real terms is a function of net investment, the retention ratio $1 - \beta$, the tax rate on rentiers' incomes and their propensity to save.

From equations (3.1)–(3.6) we obtain an expression relating the mark-up and employment to pre-tax profits:

$$\frac{\lambda}{1 + \lambda}aL = \frac{\Pi}{p} + \bar{D} \qquad (3.12)$$

In the special case when the government budget is assumed to be in balance in each period, the short-period equilibrium distribution of income between profits and wages in this Keynesian model is determined by the requirement that desired private saving be equal to the intended level of investment.[16] The differences in government policy we are considering thus alter the distribution of post-tax income to the extent required to maintain the equality between desired saving and intended investment. These required changes in distribution can be inferred from equation (3.11) if β and s_r are assumed to be unchanged. Corresponding to the change in pre-tax profits required for short-period equilibrium, there is a change in the value for the mark-up or in total employment or in both, as shown by equation (3.12). Changes in the mark-up required by this relation will affect the purchasing power of the fixed money wage rate.

Results for the competitive version

The way in which expressions (3.11) and (3.12) can be used to estimate the incidence of tax changes may be indicated by considering the effects of an increase in the tax on profits, with the tax on consumption and the tax on rentiers' incomes unchanged and the tax on wages a dependent variable. The term on the right-hand side of equation (3.11), net investment (including stock-building) in real terms, is assumed to be given for the particular short period examined and, since on the left-hand side the term $(1 - \beta) + s_r(1 - t_r)\beta$ is also unchanged in this case, after-tax profits in real terms must be unchanged. Rentiers' consumption

$$(1 - s_r)(1 - t_r)(1 - t_r) \frac{\beta \Pi}{p(1 + t_c)},$$

a function of after-tax profits, is therefore also unchanged, as is workers' consumption in real terms since it is equal to the difference between the unchanged amount available for consumption (determined by the normal productive capacity operation of all available plant and the assumedly fixed amount taken up by investment and government expenditure) and the unchanged rentiers' consumption. Since profits (before tax) in real terms must be higher, it can be seen from equation (3.12) that the mark-up is higher (due to higher market prices). The pre-tax real wage rate must therefore be lower but the tax rate on wages, a dependent variable here, is also lower, fully compensating for this change. In this model, therefore, taxes on profits or wage incomes are equivalent ways, from the point of view of the incidence of a given tax bill, of financing government expenditures.[17] The *money* value of government expenditure will be higher because of the higher mark-up.

The effects of substitution between tax rates for this version of the model are summarized in table 3.1. A shift from taxing rentiers' incomes to taxing profits (case (ii)) would lead to lower after-tax profits, in spite of an increase in the mark-up which would reduce workers' consumption, while a shift from a tax on consumption to a profits tax (case (iii)) would lead to a rise in the mark-up which would on balance leave firms no worse off, rentiers better off and workers worse off.[18] In the former case, the after-tax profits of firms required for equilibrium would be lower since saving by rentiers would be higher. Consumption of rentiers would also be higher because of their higher after-tax incomes and this means fewer goods would be available for consumption by the workers.[19] In the latter case, after-tax profits in terms of the factor-cost price of the good must be unchanged, given a constant retention ratio, propensity to save of rentiers and tax rate on rentiers' incomes, but the incomes of rentiers in terms of the market price of the good, and their consumption, are higher. Workers are worse off because the higher mark-up more than offsets the lower tax on the consumption good.[20] The ambiguous result in case (v) arises because the decrease in the tax rate on rentiers' incomes increases their incomes in terms of the factor price of output, but since the increase in the consumption tax raises the market price relative to the factor price, their incomes in terms of the market price, and thus their consumption, may not have increased.[21]

Firms and workers tend to be worse off when one of the three other tax rates is raised to compensate for a lower tax rate on rentiers' incomes.[22]

Our model can also be used to examine the effects of an increase in one of the tax rates to cover the cost of higher government expenditure in real terms. These effects are summarized in table 3.2. The distribution among groups of the benefits of the higher government expenditure is ignored for purposes of this comparison. The market price of the good would be higher in all but one of the cases. Financing the increase in government expenditure by a higher tax on wage incomes would not raise price, since this entails no change in the money value of the aggregate demand.

Table 3.1 Short-period effects of compensating changes in tax rates (competitive version of the model)

	After-tax profits (real terms)	Profits (real terms)	Rentiers' consumption (real terms)	Wage rate, post-tax (real terms)[a]	Mark-up
			Change in		
(i) $\Delta t_f > 0$; $\Delta t_r = \Delta t_c = 0$ $\Delta t_w < 0$	0	+	0	0	+
(ii) $\Delta t_f > 0$; $\Delta t_c = \Delta t_w = 0$ $\Delta t_r < 0$	−	+	+	−	+
(iii) $\Delta t_f > 0$; $\Delta t_r = \Delta t_w = 0$ $\Delta t_c < 0$	0	+	+	−	+
(iv) $\Delta t_c > 0$; $\Delta t_f = \Delta t_r = 0$ $\Delta t_w < 0$	0	0	−	+	0
(v) $\Delta t_c > 0$; $\Delta t_f = \Delta t_w = 0$ $\Delta t_r < 0$	−	−	?	?	−
(vi) $\Delta t_w > 0$; $\Delta t_c = \Delta t_r = 0$ $\Delta t_f < 0$	−	−	+	−	−

[a] Also consumption by wage-earners.

Principal assumptions:
1. The budget is balanced and government expenditure is given in real terms.
2. Investment in real terms (including stock-building) is equal to the amount planned in a prior period.
3. The money wage is unaffected by the changes in tax rates but prices are completely flexible.
4. The retention ratio and saving propensities are unaffected by tax changes.
5. The levels of employment and output are unaffected by tax changes.

Table 3.2 Short-period effects of higher tax rates matching higher government expenditure in real terms – competitive version

	Change in				
	After-tax profits (real terms)	Profits (real terms)	Rentiers' consumption (real terms)	Wage rate, post-tax (real terms)[a]	Mark-up
(i) $\Delta t_f > 0; \Delta t_w = \Delta t_r = \Delta t_c = 0$	0	+	0	−	+
(ii) $\Delta t_w > 0; \Delta t_f = \Delta t_r = \Delta t_c = 0$	0	0	0	−	0
(iii) $\Delta t_r > 0; \Delta t_f = \Delta t_w = \Delta t_c = 0$	+	+	−	−	+
(iv) $\Delta t_c > ; \Delta t_f = \Delta t_w = \Delta t_r = 0$	0	0	−	−	0

[a] Also consumption by wage-earners.

Assumptions as for table 3.1.

Extensions of the competitive version

The above results were based on comparisons of situations of short-period equilibrium with constant values for some of the variables, such as the money-wage rate, the retention ratio and the propensity to save of rentiers. Changes in these values, in response to changes in taxes, may affect the conclusions drawn from our model. Our results would also differ if the situations compared were not ones of short-period equilibrium. Some of these possible differences will now be briefly discussed.

When rentiers, acting individually, respond to an increase in the tax rate on their incomes by lowering their propensity to save in order to prevent the drop in their consumption that would otherwise occur, the incidence of this tax change will be shifted. For example, consider an increase in t_r and a compensating reduction in t_w (the converse of case (vi) in table 3.1). With a constant value for s_r, after-tax profits and the after-tax real wage rate would be higher while rentiers' consumption would be lower. If, however, rentiers maintained their consumption, after-tax profits in real terms would have to be still higher, leading to still higher real dividends, to generate the required savings by firms and rentiers. The increase in the after-tax real wage rate would be wiped out by the higher mark-up. Since investment in real terms is the same in the situations compared, total saving must be the same. The decrease in rentiers' saving out of income is equal to the increase in retained earnings of firms. The rentiers' net worth would be unaffected by this substitution if the value of their shares reflected fully the increased retained earnings of firms. Similarly, in case (iii) of table 3.2, they can place the entire burden of the increased governmental expenditure on workers' consumption by maintaining their own consumption. This possible response of rentiers to taxation affects the detail of our results rather than their main thrust, which indicates that the short-period economic incidence of taxation may differ from the legal incidence. Indeed, the extent of this difference is increased by such response.

Changes in the retention ratio $1 - \beta$ may also affect the incidence of taxation. Increases in this ratio, since they tend to raise the propensity to save in the economy, lower required after-tax profits in real terms (net investment in these terms being unchanged). For example, in case (ii) of table 3.1, where t_f is raised and t_r is lowered, after-tax profits in real terms are lower, rentiers' consumption is higher and that of workers is lower; if firms reduced their distributions sufficiently they would be able to keep the real value of their retained profits unchanged but they would lower after-tax profits still more in the process.[23] Rentiers' after-tax incomes would as a result be equal to their initial values. The lower tax rate on their incomes is offset by the higher retention ratio and the lower after-tax profits – and thus both their consumption and that of workers would be unchanged.

Higher money wages will only affect the burden on workers of a higher tax on their incomes in short-period equilibrium situations if the resulting increase in prices leads to a fall in investment and/ or rentiers' consumption in real terms. There may be time lags, however, in the response of prices to changes in money wage rates. In itself, such a time lag clearly raises the real wage and reduces profits (if these are measured on a replacement-cost basis): in the absence of some action by the government on taxation, total consumption will rise and inventories fall below the planned level.

Once we depart from comparisons of short-period equilibrium with actual investment not equal to intended investment and/or saving not in the desired relation to income, the range of possible results is greatly widened. The equation for after-tax profits in real terms has added to it, in such cases, as shown in note 16, the difference between unintended changes in inventories and disequilibrium saving in real terms. Inability to forecast and adjust immediately to the effects of changes in government policy may lead to non-zero values for $\bar{U}$. Similarly, the time required for desired saving to adjust to changes in after-tax incomes might mean that in the short period immediately after the change in policy, on which our analysis is based, S^* is not equal to zero. The short-period effects of tax changes can still be solved. Our model can, formally, determine the short-period effects of tax changes in such situations, since it can be solved when the values of $\bar{U}$ and S^*/p are specified. But an important limitation of the model is its inability to determine the values for $\bar{U}$ and S^*/p. For example, consider case (i) in table 3.1, where the profits tax is increased and the tax on wage incomes is lowered. If there is some disequilibrium saving, because workers' consumption responds to higher after-tax income only after a time lag, then after-tax profits are lower than they would otherwise have been.[24] The economic incidence of the tax change then bears some relation to the legal incidence. This would not be the end of the story, however, because in subsequent periods workers' expenditure would presumably come into line with their post-tax incomes. We cannot pursue the matter any further than the end of the first period, however, because this would require, *inter alia*, an analysis of how the level of investment decisions would change between the prior period and the one under review.

Comparison with neoclassical models

The competitive version of our model was developed at some length because it facilitates comparisons with the results obtained by those working with neoclassical models. They assume commodity markets to be perfectly competitive, and full employment is 'automatically achieved through wage and price flexibility' (Mieszkowski, 1969, p. 1104). In the competitive version of our model employment is constant and this constant level can be identified with the full employment level for purposes of this comparison (if we assume that there is just sufficient productive capacity to employ the total labour force[25]). From the neoclassical models it is concluded that the burden of an increase in profits tax to finance an increase in government expenditure falls on profits when equilibrium positions are compared. This contrasts with the conclusion of our basic model (table 3.2, case (i)) that it will fall on real wages.

This difference in conclusions arises because the distribution of income is assumed to be determined in different ways in the two models. Neoclassical incidence theory is based on the marginal productivity theory of distribution – the real wage rate (pre-tax) is determined in the labour market as part of the automatic process that results in full employment. When the government increases the tax rate on profits and spends the proceeds the real wage rate is unchanged.[26] Pre-tax profits must be unchanged since the output, employment and the wage bill are constant, and thus the burden of the profits tax falls solely on profits.[27] Private investment and capitalists' consumption, which are dependent variables, would be lower in the short period as a result of this tax, and they would be replaced by government expenditure. In our model, on the other hand, investment is assumed to be an independent variable in the short period and it, along with the saving propensities, determines the short-period equilibrium distribution of income. After-tax profits are determined by the requirement (for short-period equilibrium) that savings must be in the desired relation to income, and be equal to investment. The real wage rate takes on the value that is consistent with this level of profits. It is determined by conditions in the commodity market.[28]

Non-competitive version with employment a dependent variable

In the non-competitive version of our model, the factor-cost price of output is set by price-leaders who apply a fixed mark-up over their prime costs when plant is operated at a standard or target rate of utilization which is less than normal productive capacity. The distribution of output over different plants is assumed to be constant at all levels of plant utilization considered, and the average realized mark-up is also constant. It is determined by the price set by the price-leaders, the technical characteristics of all the plants and the output share of each plant. There are unemployed resources in all the situations compared – both labour and productive capacity equal in average quality to that employed are available. The set of equations (3.1)–(3.10) again describes the model but here the mark-up λ is predetermined (and operates without any time lag) and its place as an unknown is taken by L, total employment.

We proceed as before, considering first compensating changes in tax rates and then the effects of balanced changes in government expenditure and taxation. Equations (3.11) and (3.12) are again used to sort out the effects of the various changes.

With employment and the degree of utilization of plant being dependent variables it is possible for compensating changes in tax rates to make some groups better off without making others worse off, by spreading the burden of a tax bill that is fixed (in real terms) over a larger total output, and vice versa. For example, substitution of a profits tax for a tax on wage incomes can have

Table 3.3 Short-period effects of compensating changes in tax rates (non-competitive model with employment variable)

	Change in				
	After-tax profits (real terms)	Profits (real terms)	Rentiers' consumption (real terms)	Wage rate, post-tax (real terms)[a]	Employment and output
(i) $\Delta t_f > 0$; $\Delta t_r = \Delta t_c = 0$ $\Delta t_w < 0$	0	+	0	+	+
(ii) $\Delta t_f > 0$; $\Delta t_w = \Delta t_c = 0$ $\Delta t_r < 0$	−	+	+	0	+
(iii) $\Delta t_f > 0$; $\Delta t_w = \Delta t_r = 0$ $\Delta t_c < 0$	0	+	+	+	+
(iv) $\Delta t_c > 0$; $\Delta t_f = \Delta t_r = 0$ $\Delta t_w < 0$	0	0	−	+	0
(v) $\Delta t_c > 0$; $\Delta t_f = \Delta t_w = 0$ $\Delta t_r < 0$	−	−	?	−	−
(vi) $\Delta t_w > 0$; $\Delta t_f = \Delta t_c = 0$ $\Delta t_r < 0$	−	−	+	−	−

[a] Also consumption by wage-earners.

Principal assumptions:
1. The budget is balanced and government expenditure is given in real terms.
2. Investment in real terms (including stock-building) is equal to the amount planned in a prior period.
3. The money wage and factor-cost price are unaffected by the change in tax rates.
4. The retention ratio and saving propensities are unaffected by tax changes.

beneficial effects, as shown in table 3.3. From equation (3.11) it can be deduced that in this case (case (i)) after-tax profits must be unchanged since the required saving is unchanged and the saving propensities and the tax rate on rentiers' incomes are constant. With the lower tax on wage incomes the post-tax real wage rate is higher and thus effective demand is higher resulting in higher employment and output. The effects on rentiers' consumption of substituting a higher tax rate on consumption for a lower tax rate on rentiers' incomes (case (v)) is ambiguous here as it was for the competitive version. The amount of the consumption output which the higher post-tax money income of rentiers could purchase depends on the extent of the increase in the market price of the consumption goods.[29]

The effects of a balanced increase in government expenditure and taxation are summarized in table 3.4. In two of the four cases listed in the table at least part of the burden of higher government expenditure is absorbed by higher output. An increase in the tax on profits is clearly a better way than raising the tax on wage incomes of meeting the cost of higher government expenditure, because of the differences in the propensities to save out of these two categories of incomes. The results obtained by raising the extra taxation from higher tax rates on workers' incomes and consumption are the same as in the competitive version since total output is unchanged by the balanced increase in the government's budget.

Rentiers are made worse off when the higher government expenditure is financed by a higher tax rate on their incomes if the propensity to consume is unchanged. If, however, they maintain their consumption, the expansionary effects on employment, output and profits would be greater than those indicated in table 3.4. No one would then be worse off as a result of the increase in taxation and government expenditure; the lower personal saving of rentiers would be offset by the higher profits and retained earnings of firms. In so far as the value of their share holdings are higher because of the higher saving of firms their wealth will be unaffected by this tax on their incomes.[30]

Non-competitive version with fixed employment

A fixed level of employment of labour (which may be 'full employment') is assumed to be maintained by appropriate

Table 3.4 Short-period effects of higher tax rates matching higher government expenditure in real terms – non-competitive, employment variable version

	Change in				
	After-tax profits (real terms)	Profits (real terms)	Rentiers' consumption (real terms)	Wage rate, post-tax (real terms)[a]	Employment and output
(i) $\Delta t_f > 0$; $\Delta t_w = \Delta t_r = \Delta t_c = 0$	0	+	0	0	+
(ii) $\Delta t_w > 0$; $\Delta t_f = \Delta t_r = \Delta t_c = 0$	0	0	0	−	0
(iii) $\Delta t_r > 0$; $\Delta t_f = \Delta t_w = \Delta t_c = 0$	+	+	−	0	+
(iv) $\Delta t_c > 0$; $\Delta t_f = \Delta t_w = \Delta t_r = 0$	0	0	−	−	0

[a] Also consumption by wage-earners.

Assumptions as for table 3.3.

government fiscal policy, but the oligopolistic firms in the model maintain some excess productive capacity. The government's budget surplus or deficit takes on whatever value is consistent with the maintenance of the target level of employment. Equation (3.8) is thus dropped, leaving equations (3.1)–(3.7) and (3.9) and (3.10) to describe this version.[31] Both the mark-up λ and total employment L are predetermined and they, along with the given value of average output per man, determine the pre-tax distribution of income as shown by equation (3.12). Thus changes in tax rates, with λ given, cannot be shifted and the legal and economic incidence of taxation coincide in the short period when there are constant values for the independent variables, as indicated in table 3.5.

For this version of the model the increase in a tax rate that maintains a constant level of employment when some other tax rate is lowered, or when government expenditure is increased, is borne by the group whose tax has been raised. This result, that with parameters unchanged the legal and economic incidence of taxation is the same in the short period, resembles that obtained for the competitive neoclassical models. The reason for this similarity is that the formal structures of these models preclude changes in government expenditure and taxation from affecting the distribution of pre-tax incomes and total employment. One important difference between our Keynesian model and the neoclassical models is that investment in real terms is exogenous and one of the government variables must be endogenous to maintain a fixed level of employment in our model whereas, in neoclassical models, the endogeneity of investment in real terms maintains full employment automatically. Another difference between our non-competitive Keynesian model and these competitive neoclassical models is that there is scope in ours for the actions of particular groups to alter the parameters (i.e. to change the values of the independent variables that determine the results in tables 3.5 and 3.6) in such a way as to shift the tax burden. Some of these possibilities will be considered in the following section.

Table 3.5 Short-period effects of compensating changes in tax rates with constant employment (non-competitive firms, and possibly unbalanced budget)

	Change in			
	After-tax profits (real terms)	*Rentiers' consumption (real terms)*	*Wage rate, post-tax (real terms)*[a]	*Budget balance $p\bar{G}-T$*
(i) $\Delta t_f > 0$; $\Delta t_r = \Delta t_c = 0$ $\Delta t_w < 0$	−	−	+	−
(ii) $\Delta t_f > 0$; $\Delta t_w = \Delta t_c = 0$ $\Delta t_r < 0$	−	0	0	−
(iii) $\Delta t_f > 0$; $\Delta t_w = \Delta t_r = 0$ $\Delta t_c < 0$	−	−	+	−
(iv) $\Delta t_c > 0$; $\Delta t_f = \Delta t_r = 0$ $\Delta t_w < 0$	0	−	+	0
(v) $\Delta t_c > 0$; $\Delta t_f = \Delta t_w = 0$ $\Delta t_r < 0$	0	+	−	+
(vi) $\Delta t_w > 0$; $\Delta t_f = \Delta t_c = 0$ $\Delta t_r < 0$	0	+	−	+

[a] Also consumption by wage-earners.

Principal assumptions:
1. Government expenditure is given in real terms.
2. Investment in real terms (including stock-building) is equal to the amount planned in a prior period.
3. The money wage and factor-cost price are unaffected by the change in tax rates.
4. The retention ratio and saving propensities are unaffected by tax changes.
5. The levels of employment and output are unaffected by tax changes.

Extensions of the non-competitive versions

Employment variable, government budget balanced

Our results for the incidence of tax changes in the non-competitive versions of the model may be altered if these taxes are allowed to

Table 3.6 Short-period effects of higher tax rates assuming constant employment with higher government expenditure in real terms (non-competitive firms, and possibly unbalanced budget)

	Change in			
	After-tax profits (real terms)	*Rentiers' consumption (real terms)*	*Wage rate, post-tax (real terms)*[a]	*Budget balance $p\bar{G}-T$*
(i) $\Delta t_f > 0$; $\Delta t_w = \Delta t_r = \Delta t_c = 0$	–	–	0	–
(ii) $\Delta t_w > 0$; $\Delta t_f = \Delta t_r = \Delta t_c = 0$	0	0	–	0
(iii) $\Delta t_r > 0$; $\Delta t_f = \Delta t_w = \Delta t_c = 0$	0	–	0	–
(iv) $\Delta t_c > 0$; $\Delta t_f = \Delta t_w = \Delta t_r = 0$	0	–	–	0

[a] Also consumption by wage-earners.

Assumptions as for table 3.5.

affect the values of some of the variables which so far have been assumed to be independent of the model. Thus changes in after-tax profits might lead to a change in mark-ups, and such changes could then affect the incidence of taxation. For example, in case (ii) of table 3.3 where the tax on profits is raised and the tax on rentiers' income is lowered, firms might attempt to recover the position they held before the tax changes by raising mark-ups. Equation (3.11), which does not involve the mark-up λ, shows that this attempt cannot alter the post-tax level of profits in real terms, if net investment in real terms really is unchanged. It will make the position of workers worse, however, since the price of the consumption good is higher with the higher mark-up. The increase in employment that would otherwise occur in this case if mark-ups were unchanged might be wiped out if firms tried to maintain their post-tax profits by raising mark-ups.

Pressures from workers for lower mark-ups may arise as they try to shift the direct burden of higher government expenditure financed, say, by a tax on the consumption good. Higher money wage rates obtained through collective bargaining will lead to an erosion of true mark-ups, at least for some time, if the mark-ups are applied by the firms on the basis of historical costs and only the increase in direct costs is passed on in higher prices. If mark-ups are lowered as part of the process of adjustment to tax changes but total private investment in real terms is unaffected, the position of workers will be improved.[32] Total profits in real terms will be unchanged, but the profits share will be lower since total output and employment will be higher.

Attempts by firms to maintain their retained earnings unchanged in real terms by raising their retention ratio, when after-tax profits are lower, could succeed only by lowering after-tax profits still further. This result follows because their action increases the overall propensity to save in the economy and thus lowers the level of after-tax profits required to achieve short-period equilibrium.

Rentiers can again shift the burden of changes in government policy by maintaining their consumption as in the competitive version of this model. This response of rentiers to lower after-tax incomes can also benefit the unemployed. For example, in table 3.3, case (iv), where $\Delta t_c > 0$, $\Delta t_w < 0$, a lower propensity to save of rentiers would lead to higher after-tax profits and employment. Similarly, in table 3.4, case (iii), where larger government purchases are financed by means of a higher tax on rentiers' incomes, this behaviour ensures that the government demand is supplied out of increased output, if unemployed resources are available.

Employment fixed, government budget may not be balanced

The short-period equilibrium results of tax and expenditure changes may differ from those summarized in tables 3.5 and 3.6, by successful attempts to shift the legal incidence of taxation. These attempts would result in changes in the government's budget balance and in struggles over the mark-up. For example, firms may try to maintain the real value of their retained earnings in the face of lower after-tax profits, as in case (i) in table 3.5, by raising the retention ratio. With the propensity to save of rentiers unchanged, there can be a further reduction in the tax on workers' incomes, increasing the government's deficit (or decreasing its surplus). Any corresponding move by rentiers to maintain their consumption, thus lowering their (and the private sector's) propensity to save, will require higher public saving in the new short-period equilibrium position. Regardless of what the firms do to their retention ratio, if the rentiers succeed in maintaining their consumption in real terms at the pre-tax change level, then workers' consumption in real terms must also be unchanged. They not only would not gain from any increase in the retention ratio; they would also not obtain the higher consumption shown in table 3.5.

Firms, when their after-tax profits are lower, say, as a result of an increase in the tax on profits accompanying an increase in government expenditure, can only restore post-tax profits by obtaining higher mark-ups. In this new short-period equilibrium position price would not only be higher, it would be increased relative to the money wage rate. Firms would in this way shift the burden of higher government expenditure to workers. In a similar situation workers might try to shift the incidence of higher taxes on their incomes or on the consumption good by bargaining for higher money wage rates. They can succeed in this way only if mark-ups are reduced, as would happen if there were a lag in the raising of prices. Price would in this case have increased in the new short-period equilibrium but in a smaller proportion than the money wage rate. These conflicts over the sharing of the burden of higher government expenditure may lead not to a new short-period equilibrium but to continuing price increases. The originating impulse, after the government fiscal changes, may come either from higher prices or higher money wage rates depending on the tax that was increased. The process, however, would be the same: workers would respond to higher prices by obtaining higher money wages which would lead to still higher prices etc. But that is another story.[33]

Conclusions

This examination of the short-period incidence of changes in taxation with a balanced budget has shown that, on certain of our assumptions, the actual and legal incidence may differ. These differences occur when we assume that investment (including stock-building) is unaffected in real terms by these changes, and further assume that the changes affect pre-tax incomes by altering the price (mark-up), as in the competitive version of our model, or by altering the level of employment as in the non-competitive version with unemployed labour.[34] In each case our results differ from those obtained from neoclassical models because of the different explanations of distribution.

However, we find that, if it is assumed that the government tries to maintain full employment by fiscal measures, which may lead to a surplus or a deficit, then our basic model for the non-competitive version shows the incidence of taxation as very similar to that derived from neoclassical competitive models.

We have obtained results on the incidence of taxation by concentrating on situations of short-period equilibrium. This is appropriate for comparisons with the neoclassical models because they deal only with equilibrium positions, and it is in line with Kalecki's work in this area. It is only a first step, however, and a fuller treatment of the subject would require the tracing of the effects of tax changes over time. A change in tax at the beginning of a short period, even if we assume that it does not affect current investment, would probably work itself out over more than one short period. The resulting changes in output, prices, profits etc. will affect investment decisions and these will lead to further changes. In order to assess the longer-term effects of tax changes the analysis must be carried out within the context of a fully articulated growth model that permits the effects of the changes to be traced out over time.

Notes

1 Earlier drafts of this chapter were written while the authors were in Cambridge, Asimakopulos at Clare Hall and Burbidge at King's College. We are grateful to C. Green, F. H. Hahn, G. C. Harcourt, Lord Kahn, M. King, R. R. Neild, W. B. Reddaway and J. C. Weldon for comments on earlier drafts of this chapter. We are also grateful to J. Eatwell for allowing us to see an unpublished paper on the subject of our article.

2 A notable exception to this is the work of Eatwell, both in his

published article (1971) and in his unpublished paper. Professor Kaldor (1955–6) has referred to his own attempt 'to analyse the ultimate incidence of profits taxation under full employment conditions in a paper prepared for the Royal Commission on Taxation in 1951' (p. 94, n.3) in a Keynesian framework. He briefly contrasted incidence of taxation in a Ricardian model as opposed to a Keynesian model (p. 96).

3 For a review of this work see Mieszkowski (1969). This review article does not refer to Kalecki's important 1937 paper, reprinted in Kalecki (1971b).

4 For a brief discussion of investment decisions in a similar context see Asimakopulos (1971).

5 Versions of the model with a positive propensity to save out of wage incomes have also been developed. The basic results are unchanged as long as a Keynesian theory of distribution can be obtained, i.e. if conditions similar to the one for an economy with no government, where the propensity to save out of wages must be less than the propensity to save out of profits, are satisfied.

6 Situations with changing money wage rates could be handled by measuring values in wage units rather than in money terms. Some of the possible effects of changes in money wage rates following tax changes are considered below.

7 The differences in results obtained from our one-sector model and from models with separate consumption and investment goods sectors arise because in the two-sector versions changes in tax rates may affect the relative prices of consumption and investment goods. This would affect the relative incomes (in terms of the consumption good) of rentiers and workers and the relative profits made in the two sectors. There may be long-period consequences on the inducement to invest and on relative costs in the two sectors because of the differential effects on their profitability noted in our discussion of the competitive version. These differences do not alter the general conclusions of our paper that the short-period incidence of taxation may differ from the legal incidence.

8 The assumptions made here with respect to the nature of output have been described in Asimakopulos (1969, 1970). As soon as the output is set aside for investment in plant and equipment the characteristics of this good change (with no additional expenditure of labour), and it is formed into plants which are produced by accumulating this good over time.

9 Plants are assumed to employ only direct labour – labour whose employment varies directly with the degree of utilization of plant.

10 A more general approach would be to assume both that individual plants can be worked at above normal capacity, even though at

sharply increasing costs, and that the number of existing plants utilized in the current short period depends on the value of the wage rate in terms of the product. The higher this value is, the smaller is the number of existing plants that could cover their variable costs. Average output per man in the economy would thus be an increasing function, and employment made possible by the existing plant a decreasing function, of the wage in terms of the product. The changes in our results if this more general vintage approach were adopted will be noted.

11 This tax equation embodies 'double-taxation' of the income of the rentiers. We have worked out the incidence of changes in government policy in models where the corporate income tax is fully integrated into the personal income tax structure. The tax equation would then be

$$T = t_w wL + t_f(1 - \beta)\Pi + t_r\beta\Pi + t_c p\bar{C}$$

12 Kalecki (1937b) analyses the effects of taxation changes under this assumption. Our model can be readily extended to deal with unbalanced budgets. In the case presented below where firms are oligopolistic and the government acts to maintain a fixed level of employment for the short period, deficits or surpluses occur in the government's budget if they are required by its employment policy. The achievement of a balanced budget depends on the ability of the government to make continuous and accurate forecasts of what is going to happen when it changes one of the variables under its control, and to make suitable adjustments in tax rates. Errors in forecasting that result in budget surplus (deficits) are similar in their effects on our results to disequilibrium private saving (dissaving), discussed below.

13 This formulation implies that rentiers' consumption is normally a function only of their incomes. The effects on the results of assuming that consumption is also dependent on wealth, and may be invariant to short-period changes in income, will be considered below.

14 In the more general vintage version of the model mentioned in note 10, both output per man and total employment are dependent variables, along with the average mark-up. The model is closed in this case by the addition of two equations. One relates output per man to the level of employment, and the other the level of employment offered to the wage in terms of the product. That is, (a) $a = a(L)$ where $da/dL < 0$ and (b) $L = L(w/p)$ where $dL/d(w/p) < 0$.

15 With the fully integrated tax structure mentioned in note 11, the corresponding equation would be

$$\frac{\Pi}{p}[(1 - t_f)(1 - \beta) + s_r(1 - t_r)\beta] = \bar{I} - \bar{D}$$

Our results would be largely unchanged if full integration were assumed.

16 In the general case – when the government's budget is not necessarily in balance and the situation may not be one of short-period equilibrium – we obtain, for after-tax profits in real terms, in place of equation (3.11),

$$(1 - t_f)\frac{\Pi}{p}[(1 - \beta) + s_r(1 - t_r)\beta] = \bar{I} - \bar{D} + \bar{U} + \bar{G} - T/p - S^*p$$

The distribution of income between profits and wages is determined by the requirement that desired private saving in real terms be equal to the actual level of investment in real terms plus the government's budget balance in real terms, minus the amount by which actual saving differs from this desired private saving in real terms.

17 In the more general vintage approach discussed in notes 10 and 14, where utilization of plant is a function of the wage rate in terms of the product, there would be some beneficial effects for workers of a switch to a higher profits tax. The higher market price would result in somewhat higher employment and output, and the after-tax real wage rate of the workers would be higher. Firms and rentiers would be no worse off but workers would be better off.

Any reduction in rentiers' consumption, e.g. if their incomes are a lagged function of profits and they consume less when current price is higher, would destroy the equivalence of taxes on profits and wage incomes. Part of the short-period incidence of a given real tax bill would, in this case, be shifted to firms in the form of lower after-tax profits, when the tax on profits is raised and the tax on wage incomes is simultaneously lowered. Equation (3.11) would be replaced by

$$(1 - t_f)\frac{\Pi}{p} = \bar{I} - \bar{D} + [1 - s_r(1 - t_r)](1 - t_{f-1})\beta_{-1}\frac{\Pi_{-1}}{p}$$

where the subscript -1 indicates values for the immediately preceding period. A higher value for p would reduce rentiers' consumption, if their propensity to save is unchanged, and thus lower after-tax profits in real terms.

18 Indications of the short-period equilibrium effects of substituting equal changes in two tax rates for some other tax rate can be obtained by combining the cases listed in table 3.1 (or their converses).

19 This decrease in the real wage rate would be smaller (but still present) with the more general vintage approach because of the higher employment and output accompanying the lower real wage rate.

20 This conclusion may be reversed under certain conditions with the more general vintage approach. The higher output accompanying the higher factor-cost price of output may result in a higher real wage

rate, given the lower tax rate on consumption.

21 Their consumption, in real terms, is greater or smaller as $(1 - \beta)wL$ is greater or less than $s_r(1 - t_r)\beta\Pi$.

22 This analysis could also be extended to allow for the taxation of rentiers' wealth. A decrease in the tax on rentiers' wealth would have the effects associated above with a lower tax rate on rentiers' incomes. Kalecki's examination of the effects of capital taxation (Kalecki, 1971b, pp. 41–2) thus corresponds to our examination of the effects of taxation of rentiers' incomes.

23 It is suggested in Kaldor (1955, p. 161) that firms may try to maintain the value of retained earnings when a higher tax rate is imposed on profits. '. . . there is a certain amount . . . which it is considered necessary to set aside for purposes of renewals and expansion, and every rise in taxation reduces the proportion that can be "safely" distributed without impinging on these financial requirements.'

24 A similar result would occur in case (i) of table 3.1 if prices rose with a time lag after demand increased, and the initial burden of adjustment was borne by a fall in inventories.

25 For purposes of this comparison labour will be assumed to be in perfectly inelastic supply. This is the assumption made by Mieszkowski (1969, p. 1103) in his presentation of the neoclassical model. This neoclassical model can be obtained from the competitive general vintage version of our model mentioned in notes 10 and 14 by adding the assumption of full employment as an additional equation, $L = L_f$, to the 12 equations for this version. They are (3.1)–(3.10) plus $a = a(L)$ and $L = L(w/p)$. The 13 dependent variables in the neoclassical model are the 12 in our general vintage version plus the level of investment $\bar{I}$ in real terms. The demand for labour equation, $L = L(w/p)$, and the assumption of full employment determine the pre-tax real wage rate. Thus both the pre-tax distribution of income and total output, given the available productive capacity, are determined by the assumed conditions in the labour market. Investment is equal to whatever private saving is forthcoming from the corresponding full-employment income.

26 For this result to hold when there are two or more production sectors the government must spend the proceeds in a neutral manner, i.e. in the way those being taxed would have spent them. Harberger (1962, p. 224) assumes that the government acts in this way in his analysis of the incidence of the corporate profits tax.

27 This argument shows, in fact, that any change in government policy, as long as it does not affect the demand or supply curves of labour when it is assumed that the real wage rate is determined in the labour market, will leave pre-tax profits and the pre-tax wage bill unchanged.

Therefore the actual incidence of any such change in government policy is the same as the legal incidence.

28 The differences in our results from those obtained in the neoclassical models do not depend on the assumptions made with respect to the nature of cost curves. Even if they were U-shaped (a special case of the general vintage model referred to in notes 10, 14 and 25) with the *real wage rate equal to the marginal product of labour*, the economic incidence of the tax would still differ from the legal incidence because of the factors determining the short-period equilibrium distribution of income. Higher government expenditure financed by a higher tax rate on profits would result in a lower real wage rate since after-tax profits in real terms must be unchanged in short-period equilibrium. Not only would the real wage rate be lower but employment and output would also be higher. In the new short-period equilibrium the higher price of output in terms of the money wage rate means that firms would be operating plants, already being utilized, more intensively where this was feasible and plants may be brought into operation for which average variable costs could not previously have been covered.

If employment cannot be higher because the initial situation is one of full employment of labour, even though productive capacity is available to produce more at a lower real wage rate, the effects of an increase in the tax rate on profits to finance higher government expenditure cannot be readily determined in a Keynesian model. With the lower real wage rate required for short-period equilibrium when investment in real terms is unchanged, the firms' demand for labour would be higher. The bidding by employers for workers would increase money wage rates, thus tending to prevent the fall in the real wage rate required for equilibrium. There may be many possible courses and outcomes of this inflationary situation. Only if it leads to precisely the reduction in private investment in real terms that eliminates the inflationary pressures and maintains full employment will after-tax profits be lower by the amount of the profits taxation, thus making the legal and economic incidence the same. This result may be brought about temporarily by the fall in inventories, as indicated in note 24. But this would not be a position of short-period equilibrium unless firms, even in the face of high demand, accepted this lower actual level of investment as their new planned level. Alternatively, inflationary pressures may be suppressed by firms refraining, after price has increased relative to the money wage rate to restore post-tax profits in real-terms, from bidding up money wage rates. They would remain off their demand curves for labour and, if their investment in real terms were unchanged, the burden of the tax would be placed on the workers. Intermediate outcomes would have decreases in both investment and real wage rates with the burden of taxation shared between capitalists and workers. More extreme responses might also occur; the inflationary situation might have adverse effects on business confidence leading to a sharp decline in investment and lower employment.

29 Rentiers are better or worse off according as $\lambda(1 - \beta) (1 - t_w)wL$ is greater or smaller than $s_r(1 - t_r)\beta\Pi[\lambda(1 + t_c) + (t_w + t_c)]$.

30 A tax on rentiers' incomes is equivalent in its effects to a wealth tax as noted in note 22. Our conclusions are the same as those reached by Kalecki (1971b, pp. 41–2) when he considered capital taxation. He assumed that capitalists' consumption was unaltered and thus gross profits would be, initially, increased by the amount of taxation. Kalecki went on to consider the effects of this policy on the inducement to invest. He concluded that since the net profitability of investment is unaffected by capital taxation, the higher gross profits would result in a stronger inducement to invest. There would thus be a further boost to employment, output and profits in future short periods as a result of higher investment.

31 The real value for the government's budget balance, the value of expenditure minus taxation, would appear on the right-hand side of equation (3.11) for this model.

32 Kalecki, in his 1971b paper (pp. 161–3), argued that trade union power restrains mark-ups and this affects the distribution of income by leading to higher total output and employment. He also noted that an alternative way of improving labour's share would be through 'subsidising of prices of wage goods which is financed by direct taxation of profits' (p. 164). Kalecki stated that aggregate net profits will not be affected by such an operation. In terms of our model, subsidization of wage goods is equivalent to a reduction in t_c financed by an increase in t_f as in case (iii) of table 3.3. Our conclusions are the same as Kalecki's.

33 For an examination of this question see Hotson (1971).

34 In the general vintage competitive version of the model, mentioned in note 10, both price and employment may be affected.

4

Kalecki on the Determinants of Profits

Kalecki, in the introduction to his selected essays on the dynamics of the capitalist economy, noted that his views on the distribution of income remained unchanged from his first writings on this topic in 1933, while 'there is a continuous search for new solutions in the theory of investment decisions' (Kalecki, 1971b, p. vii). There was one aspect of his approach to investment decisions, however, that also remained unchanged, i.e. the positive role of current profits on current investment decisions through their effects on the expectations of profitability of new investment. Embedded in Kalecki's approach to the cyclical behaviour of a capitalist economy is the double-sided relation between profits and investment. Current investment expenditures, which are based on investment decisions made in the past, are an important element in the determination of current profits, while current profits influence current investment decisions and thus future investment expenditures. This double-sided relationship leads naturally to an attempt to trace the business cycle by linking successive short periods as events in preceding short periods feed into succeeding short periods etc. The trend would emerge in such an approach as, in Kalecki's words, 'but a slowly changing component of a chain of short-period situations; it has no independent entity . . .' (p. 165). The extent to which current profits affect current investment

I am grateful to J. Pöschl for comments on an earlier draft. He is not, of course, responsible for the interpretation of writings, or any errors, contained in this chapter.

decisions could differ in different short periods depending on 'economic, social and technological developments' (p. 183), so that any set of equations with fixed coefficients that purports to explain the trend and cycle would not be consistent with Kalecki's mature view of the development of a capitalist economy.

The time sequence of the investment process for capital goods – from investment decisions to investment activity to the eventual delivery of completed equipment – plays an important role in Kalecki's analysis of the business cycle, but the time lag between investment decisions and actual investment is also an important element in his causal explanation of the determination of profits. The significance of this role may not be evident to a reader of Kalecki's characteristically brief comments on this point.[1] A careful examination of his position on this topic can thus be instructive.

As an illustration of Kalecki's general approach, a profits equation for the United States economy is obtained and quarterly national accounts data make it possible to trace the relative importance of the various determinants of profits over the post-war period.

A causal explanation of profits

Kalecki first examined the determinants of profits in a simplified model of a closed economy in which government expenditure and taxation are negligible.[2] The analysis begins with the national income identity between gross national product, which in this special case is equal to the sum of gross profits P and of wages and salaries W, and gross national expenditure, which is equal to the sum of gross investment I, of capitalists' consumption C_c and of workers' consumption C_w. Kalecki then makes the further assumption that workers do not save and, by cancelling W and C_w, he arrives at the equation

$$P = I + C_c \qquad (4.1)$$

Although one of the bases for the derivation of equation (4.1) is an identity, it also embodies a behavioural assumption – that the propensity to save of workers is zero – and a short-period equilibrium assumption, that the saving of workers in the period of time being examined is in the desired relation to their incomes. In his 1933 study of the business cycle, Kalecki's use of his profits equation was based on the implicit assumption of short-period equilibrium, since at each point in time actual investment was equal to planned investment and the actual consumption expenditures of both capitalists and workers were in the desired relations to their incomes. The assumption of short-period equilibrium means that the full multiplier effects of any change in investment that might have occurred must have been completed within the interval of time for which the data in equation (4.1) are relevant. The completion of the full multiplier effects requires the passage of time, but this can easily be overlooked when the starting point is equation (4.1), because it contains no explicit reference to time. For example, an increase in investment expenditures, assuming the consumption expenditures of capitalists are unchanged, will only increase profits by an equal amount after a series of rounds with workers being hired, their wages being spent on commodities, leading to the hiring of more workers etc. This was recognized by Kalecki in his 1933 study of the business cycle. 'When production of investment goods rises . . . the levels of aggregate production and of the profit per unit of output will *ultimately* rise to such an extent that the increment in real profits is equated to the increment of the production of investment goods' (Kalecki, 1971b, p. 12 (my italics)). It is important when working with equation (4.1) to keep its behavioural and special equilibrium characteristics in mind.[3] No *actual* short period of time in a changing economy can be expected to satisfy the implied equilibrium conditions of equation (4.1).

Kalecki considers the possible causal significance of equation (4.1), i.e. whether it should be read as meaning that current profits 'determine capitalists' consumption and investment, or the reverse of this' (Kalecki, 1971b, p. 78). His initial answer is based on a consideration of which of the items in the equation are directly subject to the decisions of capitalists. He concludes that 'it is clear that capitalists may decide to consume and to invest more in a given period than in the preceding one, but they cannot decide to earn more. It is, therefore, their investment and consumption decisions which determine profits, and not vice versa' (pp. 78–9). The reason given by Kalecki is not sufficient to determine a one-way causation between current capitalists' expenditures and current profits, since it does not exclude the possibility that these decisions may be a function of current profits, thus allowing for a mutually interdependent relationship. What is needed to arrive at Kalecki's conclusion is not only that capitalists' expenditures, and not profits, are directly subject to their decisions but that in the particular period examined these expenditures are independent of profits.

Since the two sides of equation (4.1) must be equal, and the items on the right-hand side are independent of current profits, then it must be that they are the immediate determinants of these profits. The attribution of one-way causality to equation (4.1) thus depends on the time lag in the implementation of investment decisions and the length of the time period covered by the data in that equation.

There is, perhaps, implicit recognition by Kalecki of the essential role of the length of the time period for his causal attribution, because he goes on to make a statement about the determination of profits when the period of time for equation (4.1) is 'short' – a statement that makes a causal connection between capitalists' investment and consumption decisions taken in the *past* and *current* profits. 'If the period which we consider is short, we may say that the capitalists' investment and consumption are determined by decisions shaped in the *past*. For the execution of investment orders takes a certain time, and capitalists' consumption responds to changes in the factors which influence it only with a certain delay' (p. 79). But if this period is short, then *current* capitalists' expenditures (whether they are fully determined by *past* investment decisions or not) can be said to determine *current* profits, and not the reverse, because there is insufficient time for current profits to influence these values.[4] Such a causal interpretation of equation (4.1) would hold, given that the period of time is short, even if conditions were stationary, because the time lags are operative even though it just so happens that when values are constant over time the effects of these lags are not apparent. Kalecki observed for stationary conditions that 'In such a case profits would remain stationary, and the problem of interpreting [equation (4.1)] would lose its importance' (Kalecki, 1971b). It would be inconsistent with the structure of Kalecki's theory to interpret this statement to mean that the causal explanation for profits provided by equation (4.1) does not hold under stationary conditions. The word 'importance' in Kalecki's statement presumably refers to the point that equation (4.1) can no longer be part of an explanation of the fluctuations in an economy – fluctuations that are excluded under stationary conditions – rather than being a denial of the causal interpretation of that equation under stationary conditions.[5]

Kalecki recognizes that actual investment in a particular period may differ from the investment planned for that period because of mistaken short-term expectations of sales that result in 'unexpected accumulation or running down of stocks' (Kalecki, 1971b). Further, he believes 'that consumption and investment decisions will usually be made in real terms and in the meantime prices may change', so that he writes the profits equation using constant prices for investment and consumption expenditures in order to get a relation between expenditure *decisions* and profits. He thus concludes 'that the real gross profits in a given short period are determined by decisions of capitalists with respect to their consumption and investment shaped in the past, subject to correction for unexpected changes in the volume of stocks' (pp. 79–80). A different statement that points to actual capitalists' expenditures as the determinants of profits would be consistent with Kalecki's if it shares the assumption that current capitalist expenditures are not dependent on current profits, and that all wages are spent. This statement has gross profits in a short period of time being determined by capitalists' expenditures in that period. (Both sides of the equation can be expressed in current prices or they can be deflated by some index of prices.) Since no actual period of time would be characterized by short-period equilibrium, it is necessary to recognize that profits in such a period cannot be fully explained by decisions made in the past. They would also be affected by unanticipated changes in inventories and disequilibrium savings of workers that reflect the incomplete working out of the multiplier.

It may be useful to emphasize again that the explanation of profits in a short period as a result of capitalists' expenditures in that period does not deny the existence of a complex relationship between profits, the expectations of the profitability of investment and the investment decisions that guide future investment expenditures. The concentration on the immediate determinants of current profits in the short period is just the first step in the analysis of a complex reality that evolves over time.

An erroneous interpretation of Kalecki's profit equation

Sawyer provides an interpretation of Kalecki's statement about the loss of 'importance' of the profits equation under stationary conditions that differs from the one given above. He writes that in a stationary 'equilibrium it would not be possible to say which side of equation [(4.1)] determined the other. Indeed in such an equilibrium, equation [(4.1)] is little more than a consistency requirement under the assumption that workers' savings are zero' (Sawyer, 1985, p. 76). There is here a misunderstanding of the nature of equation (4.1), an equation that always holds (when workers' savings are zero) – it is part of a consistency requirement – even though the economy is not stationary. It is only the assumption of time lags in the relations that connect capitalists' expenditures to profits that makes possible a statement of one-way causality from current capitalists' expenditures to current profits. This statement is not dependent on the presence of fluctuations in the economy.

There is also a problem with Sawyer's interpretation of Kalecki's earlier statement quoted above, 'that capitalists may decide to consume and to invest more in a given period than in the preceding one, but that they cannot decide to earn more' (Kalecki, 1971b, pp. 78–9). Sawyer argues that an 'implication of that statement is the view of underlying, if not precise, profit maximization in the sense that Kalecki argued that firms cannot decide to earn more profits. If firms were consciously foregoing profits (say, in the interests of increasing market shares) then even if the opportunities available to the firms did not change, the firms could decide to earn more profits' (Sawyer, 1985, pp. 74–5). This observation reveals a basic misunderstanding of the nature of equation (4.1). It is a macroeconomic equation and it does not reveal anything about microeconomic motives. It shows net effects on total gross profits in the particular period of all spending decisions as they affected capitalists' expenditures in that period (assuming as always that all wages are spent). There is no possibility for firms to have earned more profits under the given conditions of that period, nor is there any implication in Kalecki's statement about the firms' attitudes to profit maximization. Even if, for example, individual firms were charging lower prices than those that would maximize their short-period profits in order to forestall entry into their markets, the total profits earned by all firms would be unaltered by this policy, as long as total capitalists' expenditures remain unchanged. The effect of the lower prices would be to increase real wages and the levels of output and employment. Given capitalists' expenditures in a period, firms as a whole in this situation cannot, contrary to Sawyer's statement, 'decide to earn more profits'.

The distribution of national income

The explanation for the determination of profits that is reflected in equation (4.1) is basic to all of Kalecki's writings on macroeconomics; it is from this point that he goes on to infer the levels of wages, output and employment, given this total of profits. It is the 'distribution factors', among which he includes the 'degree of monopoly' (Kalecki, 1971b, p. 80), that determine the mark-ups on unit prime costs, and thus the level of output that is consistent with the given profits. The term 'distribution factors', as applied to the economy, comprises many complex and diverse forces, with different factors predominating in the determination of the price–wage cost relation in different industries. There are the important differences that Kalecki emphasized between price determination in primary goods industries and in manufactured goods industries. 'Generally speaking, changes in the prices of finished goods are "cost-determined" while changes in the prices of raw materials inclusive of primary foodstuffs are "demand-determined"' (Kalecki, 1971b, p. 43). There are also differences between the situations faced by individual industries in each of these very broad sectors. For example, some manufacturing industries that are more highly concentrated and have higher barriers to entry than others could be in a better position to build higher target rates of profits in their mark-ups and to maintain them in the face of depressed demand. For these industries a given value for profits would be accompanied by lower levels of output in a recession than in industries whose price–cost margins are more easily eroded in cyclical downturns, assuming, for purposes of this comparison, that both groups started with the same profit margin and levels of output. The relation between any level of profits in the economy and its corresponding level of output would thus depend, among other things, on the distribution of total demand between different sectors and industries. One of the 'other things' affecting this relation would be the phase of the business cycle in which the economy finds itself because of the differential effects of fluctuations in demand on the average mark-ups in different industries. A detailed investigation of the forces at work at the industry level would have to be part of any study of changes in profit shares in a particular economy.

Kalecki's explanation of the determination of prices in manufacturing industries leads to a formula (Kalecki, 1971b, p. 53) for the wage share in the manufacturing sector's value added that relates it inversely to the mark-up on unit prime costs and to the ratio of the cost of raw materials to the wage bill (with both of these values being weighted averages of comparable industry values).[6] This wage share is based only on part of labour income, that part which is included in prime costs.

The two broad categories of factor incomes in Kalecki's model are gross profits (including interest, rent and perhaps the salaries 'of higher business executives' (p. 76n.)) and wages and salaries (except for those noted). The firm is assumed to mark-up unit prime costs (see, for instance, Kalecki (1971b, pp. 45–7)) after taking into account the average price in the industry and the strength of 'the various forces which protect the firm's competitive position which Kalecki collected in the term "degree of monopoly"' (Basile and Salvadori, 1984–5, p. 259). In considering the distribution of national income it is implicitly assumed by Kalecki (1971b, p. 62) that aggregate wages are all included in prime costs,[7] and that they are marked up (along with materials costs) in order to arrive at total proceeds. This procedure abstracts from the wages and salaries portion of overhead costs and what Kalecki's analysis can at most provide is, as he recognized in his 1968 trend and business cycle article, 'the relative share of labour prime costs in the national income . . .' (Kalecki, 1971b, p. 168). It can readily be inferred that the presence of wages and salaries in overheads results in pro-cyclical movements in the profit share, even though there are fixed mark-ups on constant unit prime costs (Asimakopulos, 1975, p. 327).[8] Kalecki's 'degree of monopoly', even when it is broadly interpreted (as in the above quotation from Basile and Salvadori) in order to explain the mark-ups in the manufacturing sector, does not determine factor shares. The proportion of total factor income accounted for by overhead wages and salaries depends, in part, on the level of output. Capitalist expenditures that are, as we saw, the determinants of profits in this simplified model thus also have a role in the determination of factor shares through their influence on effective demand and total output.

Profits in an open economy with government expenditure and taxation

Kalecki, in his examination of the determinants of profits, turns from his simplified model to a more general one with international trade, and government taxation and expenditure. The national accounts identity now includes, on the left-hand side, the sum of after-tax gross profits, after-tax wages and salaries, and direct plus indirect taxes, while on the right-hand side there is the sum of gross investment, the export surplus, government expenditures on goods and services, and total consumption expenditures. The equality between these two sides is unaffected if transfer payments are added on one side to workers' incomes and on the other to government expenditures. With workers' incomes (adjusted in this way) and total taxes subtracted from both sides of the equation, we arrive at Kalecki's equation for gross profits net of taxes (P^*) for this case. It can be written as

$$P^* = I + \text{GD} + \text{IS} + C_c - \text{WS} \qquad (4.2)$$

where GD is the government deficit, IS is the export surplus (or net foreign investment on a national accounts basis) and WS is saving by workers.

Equation (4.2) is consistent with that derived for the simplified model, with gross profits after taxes shown as being equal to the sum of gross investment and capitalists' consumption when the government budget and foreign trade are balanced and workers do not save. Starting from the latter form, if capitalists' consumption is subtracted from both sides, we obtain an equality between gross savings and gross investment. (This equality is also implicit in equation (4.2), and it can be shown by subtracting the term GD

+ C_c – WS from both sides of the equation.) Kalecki's comments on this relation reflect some confusion between the necessary (definitional) equality of savings and investment and their equality when the period examined also happens to be characterized by short-period equilibrium. He states that, 'It should be emphasized that the equality between savings and investment plus export surplus plus budget deficit in the general case – or investment alone in the special case – will be valid under all circumstances' (Kalecki, 1971b, p. 83). The phrase 'valid under all circumstances' presumably recognizes that the equality between gross saving and investment must hold even if the period of time considered is not one of short-period equilibrium. But two important elements of a short-period equilibrium situation have already been included by Kalecki in his statement of this equality, so that the particular form he uses is not 'valid under all circumstances'. Firstly, a value of zero for saving by workers is a reflection of their propensity to save, so that their consumption is in the equilibrium relation to income and this source provides no further multiplier effects for any increases in investment that might have occurred. Secondly, it appears that actual investment is equal to planned investment, with no unexpected accumulation or running down of stocks that could lead to further output changes.

Kalecki's final comment in this section that 'investment "finances itself"' (p. 84) is also valid only for a situation of short-period equilibrium. It follows the observation that 'If additional investment is financed by bank credit, the spending of the amounts in question will cause equal amounts of saved profits to accumulate as bank deposits. The investing capitalists will thus find it possible to float bonds to the same extent and thus to repay bank credits'. But, as we saw in explaining the significance of equation (4.1) and in note 3, profits will only increase by the increase in investment *after* the completion of the full multiplier process; it does not occur as soon as the additional investment finance is expended. Kalecki's conclusion from the necessary equality between saving and investment, which is 'valid under all circumstances', that '. . . investment, once carried out, automatically provides the savings necessary to finance it' (Kalecki, 1971b, p. 83) thus appears to confuse this necessary equality with an equilibrium relation.[9] This equality, unless the period is also one of short-period equilibrium, does not provide saving that is available to purchase all the bonds of investing firms. For example, if the increase in investment is equal to the planned increase but the newly hired workers have not yet spent all their wages, so that the full multiplier effects of this increase have not been completed, then the workers' 'disequilibrium' saving is *not* available for the purchase of bonds issued by the investing firms.

Kalecki often emphasized (e.g. Kalecki, 1971b, pp. 80–1) the two 'stages' of his theory of distribution for the simplified model of a closed economy with no government taxation and expenditure. It was only capitalists' expenditures that determined profits while, given this level of profits, the profit margins that firms were able to establish determined output and the profit share. This result has then been taken to be the case for his theory of distribution in general. For example, Joan Robinson stated that in Kalecki's theory of distribution 'we find the very striking proposition that firms, considered as a whole, cannot increase their profits merely by raising prices. Raising profit margins reduces real wages and consequently employment in wage-good industries. The *share* of profit is increased but the total profits remain equal to the flow of capitalists' expenditure' (Robinson, 1980b, p. 192). Insufficient attention has been paid to the general model where higher mark-ups and prices can increase profits, as well as the profit share, by affecting the items other than capitalists' expenditures on the right-hand side of the profits equation (see note 11).

A profits equation for the United States economy, 1950–1985

Kalecki's explanation of the determination of profits can be used to obtain an overall view of developments in a particular economy. This will be illustrated here for the case of the United States economy for the period 1950–85. The discussion above pointed out that, in order for the values on the right-hand side of the profits equation to be considered as part of a causal explanation of current profits, they must be independent of current profits. This means that the unit period of time in this analysis should be short in order to minimize the feedback from profits to capitalists' expenditures. The unit time period in our analysis is a quarter of a year. Investment expenditures in a particular quarter can be reasonably assumed to be independent of profits in that quarter because of the time lag between investment decisions and actual expenditures. The differences between investment expenditures in a quarter and planned expenditures for the quarter that are due to mistaken short-time expectations, with consequent unexpected changes in inventories, do not weaken this independence, because they are not functionally related to current profits. Capitalists' consumption expenditures in a particular quarter are also largely independent of profits in that quarter. These expenditures, as Kalecki observed, have a significant autonomous component, and even the incomes which influence them tend to follow profits by at least one quarter. Dividends are generally paid after profits have been earned, while interest income depends on the terms at which loans were made in earlier periods. The other components of the profits equation – the government deficit, the international surplus and saving by workers – are also largely independent of current profits. This does not mean that there might not be some minor feedback from current profits to these items, e.g. the national accounts' estimates of government revenues might include anticipated or imputed taxes on current profits, but the large causal arrow is from the items on the right-hand side of the equation to profits.

The use of available national accounts data for the profits equation makes it necessary to adapt Kalecki's version of this equation. Capitalists' and workers' consumption expenditures are not listed separately, so that use must be made of total personal expenditure on consumer goods and services. A decision also has to be made on how the net income of unincorporated business should be treated since any breakdown of this total into 'wages' and 'profits' is arbitrary.[10] The choice made here is to restrict the profits term to gross retained earnings P' of the corporate sector with dividends, interest and rent payments to individuals, as well as net income in the incorporated business sector, being included as part of personal income. This revised profits equation can be written as

$$P' = I + GD + IS - PS \qquad (4.3)[11]$$

where PS is total personal saving. Data for all these items can be readily found in the United States national accounts.

The values for the determinants of current profits, shown on the right-hand side of equation (4.3), may be interrelated, and the net effect on profits of a change in one of these values will depend on how this change affects the other items. For example, a given increase in gross investment in a particular quarter will generally increase profits in the quarter by less than this amount, since part of investment expenditures will be directed to imported goods, while the boost to economic activity provided by higher investment will also affect the government deficit and personal saving. Thus while quarter-to-quarter changes in the values for the determinants of profits indicate the contribution of each to the total change in profits, they do not reveal whether, or to what extent, they are the result of independent changes in the parameters affecting these values. Examples of such 'independent' changes would be changes in long-term expectations that guide investment decisions, in the tax-expenditure structure of the government budget, in the international competitiveness of the economy and in the propensity to save. A detailed study of the economy would be needed to trace the reasons for the changes in the values for the determinants of profits. Even at the very broad level of these macroeconomic variables, however, structural changes in the economy will be indicated by comparisons of the relative importance of each of these items as contributors to profits over periods of time that cover more than one cycle. A comparison of quarter-to-quarter changes over each cycle can be used to check for regularities in the cyclical patterns of changes in each of these determinants.

The quarterly data for profits and its determinants examined here have been deflated by the implicit price deflator for gross private domestic fixed investment. Changes in the profits figures (gross retained earnings) thus indicate changes in their purchasing power over items included in private fixed investment.

The average deflated values for profits and its determinants are shown in table 4.1 for each expansionary and contractionary cyclical period in the interval 1950–85. The upward trend in the economy, as well as the effects of governmental stabilization policies and other cyclical changes, have considerably moderated the cyclical declines in profits. The values for gross investment show the expected cyclical pattern, being lower on average during contractionary periods than during the preceding expansionary periods, except for the long cycle from 1961 to 1970, where the

Table 4.1 Average value of deflated data, United States ($billion, 1972 prices), 1950–1985 (deflator: implicit price index for gross private domestic fixed investment)

	P' ($b.1972)	I ($b.1972 (% of P'))		GD ($b.1972 (% of P'))		IS ($b.1972 (% of P'))		PS ($b.1972 (% of P'))	
Cycle 1: 50:1ᵃ→54:2; expansion A, 50:1→53:2; contraction B, 53:3→54:2									
1	58.6	88.8	(151.5)	0.1	(0.2)	−0.6	(−1.0)	26.2	(44.7)
A	58.0	91.2	(157.2)	−4.0	(−6.9)	−0.6	(−1.0)	25.5	(44.0)
B	60.9	79.9	(131.2)	14.4	(23.6)	−0.8	(−1.3)	29.0	(47.6)
Cycle 2: 54:3→58:2; expansion A, 54:3→57:3; contraction B, 57:4→58:2									
2	71.9	97.6	(135.7)	−0.3	(−0.4)	3.2	(4.5)	29.0	(40.3)
A	72.2	100.6	(139.3)	−3.4	(−4.7)	3.2	(4.4)	28.5	(39.5)
B	70.4	84.5	(120.0)	13.1	(18.6)	2.9	(4.1)	30.9	(43.0)
Cycle 3: 58:3→61:1; expansion A, 58:3→60:2; contraction B, 60:3→61:1									
3	80.2	103.3	(128.8)	3.3	(4.1)	1.6	(2.0)	29.7	(37.0)
A	80.2	105.8	(131.9)	3.7	(4.6)	0.0	(0.0)	30.5	(38.0)
B	80.1	96.5	(120.5)	2.3	(2.9)	5.9	(7.4)	27.4	(34.2)
Cycle 4: 61:2→69:4; expansion A, 61:2→69:4; contraction B, 70:1→70:4									
4	110.0	146.1	(132.8)	3.8	(3.5)	4.4	(4.0)	43.5	(39.5)
A	109.6	144.7	(132.0)	3.0	(2.7)	4.5	(4.1)	41.5	(37.9)
B	112.9	158.4	(140.3)	10.5	(9.3)	3.6	(3.2)	61.2	(54.2)

Cycle 5: 71:1→75:1; expansion A, 71:1→73:4; contraction B, 74:1→75:1								
5	132.6	192.9	(145.5)	6.8	(5.1)	1.4	(1.1)	65.6	(49.4)
A	134.2	195.6	(145.8)	4.9	(3.7)	0.1	(0.1)	63.6	(47.4)
B	128.8	186.6	(144.9)	11.3	(8.8)	4.6	(3.6)	70.0	(54.3)
Cycle 6: 75:2→80:3; expansion A, 75:2→80:1; contraction B, 80:2→80:3								
6	164.7	209.3	(127.1)	14.8	(9.0)	−0.2	(−0.1)	58.0	(35.2)
A	163.9	210.2	(128.2)	14.0	(8.5)	−1.0	(−0.6)	58.1	(35.4)
B	172.2	200.6	(116.5)	22.7	(13.2)	8.0	(4.6)	57.5	(33.4)
Cycle 7: 80:4→82:4; expansion A, 80:4→81:3; contraction B, 81:4→82:4								
7	179.3	210.4	(117.3)	31.6	(17.6)	0.1	(0.1)	62.9	(35.1)
A	177.2	223.4	(126.1)	8.4	(4.7)	2.3	(1.3)	57.0	(32.2)
B	181.0	200.0	(110.5)	50.1	(27.7)	−1.7	(−0.9)	67.7	(37.4)
Expansion: 83:1→85:3								
8	231.3	263.7	(114.0)	60.4	(26.1)	−36.0	(−15.6)	59.3	(25.6)

The sum of the determinants may not equal the value for profits because of rounding errors and the omission of the residual error of estimate.

[a] 50:1 refers to the first quarter of 1950, and so on.

Source: See Appendix

trend growth overwhelmed this normal cyclical pattern. Similarly, values for the government deficit generally show the expected cyclical pattern, being larger in the contractionary than in the expansionary periods. There has also been an important structural change in this item – it has grown substantially over this 36-year interval. The cyclical patterns in the values for the international surplus are somewhat less clear, with special factors influencing these values in particular cycles. The large deficit in the final period is well outside the usual range. The cyclical pattern in personal saving is rather erratic, but what is particuarly striking is the relatively low values for this item as a proportion of profits in the latter part of this interval.

This average of the quarterly changes in profits and its determinants, expressed as a percentage of the previous quarter's profits, shown in table 4.2, make it easier to trace out the cyclical patterns in each of these items. In table 4.3 the data for the first seven cycles during our time interval are combined into three periods, each of which begins with an expansion and ends with a contraction. Values for the period 1983–5 are also repeated. This consolidation of data helps make clear the long-term changes in the relative values of these determinants of profits that appear to have taken place. The change in the relative values for personal saving are highlighted in the second part of this table.

Conclusion

Kalecki's causal explanation of the determination of profits is dependent on his recognition of time lags in the investment process that separate investment decisions from investment expenditures, and to time lags in the response of capitalists' consumption expenditures to changes in profits. In order for these time lags to be effective for this purpose, the unit period of time for which profits are to be explained must be relatively short. It is only in such a case that the necessary equality between profits and capitalists' expenditures (in a simplified model of a closed economy with no government expenditure and taxation, and no workers' saving) can be turned into a causal explanation for profits. For a unit time period that is lengthy, capitalists' expenditures in the period would be affected by profits during the period and it would not be possible to attribute one-way causation from current capitalists' expenditures to current profits. In such a case current expenditures and current profits would be mutually determined.

The particular short period being examined need not be one of short-period equilibrium, given the required assumptions about time lags, for this attribution of causality from capitalists' expenditures to profits. This equilibrium is required, however, for the validation of Kalecki's further statement that 'investment "finances itself"', in the sense that he used it, with 'investing capitalists . . . finding it possible to float bonds to the same extent and thus to repay the bank credits' (Kalecki, 1971b, p. 84).

In a more general model of an open economy with government expenditure and taxation that is not restricted to short-period equilibrium, profits in a particular quarter can be said to be determined by investment, the government deficit, the international surplus and (negatively) by personal saving. The attribution of causality requires, as before, that the values of these items in a particular quarter be independent of the current value for profits. The mark-ups that firms manage to obtain on their costs can affect profits in real terms in this model (unlike the situation for the simplified model), even though capitalists' expenditures are fixed in real terms because of their possible effects on other items in the profits equation.

Appendix

The data on our variables for the United States for the period 1950–76 were obtained from *The National Income and Product Accounts of the United States, 1929–76, Statistical Tables*, a supplement of the *Survey of Current Business* (US Department of Commerce, Washington DC, September 1981). For the period 1977–81 they were obtained from *Survey of Current Business*, July 1982, and for 1982 from *Survey of Current Business*, April 1983. For the first three quarters of 1983, they were obtained from the *Survey of Current Business*, for 1983:4 to 1984:4 the March 1985 issue of that publication was used, and the 1985 data were obtained from the November 1985 issue. Data on gross private domestic investment, the total government deficit, the international surplus (or net foreign investment) and personal saving are reported in these sources. The values for gross retained earnings are obtained

Table 4.2 Average values of changes, as a percentage of the previous quarter's value for gross retained earnings ($billion, 1972 prices), United States, 1950–1985)

	P' (% of P'_{-1})	I (% of P'_{-1})	GD (% of P'_{-1})	IS (% of P'_{-1})	PS (% of P'_{-1})
Cycle 1: expansion A; 50:2→53:2; contraction B; 53:3→54:2					
1	1.3	0.5	0.0	0.4	−0.3
A	1.3	1.8	−0.5	0.0	0.3
B	1.4	−3.9	1.7	1.5	−2.1
Cycle 2: expansion A; 54:3→57:3; contraction B; 57:4→58:2					
2	0.6	0.2	0.6	0.1	0.4
A	1.1	2.4	−1.6	0.7	0.7
B	−1.6	−9.6	10.3	−2.6	−0.7
Cycle 3: expansion A; 58:3→60:2; contraction B; 60:3→61:1					
3	1.2	1.9	−1.6	0.6	−0.1
A	0.8	4.5	−4.2	0.2	−0.6
B	−0.3	−5.1	5.4	1.7	1.2
Cycle 4: expansion A; 61:2→69:4; contraction B; 70:1→70:4					
4	0.9	1.7	0.3	−0.1	0.9
A	1.1	2.1	−0.4	−0.1	0.6
B	−0.4	−2.0	6.7	0.0	3.1

Cycle 5: expansion A; 71:1→73:4; contraction B; 74:1→75:1					
5	1.0	-0.2	0.6	0.5	-0.4
A	2.0	4.4	-1.8	0.5	1.1
B	-1.4	-11.4	6.4	0.6	-3.9
Cycle 6: expansion A; 75:2→80:1; contraction B; 80:2→80:3					
6	1.3	1.5	-0.2	-0.1	0.1
A	1.4	2.5	-0.8	-0.5	-0.1
B	0.3	-8.2	5.3	3.8	1.9
Cycle 7: expansion A; 80:4→81:3; contraction B; 81:4→82:4					
7	0.9	-0.8	3.2	-1.2	0.2
A	1.3	5.1	-1.7	-1.5	0.8
B	0.5	-5.6	7.2	-1.0	-0.3
Expansion (83:1→85:3)					
8	3.2	4.3	-0.5	-2.0	-1.0

The sum of the changes in the determinants may not equal the value for the change in profits because of rounding errors and the omission of changes in the residual error of estimate.

Source: See Appendix

Table 4.3 Average values and ratios of profits and their determinants ($ billion, 1972 prices), United States, 1950–1985

Interval		P' ($b.1972)	I ($b.1972 (% of P'))		GD ($b.1972 (% of P'))		IS ($b.1972 (% of P'))		PS ($b.1972 (% of P'))	
I	1950:1→1961:1	68.6	95.5	(139.1)	0.7	(1.0)	1.3	(1.0)	28.1	(41.0)
II	1961:2→1975:1	116.9	160.3	(137.1)	4.7	(4.0)	3.5	(3.0)	50.2	(42.9)
III	1975:2→1982:4	168.9	209.6	(124.1)	19.7	(11.7)	-0.1	(-0.1)	59.4	(35.2)
IV	1983:1→1985:3	231.3	263.7	(114.0)	60.4	(26.1)	-36.0	(-15.6)	59.3	(25.6)

Interval		P'/PS	I/PS	GD/PS	IS/PS
I	1950:1→1961:1	2.44	3.40	0.02	0.05
II	1961:2→1975:1	2.33	3.19	0.09	0.07
III	1975:2→1982:4	2.84	3.53	0.33	0
IV	1983:1→1985:3	3.90	4.45	1.02	-0.61

Source: See Appendix

Table 4.4 Gross retained earnings and their determinants, United States, 1983:1 to 1985:3, ($billion, 1972 prices)

Date	P'	I (% of P')	GD (% of P')	IS (% of P')	PS (% of P')
1983:1	193.4	187.8 (97.1)	70.4 (36.4)	-1.9 (-1.0)	59.4 (30.7)
1983:2	205.9	209.7 (101.8)	57.6 (28.0)	-14.4 (-7.0)	45.1 (21.9)
1983:3	217.5	227.7 (104.7)	61.8 (28.4)	-19.2 (-8.8)	55.1 (25.3)
1983:4	223.4	248.0 (111.0)	59.4 (26.6)	-27.1 (-12.1)	59.1 (26.5)
1984:1	230.3	288.0 (125.1)	49.6 (21.5)	-35.9 (-15.6)	70.4 (30.6)
1984:2	235.7	286.8 (121.7)	50.0 (21.2)	-38.9 (-16.5)	66.2 (28.1)
1984:3	239.6	302.4 (126.2)	60.7 (25.3)	-54.5 (-22.7)	74.9 (31.3)
1984:4	243.8	289.8 (118.9)	64.3 (26.4)	-41.6 (-17.1)	74.1 (30.4)
1985:1	244.7	291.2 (119.0)	50.2 (20.5)	-47.1 (-19.2)	53.4 (21.8)
1985:2	250.4	289.2 (115.5)	73.7 (29.4)	-55.9 (-22.3)	62.7 (25.0)
1985:3	259.7	280.7 (108.1)	67.3 (25.9)	-59.3 (-22.8)	32.8 (12.6)

The use of the values for I, GD, IS and PS in equation (4.3) does not lead to the precise value for P', because of residual errors of estimate in the national accounts.

by taking the sum of undistributed profits with inventory valuation and capital consumption adjustments, and capital consumption allowances. The quarterly data for the items in equation (4.3) are reported in Asimakopulos (1983a), while those for 1983:1 to 1985:3 are presented in table 4.4.

Notes

1 It is pointed out below that the implications of Kalecki's profits equation are misunderstood by Sawyer (1985).
2 This was the only model in his 1933 study of the business cycle (Kalecki, 1971b, chapter 1) and it also appeared in his consideration of the determinants of profits in Kalecki (1942) that comprised the first part of chapter 3 of Kalecki (1954), and which was later incorporated into chapter 7 of Kalecki (1971b).
3 This appears to have been forgotten by Kalecki in his 1937 article on taxation when he used an extended form of equation (4.1) to investigate the effects of an increase in the tax T_i on capitalists' incomes, with the resulting tax revenue being used to increase payments to the unemployed which are then spent on commodities. He concluded that '. . . the immediate result of an increased income tax is a rise of gross profit . . . the gross profit is greater by the amount of the increment of T_i.' (Kalecki, 1971b, p. 39). This conclusion is incorrect. The 'immediate result' of the increased tax and the increased expenditures of the unemployed will only increase profits by the profit margins on the goods purchased. It is the resulting increase in output of consumption goods, the hiring of more workers, their increased consumption expenditures etc. that eventually leads to the increase in profits equal to the increase of taxation on capitalists' incomes. Kalecki's analysis of the incidence of taxation is based on the comparison of situations of short-period equilibrium and there is nothing in the analysis that allows an estimate of the time required to move from one position of short-period equilibrium to the other.
4 If the analysis assumes that capitalists' consumption is a function of current profits, as in Kalecki's 1933 study of the business cycle, then profits can be said to be determined in short-period equilibrium (with the workers' propensity to save equal to zero) by the sum of investment expenditures and the autonomous component of capitalists' consumption, multiplied by the reciprocal of the capitalists' marginal propensity to save.
5 A position similar to the one adopted here is expressed by Kahn in

his consideration of equilibrium growth paths. He notes that 'high profits are caused by high investment – purely as a current phenomenon' while he recognizes that when dealing with 'the expectation of capitalists' income . . . the causation is the other way round: high investment is caused by high profits . . . with equilibrium growth the future is like the present. But although the rate of profit is the same viewed in current terms as in terms of expectations, the nature of causation is still important' (Kahn, 1959, pp. 203–4).

6 Kalecki does not attempt an explanation of factor distribution in the primary goods sector other than to observe that the price–wage cost ratio moves cyclically.

7 This is at variance with the recognition in his 1933 study of the business cycle 'that a part of wages are overheads' (Kalecki, 1971b, p. 11n.).

8 Kalecki (1971b, pp. 74–7) also argues that the relative share of wages and salaries in total income would move contra-cyclically. He provides a regression equation for the United States economy for the period 1929–41 that displays this feature.

9 In Asimakopulos (1983b, pp. 224–5) it is pointed out that Kalecki in his discussion of finance (Kalecki, 1935b) implicitly assumed that short-period equilibrium was established within a year of an increase in investment.

10 Kalecki included in the concept of gross profits of his model 'withdrawals from unincorporated business' (Kalecki, 1971b, p. 78), but how these withdrawals can be estimated from available data is not clear. They include, in any case, a significant wages and salaries portion.

11 One of the differences between the more general models for which equations (4.2) and (4.3) are valid and the simplified model of equation (4.1) as noted above is that in the latter total profits, given the values for capitalists' expenditures, are independent of the values for the mark-ups, while this is not the case for the former (Asimakopulos, 1975, p. 332). For example, higher mark-ups in the more general models would tend to increase profits, even though capitalists' expenditures in real terms are unchanged, because the consequent lower real wages, output and employment could lead to higher government deficits and lower personal saving that more than outweigh any adverse effects of higher domestic prices on the international surplus. There is no reason to expect that the difference in the values for the separate items in equation (4.3) would just balance out so that, with capitalists' expenditures in real terms unchanged, profits would be unaffected by the difference in mark-ups.

5

Keynes's Theory of Effective Demand Revisited

The aggregate supply and demand functions presented by Keynes in chapter 3 of *The General Theory of Employment, Interest and Money* in order to define effective demand have continued to draw comment, criticism and suggested reinterpretation.[1] A definitive interpretation of, and commentary on, these concepts is made difficult by inconsistencies and errors in the way Keynes presented them. They make the task of unravelling what Keynes 'really' meant more difficult but, with the *Collected Writings* of Keynes now available, it is possible to trace out a consistent theory of effective demand. The key pieces fit together once it is recognized that Keynes accepted implicitly Marshall's microeconomics and that they provided the foundations for his aggregate supply function. Most of the errors that Keynes made in the first six chapters of *The General Theory* then appear as the almost inevitable result of charting new territory and grappling with unfamiliar aggregate concepts.

This chapter was written after many discussions on this topic with my colleague J. C. Weldon. Their effect on my perceptions of the issues involved were such that it is very difficult to disentangle 'prior claims' for the ideas in this chapter. In any case, Weldon first expressed in 1975 the point that Keynes's definition of the aggregate demand function on page 25 of *The General Theory* has no basis in Keynes's model. I am, of course, alone responsible for the writing of this chapter and any errors that it might contain. I also gratefully acknowledge comments on an earlier draft from G. Caravelis, D. Patinkin, J. Robinson and L. Tarshis and absolve them of any responsibility for any errors, and the interpretation of writings, in this chapter.

Keynes occasionally forgot that employment decisions are taken by competitive entrepreneurs whose expectations concern conditions in their particular markets – conditions that cannot be affected by their individual actions. His first definition of the aggregate demand function (Keynes, 1936, p. 25) is based on the erroneous assumption that the individual entrepreneurs consider that the demand they face is affected by the employment they offer. A similar confusion, between an aggregate function that is based on aggregation over a set of independent individual decisions and one that would be obtained if there was only a single giant firm in the economy, may explain the errors in the 'mysterious' footnote on page 55 of *The General Theory*, dealing with the aggregate supply function, to which Patinkin (1978, 1979) has drawn attention.

In this presentation of Keynes's theory of effective demand, the Marshallian microfoundations of his theory are respected, as are the guidelines Keynes set for himself.[2] For this reason, aggregate values are expressed only in Keynes's 'two fundamental units of value, namely, quantities of money-value and quantities of employment' (Keynes, 1936, p. 41). None of Keynes's conclusions about the factors determining the level of employment are affected by the clearing away of errors and inconsistencies in his presentation of the theory of effective demand. Whether these conclusions are useful for policy purposes is, of course, another question, and one that is not considered here.

Effective demand redefined

In Keynes's model the decisions to produce which are made by individual entrepreneurs have to be based on expectations because of the lapse of time 'between the incurring of costs by the producer (with the consumer in view) and the purchase of the output by the ultimate consumer' (Keynes, 1936, p. 46). The rates of output and employment[3] in any interval were thus said to be determined by 'short-term expectations' concerned 'with the price which a manufacturer can expect to get for his "finished" output at the time when he commits himself to starting the process which will produce it' (p. 46). Keynes insisted on the primary role of these expectations in determining employment. Each individual firm was seen as 'deciding its daily output . . . by its . . . expectations as to the cost of output on various possible scales and expectations as to the sale-proceeds of this output . . . It is upon these various expectations that the amount of employment which the firms offer will depend' (p. 47).[4] The expected 'sale-proceeds of this output' referred to by Keynes is the product of the expected price and the output at which the firm's marginal cost is equal to this expected price.

What Keynes's microfoundations thus provide him with is a relation, derived from the assumption of profit maximization for a competitive firm, between this firm's rate of output (or employment) and the expected proceeds that give rise to that output (employment). He tried to extend this relation to explain the determination of employment in the economy as a whole by means of two aggregate schedules. Keynes defined the aggregate supply price of the output of a given amount of employment as 'the expectations of proceeds which will just make it worth the while of the entrepreneurs to give that employment' (Keynes, 1936, p. 24). The aggregate supply function then shows the relationship between this aggregate supply price and employment. In an analogous fashion Keynes wrote for his second aggregate schedule 'Similarly, let D be the proceeds which entrepreneurs expect to receive from the employment of N men, the relationship between D and N . . . can be called the *Aggregate Demand Function*' (p. 25). With these functions he defined *effective demand* as 'The value of D at the point of the aggregate demand function, where it is intersected by the aggregate supply function . . .' (p. 25). This definition, however, must be restated because there is no basis in the microfoundations of Keynes's theory for this version of the aggregate demand function.[5]

Keynes's competitive entrepreneurs determine output given 'expected prices' for their output, but these expected prices are independent of their own rates of output (and employment). There is thus no individual schedule relating expected proceeds to employment offered to be used for aggregation into an aggregate demand function. Given his expected price and the corresponding output on his short-period supply curve, each entrepreneur has a single value for expected proceeds (the product of price and this short-period equilibrium output).[6] The addition of these expected proceeds (deducting user costs) determines a single point on the aggregate supply schedule, not a separate schedule.[7] Keynes's definition of effective demand should thus be altered to: *effective demand is the point on the aggregate supply function corresponding to the expectations of proceeds held by entrepreneurs.* It is these expected proceeds, as Keynes emphasized in his 1937 lecture notes, that determine output and employment.[8] The realized results, or income,[9] 'are only relevant in so far as they influence the ensuing expectations in the next production period' (Keynes, 1973b, p. 180).

The inadmissibility of Keynes's definition of effective demand because of the non-existence in his model of the 'expectational' aggregate demand function he uses has been generally overlooked in the voluminous literature on Keynes's theory.[10] One reason for this could be that there are two quite different aggregate demand functions presented in chapter 3 of *The General Theory*, with the second version having a legitimate place in the theory. This second version is based on the propensity to consume in the economy and the level of investment. It shows the equilibrium relation between consumption and income (employment) plus the volume of investment in the particular period. The existence of these two different functions was pointed out by Sir Dennis Robertson in 1936, but he did not go on to point out that the 'expectational' aggregate demand function has no basis in Keynes's model.[11]

Keynes's error in his definition of effective demand might be due to his being misled by his new terminology when grappling with the unfamiliar aggregate concepts he had constructed. Once a demand schedule, even if it is labelled 'aggregate', is specified, old habits of thought might tend to associate it with the schedule facing a single entrepreneur. Keynes makes such an error in chapter 7 of *The General Theory*, when he discusses some of the differences between his approaches to saving and investment in that book and in his *Treatise on Money*: 'As I now think, the volume of employment (and consequently of output and real income) is fixed by the entrepreneur under the motive of seeking to maximise his present and prospective profits (the allowance for user cost being determined by his view as to the use of equipment which will maximise his return from it over its whole life); whilst the volume of employment which will maximise his profit depends on the aggregate demand function given by his expectations of the sum of the proceeds resulting from consumption and investment respectively on various hypotheses' (p. 77). This is, of course, incorrect. In Keynes's model the entrepreneurs determine output (that maximizes expected profits) acting on expected prices, which are independent of their individual rates of output, and not by calculation from an aggregate demand function. The nature of Keynes's analysis would be very different if the economy had only a single firm. There would then be a basis in the model's microfoundations for Keynes's 'expectational' aggregate demand function, but no longer for the aggregate supply function.

The derivation of the aggregate supply function

Keynes's aggregate supply function is a construct derived, after several stages and special assumptions, from the individual supply curves of competitive firms. Keynes took much for granted in presenting this function; he felt that 'The aggregate supply function . . . which depends in the main on the physical conditions of supply, involves few considerations which are not already familiar. The form may be unfamiliar but the underlying factors are not new' (Keynes, 1936, p. 89). Although its foundations, the individual competitive supply curves, are very familiar, the aggregate function itself is not, as is evidenced by the confusion surrounding it in the literature and even by Keynes's occasional errors in reference to it. A careful derivation of this function, making clear its Marshallian microfoundations, is thus not out of place.

Keynes notes that in the short-period situation ('In a given state of technique, resources and costs' (Keynes, 1936, p. 23)) in which he places his analysis, an entrepreneur incurs two kinds of expenses in producing goods. There is 'first of all, the amounts which he pays out to the factors of production (exclusive of other entreprene-urs) for their current services, which we shall call the factor cost of the employment in question [i.e., the employment required to produce the goods in question] and secondly . . . the user cost of the employment in question. The excess of the value of the resulting output over the sum of its factor cost and its user cost is the profit or, as we shall call it, the *income* of the entrepreneur . . . the factor cost and the entrepreneur's profit make up between them, what we shall define as the *total income* resulting from the employment given by the entrepreneur' (p. 23). Keynes then notes that in his analysis 'It is sometimes convenient, when we are looking at it from the entrepreneur's standpoint, to call the aggregate income (i.e., factor cost *plus* profit) resulting from a given amount of employment the *proceeds* of that employment' (p. 24). He goes on immediately to define aggregate supply price in such a way that it can be used to indicate (when the entrepreneurs' short-term expectations are fulfilled) the level of income in the economy. User costs must be excluded from aggregate supply price for this purpose even though Keynes emphasizes that 'the exclusion of user cost from supply price . . . is inappropriate to the problems of the supply price of a unit of output for an individual firm' (p. 55, n.1).[12]

This exclusion of user cost from the aggregate supply price should not obscure the crucial dependence of Keynes's aggregate supply function on the supply curves of individual firms and industries. In commenting on criticisms made by Sir Dennis Robertson on a draft of *The General Theory* Keynes noted that the aggregate supply function '. . . is simply the age-old supply function . . . it is only a re-concoction of our old friend the supply function' (Keynes, 1973a, p. 513). This Marshallian underpinning is even reflected in Keynes's choice of words for the definition of aggregate supply price. He writes 'the aggregate supply price of the output of a given amount of employment is the expectation of proceeds which will just make it worth the while of the entrepreneurs to give that employment' (Keynes, 1936, p. 24). This echoes Marshall's definition of the supply price for a particular commodity, 'the normal supply price of any amount of that commodity . . . is the price the expectation of which will just suffice to maintain the existing aggregate amount of production' (Marshall, 1920, pp. 342–3). For Keynes, as well as for Marshall, the 'expectation' that is controlling the situation is an expectation of price that is held by individual entrepreneurs deciding on their individual rates of output (and employment). Where Marshall limited his aggregation to an industry and thus to an industry supply curve, Keynes went on to define an aggregate supply curve for the economy.

The aggregates Keynes needs to explain the determination of the level of employment in the economy require him to convert an expected commodity price ('which will just suffice to maintain the existing aggregate amount of production') into expected sale proceeds. With this transformation, obtained by multiplying the Marshallian supply price by the corresponding quantity and by calculating the amount of employment required to produce the specified quantity of output, Keynes can obtain flows for each industry that he can sum across industries to obtain aggregates for the economy. Even though industries produce different products, and Keynes eschews any measure of real total output, the above calculations result in identical values for each industry (e.g. dollars per week in, say, a specific year) and a measure of employment in the same units for each industry (e.g. man-hours of unskilled labour per week in the same year).

This way of moving from the expected supply price for an individual commodity to the gross proceeds used to construct Keynes's aggregate supply function is illustrated in figure 5.1. In panel A of the figure, we have a Marshallian short-period supply (SPS) curve for the industry producing good X. It shows the relationship between alternative values for expected prices and the amounts the firms in that industry would produce in the particular short period. The products of the price and output pairs on the industry supply curve give us the total sales proceeds, the expectation of which will just make it worthwhile to produce each specified rate of output. Each output rate is associated with a particular rate of employment and thus in panel B of figure 5.1

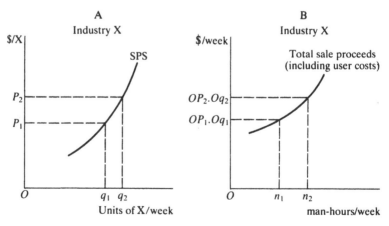

Figure 5.1 A, industry supply curve; B, industry total sale proceeds

we can show the relationship between the expected sale proceeds and the level of employment offered in that industry. Once user costs are subtracted from these total sale proceeds we arrive at this industry's aggregate proceeds function that will be an element in Keynes's aggregate supply function. It is clear from this derivation that the basis of the industry total proceeds curve is the industry (and thus the individual firm) supply curve. *The rate of output to be produced, and the employment to be offered in a given short-period situation is determined by the individual entrepreneurial expectations of price.* The various transformations required to arrive at Keynes's aggregate supply function should not obscure the fact that underlying it are a very large number of individual conceptual experiments – how much would be produced (employment provided) by the individual firms in the economy in the specific short period for alternative values of expected prices for their products?

The aggregate supply curve depends on the way the total proceeds curves for each industry are combined to form it. Keynes made brief references to this problem. The first was in a footnote on page 43 of *The General Theory* where he referred to the possibility of assuming 'that a given volume of effective demand has a particular distribution of this demand between different products uniquely associated with it'.[13] This means that in constructing the aggregate supply curve we can begin with an assumed value for the proceeds of a particular industry and then, by using the fixed proportions contributed by each industry to the total, we can obtain proceeds for each of the other industries and aggregate proceeds. (These amounts imply a particular set of expected prices for the products of these industries.) We can then sum the employment values corresponding to each of these industry proceeds to find the level of employment corresponding to each assumed value for expected aggregate proceeds. The proportion of employment contributed by each industry to total employment need not be the same at each assumed value for expected aggregate proceeds because of the differences in the industry proceeds curves.

Another procedure for going from the industry to the aggregate proceeds curve, one which kept constant the proportion of total employment rather than the proportion of total proceeds for each industry, was mentioned by Keynes on page 45 of *The General*

Theory. The aggregation here would begin with an assumed value for employment in a particular industry, and given the assumed fixed proportion of employment among industries, each industry's employment level as well as total employment would be derived. Each industry's level of employment is based on a particular value for its expected proceeds (each value would correspond to a particular expected price) and the summation of these values would provide the aggregate proceeds, the expectation of which would result in the derived level of total employment.

Two other possible rules for deriving aggregate supply curves also deserve mention. Relative expected prices for the different industry outputs may be assumed to remain constant along an aggregate supply curve. The aggregation here would proceed by first assuming a particular value for an individual price and then calculating, given the constant ratio of prices, the corresponding expected proceeds and employment for each industry.' The summation of these proceeds would be paired with the summation of the corresponding employment levels to obtain the coordinates for points on the aggregate supply curve. Finally, relative quantities produced of each commodity may be assumed to be constant at all points on an aggregate supply curve. The aggregation here would begin by first assuming a particular level of output in one industry, and then the expected prices and proceeds required to result in the assumed values of output for each industry could be obtained. The total employment required to produce these outputs could also be calculated, and it would be paired with the summation of the industry proceeds to obtain a point on the aggregate supply curve.

Each of the four methods of aggregation sketched here leads, for the same cost conditions, to different aggregate supply functions. Their purpose is to show some of the ways in which one can proceed conceptually *from the individual curves on which decisions are made to the aggregate curves used to summarize some aspects of these decision processes.* Keynes did not commit himself to any single method. He mentioned two methods to illustrate particular points, and he noted immediately that the first 'would not hold good irrespective of the particular cause of the change in demand' (Keynes, 1936, 43n.). He pointed out that this problem 'belongs to the detailed analysis of the general ideas here set forth, which it is no part of my immediate purpose to pursue'. This statement is consistent with the interpretation of the aggregate supply function presented here, in that it is a vehicle for portraying 'general ideas'.

An aggregate supply curve, specified in the units indicated by Keynes in his text (money values and units of employment), is drawn in figure 5.2. On the ordinate are measured the expected 'proceeds which will just make it worth the while of the entrepreneurs to give that employment' (Keynes, 1936, p. 24). They include all the elements, other than user costs, to be found in industry supply curves, i.e. labour, other factor costs and profits. We have seen from the steps leading to the derivation of the aggregate supply curve that the level of employment corresponding to a particular value for expected proceeds is that level which maximizes profits for competitive firms given these entrepreneurial expectations about demand conditions. Therefore Keynes's statement that at the point of effective demand 'the entrepreneurs' expectation of profits will be maximised' (Keynes, 1936, p. 25) is valid and unaffected by the change we have had to make in his definition of effective demand.[14]

The aggregate supply curve must obviously be upward-sloping, and its shape reflects what happens to labour's share in total

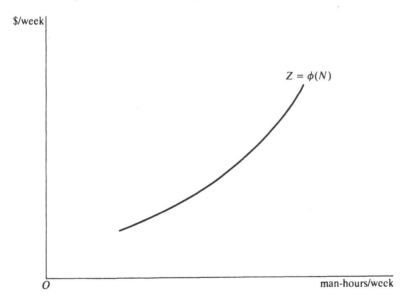

Figure 5.2 An aggregate supply curve

income at different levels of employment. The relation between the elasticity of the aggregate supply curve and the labour share in total income when employment is increased is derived in the Appendix. It is shown that this elasticity value is less than unity, unity or greater than unity as the labour share is decreased, constant or increased, respectively, when employment is higher.[15] The aggregate supply curve is generally drawn to be convex, as in figure 5.2, and certainly it must become convex at least after some point, as marginal costs increase sharply and much higher prices are required to bring forth increased output (and employment) thus lowering labour's income share.

There is one reference to the aggregate supply function in *The General Theory*, in footnote 2 on page 55, that is inconsistent with the above presentation. In this footnote, Keynes concludes that 'if wages are constant and other factor costs are a constant proportion of the wages-bill, the aggregate supply function is linear with a slope given by the reciprocal of the money-wage'. Keynes here makes two mistakes concerning his construction. He forgets that profits as well as labour and other factor costs are included in the aggregate supply price. But even if profits are excluded and 'other factor costs are a constant proportion of the wages bill', the aggregate supply function although linear would have an elasticity value of unity, and its slope (for non-zero other factor costs) would not equal the reciprocal of the money wage. For Keynes's conclusion it is necessary that 'other factor costs' as well as profits be excluded from the aggregate supply price. In the latter case the aggregate supply curve would be identical with the ray OW in figure 5.5 (see Appendix), i.e. 'the constant proportion of the wages-bill' referred to would be equal to zero.[16]

Keynes's error here might be due, as in the case of his 'expectational' aggregate demand function, to treating the aggregate schedule not as the artificially constructed schedule it is but as a curve for a single (giant) firm.[17] In the paragraph to which this footnote is appended, he drew a misleading analogy to the cost curve for an individual firm '. . . we can equate the marginal proceeds (or income) to the marginal factor cost; and thus arrive at the same sort of propositions relating marginal proceeds thus defined to marginal factor costs as have been stated by those economists who, by ignoring user cost or assuming it to be zero, have equated supply price to marginal factor cost' (Keynes, 1936,

p. 55). But the aggregate supply function is *not* a cost curve for a single entrepreneur maximizing profits on the basis of that curve. The marginal (aggregate) proceeds – the expectation of which is required to justify offering one more unit of employment – always contain a profits component. In order to obtain higher employment, expected product prices on which actual employment decisions are made must be higher and the resulting expected proceeds include higher profits.

The significance of the aggregate supply function

Running through our derivation and discussion of the aggregate supply function has been the persistent theme that, in Keynes's model, employment is the result of decisions made by individual entrepreneurs on the basis of expected prices for their individual products, given their short-period supply curves (marginal costs). For example, in figure 5.3 it is assumed that the set of expected

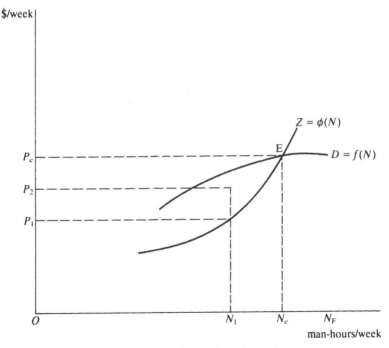

Figure 5.3 Aggregate demand and supply curves

prices, given the individual short-period supply curves at a point in time, result in expected aggregate proceeds P_1. This is the effective demand in that situation and N_1 is the level of employment.

The actual results may differ from these expectations but they will only be relevant for employment, according to Keynes, if they change expectations in subsequent production periods. In the example illustrated in figure 5.3 it is assumed that actual proceeds turned out to be P_2 when employment was N_1. Prices received by firms turned out to be higher than expected.[18] If these realized results lead to higher expected prices, then effective demand in subsequent production periods would be higher and employment would be increased. (This story could obviously be reversed if actual proceeds were lower than expected proceeds.)

An aggregate demand function reflecting the desired or equilibrium relation between consumption and income, plus the particular short period's rate of investment, is also drawn in figure 5.3.[19] (The money wage rate and other factor costs assumed in deriving the aggregate supply curve in that figure are also used for this aggregate demand function.) The realized proceeds need not lie on this aggregate demand function because of the time required for the equilibrium relation between consumption and income to be established after there have been disturbances. For example, figure 5.3 may be depicting a situation where investment has increased over its previous levels and the multiplier process is still working itself out; thus the value P_2 for the realized proceeds lies below the equilibrium aggregate demand function.[20] Whether the realized proceeds, let alone the entrepreneurs' expectations and chosen level of employment, will coincide with a point on the equilibrium aggregate demand function depends on the length of time for which the values of the factors determining the position of that function are constant. The intersection of the aggregate supply curve and the equilibrium aggregate demand function, however, was given special attention by Keynes.[21] The corresponding level of employment N_e was called 'the volume of employment in equilibrium' (Keynes, 1936, p. 29), and Keynes's summary of his theory on pages 28–32 of *The General Theory* was concerned with the factors determining it.[22]

If the realized results lie along the equilibrium aggregate demand function (a very special assumption), then the expectations of proceeds P_e and the offer of employment N_e will lead to the satisfaction of these short-term expectations. Given the fundamental factors determining this level of employment and the aggregate supply function (i.e. the capital equipment, the money wage rate and other factor prices, the propensity to consume and the volume of investment), there will be no tendency for the entrepreneurs to change the level of employment. Higher or lower values for the propensity to consume and the volume of investment will result, subject to a full-employment constraint (to be defined, along with 'involuntary unemployment', in the following section), in higher or lower values for the equilibrium level of employment. It was the large number of such 'possible positions of equilibrium',[23] marked by involuntary unemployment, which Keynes used to justify the use of the prefix *general* for his theory (Keynes, 1936, p. 3).

Definitions of involuntary unemployment and full employment

There is no separate independent demand curve for labour in Keynes's model[24] since the employment of labour (along with other factors) is determined given the expected prices and the industry short-period supply curves. An important implication of Keynes's assumption that short-period supply curves are rising ('that industry is normally working subject to decreasing returns in the short period during which equipment, *etc.* is assumed to be constant' (Keynes, 1936, p. 17)) is that higher employment is accompanied by lower real wage rates. But this inverse relationship to which Keynes drew attention should not be confused with a labour demand curve, even when it is drawn in a suggestive diagram as in figure 5.4.[25] There is no labour market in Keynes's model in which labour demand and labour supply curves interact to determine the equilibrium level of employment and the real wage rate. All that is set in his labour markets – in which there may be collective bargaining – are money wage rates, with real wages then depending on the prices determined in commodity markets by conditions of demand and supply.

This inverse relationship between the level of employment and the real wage rate can be deduced from the equality between price and marginal cost. In the short period equilibrium for the wage-good industry we have $P_w \equiv MC_w \equiv (w\Delta N_w + \Delta OPC_w)/\Delta Q_w$ where P_w and MC_w represent price and marginal cost respectively in the wage-good industry and w, ΔN_w and ΔOPC_w are the money wage rate, the increase in labour employed and other prime costs (other factor and user costs)[26] required to produce the increment in output ΔQ_w. Rearranging this expression we derive $w/P_w \equiv \Delta Q_w/\Delta N_w - \Delta OPC_w/P_w\Delta N_w$. The real wage rate is thus equal to the short-period marginal product of labour in the wage-goods industry minus the ratio of marginal other prime costs to the product of the price of the wage good and the increase in employment.[27] Keynes's assumption of decreasing returns in the short period means that the short-period marginal product of labour is decreasing, and therefore higher employment in the wage-goods industry must be accompanied by a lower real wage unless diminishing returns are offset by a sufficient decline in the other prime costs. This result also holds for other industries given the ratios of their prices relative to the price of wage goods.[28]

The inverse relation between the level of total employment and the real wage rate is derived once the rule, e.g. the ratios of expected prices are constant, for moving from the individual industry to the summary aggregate supply function is specified. This inverse relation is shown in figure 5.4. In that figure there is also a labour supply curve ($N_s = S(w/P_w)$). Keynes assumed that the labour supply to any sector is a function of the real wage rate as well as of relative money wage rates (Trevithick, 1976). The upward-sloping curve in figure 5.4 assumes that relative wages are kept constant as real wage rates are altered by changing prices relative to money wages.

If effective demand results in an employment level smaller than N_F, say N_e, then according to Keynes's definition there is involuntary unemployment. 'Men are involuntarily unemployed if, in the event of a small rise in the price of wage-goods relatively to the money-wage, both the aggregate supply of labour willing to work for the current money-wage and the aggregate demand for it at that wage would be greater than the existing volume of employment' (Keynes, 1936, p. 15). A higher expected price for wage goods with a constant money wage rate means, as we have seen from the construction of the aggregate supply curve, that output and employment offered would be higher, while the

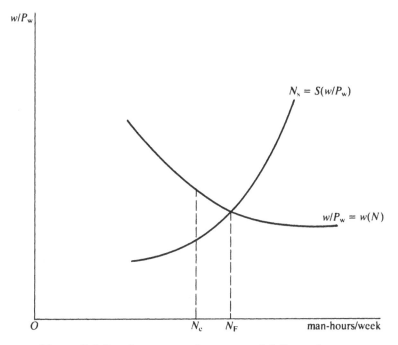

Figure 5.4 Involuntary employment and full employment

N_s curve in figure 5.4 shows that the supply of labour would still be greater than N_e.

The point N_F represents, according to Keynes's (1936, p. 26) definition, full employment: 'a situation in which aggregate employment is inelastic in response to an increase in the effective demand for its output'. An increase in effective demand – a higher point on the aggregate supply function, with price expectations borne out by events – is accompanied by a lower real wage rate. But if the initial level of employment in figure 5.4 is N_F, labour is not available at the new terms to increase output. In Keynes's model there is nothing to require that effective demand – even effective demand in a position of short-period equilibrium with firms on their supply curves[29] – be such as to result in full employment.

The aggregate supply curves drawn by Patinkin (1978, 1979) have vertical portions at the 'full-employment' levels of employment to indicate the maximum possible levels of employment in the particular situations. The drawing of these curves in this way may be misleading since the aggregate supply function is derived, as we have seen, from the industry short-period supply curves. The latter show the outputs firms would choose to produce, given alternative values for their expectations of prices and their productive capacity, without any reference to possible constraints on output due to shortages of labour or other variable inputs. These constraints would only be operative, in any case, in response to actual prices – or to prices expected by workers – and not to the prices expected by firms which govern the aggregate supply function. The value for full employment may be placed in diagrams with aggregate demand and supply functions, e.g. point N_F in figure 5.3, to indicate the full-employment position beyond which a higher level of aggregate employment cannot be maintained in response to an increase in effective demand. Such points, of course, do not affect the shapes of the aggregate supply curves.

The stability of the short-period equilibrium level of employment

Keynes (1936, p. 28) argued that in a particular short period 'given the propensity to consume and the rate of new investment', there will be only one level of employment consistent with equilibrium'. This short-period equilibrium level of employment would be N_e in figure 5.3. It is stable in that, if entrepreneurs employed more men than N_e in the expectations of proceeds higher than those shown by point E, their expectations would be disappointed and they would subsequently revise their expectations downwards. Similarly, if their expected proceeds were less than those at point E and they provided less employment than N_e, the resulting proceeds would be greater than those expected. These higher prices would lead them to increase their expectations of proceeds and the employment offered.

The involuntary unemployment that would exist if equilibrium were at N_e might result in some reduction in money wage rates. Such a reduction would shift the aggregate supply curve to the right (since the industry supply curves would be shifted to the right) and shift the aggregate demand curve downward because money incomes at any level of employment would be lower. This double movement may leave the equilibrium level of employment unchanged, but the full analysis of the effects of falling money wage rates requires consideration of its effects on the distribution of incomes, on long-term expectations and the volume of investment. Keynes's discussion of the possible effects of falling money wage rates in chapter 19 of *The General Theory* did not lead him to conclude that this was a practical method for eliminating involuntary unemployment. Critical to his conclusion is the relation between desired investment and saving. He argued that falling money wage rates, even though they might lead initially to higher output, would not be a reliable method for maintaining a higher level of employment because planned investment might not increase to cover the difference between the increase in output and the desired increase in consumption.

In contrast with his theory, Keynes (1936, p. 26) claims that 'The classical theory assumes . . . that the aggregate demand price (or proceeds) always accommodates itself to the aggregate supply price; or that, whatever the value of N may be, the proceeds D assume a value equal to the aggregate supply price Z which corresponds to N. That is to say, effective demand, instead of having a unique equilibrium value, is an infinite range of values all equally admissible; and the amount of employment is indeterminate except in so far as the marginal disutility of labour sets an upper limit. If this were true, competition between entrepreneurs would always lead to an expansion of employment up to the point at which the supply of output as a whole ceases to be elastic, *i.e.*, where a further increase in the value of effective demand will no longer be accompanied by any increase in output'. Keynes did not explain how, under these conditions, the force of 'competition between entrepreneurs' would lead to full employment.

It is not clear that, within the Marshallian framework of Keynes's analysis, this 'force of competition' would lead to full employment. The competition between entrepreneurs is fully reflected by the assumption that they are 'price takers'. If, at the set of expected prices, less than full employment is offered and with this employment realized proceeds are equal to expected proceeds, this would be an equilibrium level of employment with no tendency for this position to change. Keynes's statement about 'an expansion of employment up to the point' of full employment must be based not on 'competition between entrepreneurs' but on lower money wage rates due to competition among unemployed workers.[30] Lower money wage rates mean that individual marginal cost curves, and thus industry supply curves, are shifted downward and to the right. If expected product prices are unchanged then entrepreneurs would want to increase output and employment. With the aggregate demand accommodating itself to the aggregate supply price, their expectations would be fulfilled and the higher employment would be validated.[31] This contrasts with Keynes's theory where the two curves are distinct and the expectations of proceeds greater than those that result in the short-period equilibrium level of employment would be disappointed.

Conclusions

This restatement of Keynes's theory of effective demand has observed all the conventions of the Marshallian microfoundations on which this theory is based. From this perspective it is clear that some errors crept into the working out and explanation of his theory by Keynes. They can be seen as arising because of his pioneer work with aggregate concepts, and at times his analysis used these aggregate functions as though individual decisions were based on them. Our derivation of the aggregate supply function makes clear the importance for employment decisions in Keynes's model of individual expectations and individual supply curves. Keynes's definition of effective demand has had to be restated because the version of the aggregate demand function he used in his definition can have no meaning for the competitive entrepreneurs in his model. None of Keynes's conclusions about the factors determining the short-period equilibrium level of employment are affected by this restatement, but it helps clear up some of the misunderstandings about this theory to be found in the literature. The shape of the equilibrium aggregate demand function plays a key role in Keynes's conclusions, but its significance cannot be understood without a proper understanding of the aggregate supply function.[32]

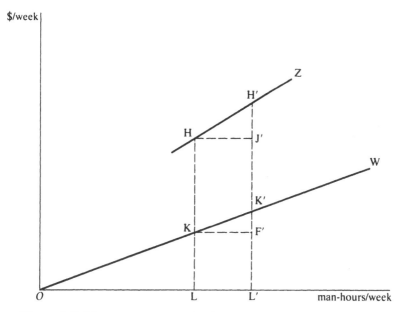

Figure 5.5 The aggregate supply function and the labour share

Appendix

In figure 5.5 the slope (with respect to the ordinate) of the ray OW is equal to $1/w$, where w is the money wage rate. The aggregate supply curve is assumed, for purposes of illustration, to have a linear portion HH'. The initial position is one with employment of OL per week, a wage bill of LK and non-labour proceeds of KH per week. If employment were OL', these values for labour and non-labour proceeds would be L'K' and K'H' respectively. The initial labour share in total income is LK/LH and, with employment OL', it is L'K'/L'H'. The labour share is increased, remains constant, or is decreased when employment is higher as $L'K'/L'H' \gtreqless LK/LH$. This can be rewritten as $L'K'/LK \gtreqless L'H'/LH$. From inspection of figure 5.5 we can see that these relations can be written as $(LK+F'K')/LK \gtreqless (LH+J'H')/LH$, or as $F'K'/LK \gtreqless J'H'/LH$. It is convenient to rewrite the latter expression as $F'K'/J'H' \gtreqless LK/LH$. The left-hand side of this expression is equal to the ratio of the slope of the Z line to the slope of OW (which equals $1/w$) both taken with respect to the ordinate (recall that the independent variable for Keynes's aggregate supply function is expected proceeds, even though he writes it as $Z = \phi(N)$). The right-hand side of the above expression is equal to initial employment OL multiplied by the wage rate, divided by initial total proceeds. The expression can be rewritten as the slope of $Zw \gtreqless OLw/LH$, and then further simplified to the slope of Z $LH/OL \gtreqless 1$. The term on the left-hand side is equal to the elasticity of the aggregate supply curve. We thus have derived the following general relation: if with higher employment the labour share in total income is higher, then the elasticity of the aggregate supply curve is greater than unity; if this share is constant then the elasticity has a value of unity, and if the labour share is decreasing then the elasticity value is less than unity. The elasticity of the aggregate supply curve at any point thus reflects the net effects of the changes in income shares that occur at the basic firm and industry levels as a result of changes in individual expectations of prices at that point.

Notes

1 Among the latest contributions are those of Roberts (1978), Patinkin (1976, 1978), Tarshis (1979), Parrinello (1980) and Casarosa (1981).

2 The derivation of the aggregate supply curve in this paper uses individual supply curves and thus differs from most of the derivations found in the literature (e.g. Wells (1960), Roberts (1978), Patinkin (1978) and Casarosa (1981)) that make use of aggregate real output. A notable exception is Weintraub (1957) who based his derivation on individual supply curves. Tarshis derives an aggregate supply function that begins with consideration of an individual firm before going on to use aggregate real output, but he assumes that the market structure is one of 'imperfect competition'. He does agree, however, with the position taken here 'that when Keynes refers to "under competition", he means in conditions of perfect – as opposed to imperfect – competition' (Tarshis, 1979, p. 365). He goes on to add 'But it is also clear that he had no real reason for assuming perfect competition'. E. A. G. Robinson, in response to Professor Tarshis's question about Keynes's role in the development of the theory of imperfect competition in Cambridge, said 'I think a quick answer to that is almost none . . . He was encouraging, he was interested, but he wasn't a partaker in that particular operation' (Patinkin and Leith, 1977, p. 79). This encouragement extended, as Harcourt (1979) has

noted, to Keynes's being a reader for Macmillan of Joan Robinson's manuscript for her *Economics of Imperfect Competition*.

In spite of Keynes's awareness of the validity of some of the criticisms that were being directed against standard marginal theory, they were not reflected in *The General Theory*. Keynes explained the approach he took on this issue in a 1935 letter to R. G. Hawtrey. 'There are, of course, some qualifications to this theory and some criticisms which can validly be made. But this is not a matter which I could very well go into in this book. I am simply accepting the usual theory of the subject without attempting to refine on it' (Keynes, 1973a, p. 615).

3 The decision on output was at the same time a decision on employment since capital equipment is given when these output decisions are taken. For Keynes 'when we say that the expectation of an increased demand . . . will lead to an increase in aggregate output, we really mean that the firms, which own the capital equipment, will be induced to associate with it a greater aggregate employment of labour' (Keynes, 1936, p. 40).

4 Keynes attached a footnote to 'daily' in this quotation to note that '*Daily* here stands for the shortest interval after which the firm is free to revise its decision as to how much employment to offer. It is, so to speak, the minimum effective unit of time'. Kregel (1976, p. 224) and Davidson (1978, p. 382) identify Keynes's 'daily' with the 'short run', a term not used by Keynes.

5 The lack of such microfoundations has been clearly noted by Parrinello (1980) and Casarosa (1981).

6 For Keynes this single value for expected proceeds should be interpreted in the light of his explanation of what he meant by an entrepreneur's 'expectation of proceeds'. 'An entrepreneur, who has to reach a practical decision as to his scale of production, does not, of course, entertain a single undoubting expectation of what the sale-proceeds of a given output will be, but several hypothetical expectations held with varying degrees of probability and definiteness. By his expectation of proceeds I mean, therefore, that expectation of proceeds which, if it were held with certainty, would lead to the same behaviour as does the bundle of vague and more various possibilities which actually makes up his state of expectation when he reaches his decision' (Keynes, 1936, p. 24, n.3). Joan Robinson (1980a, p. 57) considers that in giving such precision to expected proceeds in an uncertain world 'Keynes himself fudged his own argument'.

7 Casarosa (1981, p. 189) makes use of what he calls 'the aggregate expected demand function for entrepreneurs as a whole'. It is obtained by multiplying the expected price for output by the aggregate production function. This 'expected demand function' should not be

confused with what is usually called the aggregate demand function, which Casarosa terms the 'expenditure function'. Its role in his exposition is simply to determine the point on the aggregate supply function that maximizes the entrepreneurs' expectations of profits, given the expectations of price. But this can be done directly, as in the text above, by noting that the aggregation of the profit-maximizing proceeds for each firm (given each set of expectations about prices) determines a single point on the aggregate supply schedule.

8 This emphasis can also be found in other places in his *Collected Writings*. For example, in a November 1935 letter to Hawtrey, in response to Hawtrey's comments on the page proofs of *The General Theory*, Keynes wrote 'Effective demand always reflects the current expectation of actual demand whether it is arrived at by a careful attempt at elaborate foresight on the part of the entrepreneurs, or merely by revision at short intervals on the basis of trial and error' (Keynes, 1973a, p. 603).

9 'Income, i.e. realised results as distinct from effective demand, only exists for entrepreneurs and for them is relevant only because it reacts on their subsequent determination of effective demand and on their personal consumption' (Keynes, 1973b, p. 180).

10 In addition to Parrinello (1980) and Casarosa (1981), Patinkin (1979, pp. 172–4) noted that the aggregate demand function is not perceived by entrepreneurs in competitive industries 'contrary to Keynes'.

11 'Mr Keynes . . . oscillates between using "aggregate demand price' to mean what he has defined it to mean, *viz.* what entrepreneurs *do* expect to receive, and using it to mean what they "can expect" to receive, *i.e.* what they can legitimately expect to receive, because that, whether they expect it or not, is what they *will* receive. In a world in which errors of anticipation are common, the distinction is not unimportant' (Robertson (1936), reprinted in Robertson (1940, p. 115)). Robertson (1955, p. 476) again drew attention to these two versions. They were noticed by Wells (1962), who distinguished between an 'expected proceeds' function and the aggregate demand function.

12 See also '. . . the short-period supply price of a unit of a firm's saleable output . . . is the sum of the marginal factor cost and the marginal user cost' (p. 67).

13 This assumption was repeated on pages 280 and 286 of *The General Theory*.

14 The question of whether profits are to be included in the aggregate supply function, and their maximization at the point of effective demand, has been commented on extensively in the literature (e.g. de Jong (1954), Patinkin (1976, 1978, 1979), Harcourt (1977)

and Casarosa (1981)). Keynes confused careful readers when he misinterpreted his own construct and treated it as a cost curve for an economy-encompassing firm (see below).

15 Cf. Marty (1961) who obtains the inverse of this relationship because he derives the elasticity with respect to the abscissa. Marty, and many others trying to establish the shape of the aggregate supply curve (e.g. H. G. Johnson in Robertson (1955) and Wells (1960)), use aggregate real output.

16 Patinkin (1978, 1979) has referred to this footnote and notes its exclusion of profits from the aggregate supply curve. He is prepared to accept the implication that labour is the sole variable factor of production, but this is inconsistent with Keynes's position on this matter (see note 26).

17 Support for this view could be found in the contents of a letter Keynes wrote to Kahn in April 1934. He provided a definition of effective demand as follows: 'Let W be the marginal prime cost of production when output is O. Let P be the expected selling price of this output. Then OP is effective demand' (Keynes, 1973a, p. 422). At this stage of working out his theory Keynes was implicitly assuming a single economy-wide firm (its output O was determined by equating the expected selling price P to marginal prime cost W), and the position here is that he did not succeed in eliminating all vestiges of this approach in the final draft of *The General Theory*.

18 In Keynes's competitive model firms were basically price takers producing on the basis of expected prices, but they were producing manufactured goods and a temporary stickiness of prices seems to have been allowed. There might be an 'accumulation of stocks *before* prices have fallen' (Keynes, 1936, p. 51n.) and conversely, a decumulation of stocks before prices are raised. But in terms of latter terminology (Hicks, 1974) Keynes did not have a 'fix-price' theory since firms adjusted output in line with expected prices. Leijonhufvud (1974, p. 169) makes this point very firmly: 'In the "shortest run" for which system behaviour can be defined in Keynes' model, output prices *must* be treated as perfectly flexible. The Marshallian ground rules of his analysis will not accomodate a still shorter Hicksian "fix-price market day".'

19 The existence of such an equilibrium function, relating consumption to income, was strongly implied in *The General Theory*, e.g. 'The relationship between the community's income and what it can be expected to spend on consumption . . . will depend on the psychological characteristic of the community, which we shall call its *propensity to consume*. That is to say, consumption will depend on the level of aggregate income and, therefore, on the level of employment N,

except when there is some change in the propensity to consume'
(Keynes, 1936, p. 28). Keynes was much more circumspect in the
notes for his 1937 lectures: 'Propensity to consume [i.e. consumption
(?)] is determined *solely* by a psychological composite of actual and
expected income and is determined neither by effective demand at a
definite date nor by income at a definite date' (Keynes, 1973b, p.
180).

20 P_2 could be made to lie on some sort of aggregate demand function
by drawing aggregate demand functions in figure 5.3 that show
varying degrees of adjustment of consumption and investment to their
short-period equilibrium values. The multiplicity of 'aggregate demand
functions' that would result might be a greater source of confusion
than of understanding.

21 Keynes did not appear to distinguish between the realized proceeds
from a given level of employment and the corresponding proceeds
on the equilibrium aggregate demand curve. This was a symptom of
his neglect of time in much of his presentation of the multiplier (cf.
Hicks, 1974, chapter 1). In the notes for the 1937 lectures, the
disappointment of short-period expectations meant expectations of
proceeds other than those given by the point of intersection of the
equilibrium aggregate demand function and the aggregate supply
function. 'I now feel that if I were writing the book again I should
begin by setting forth my theory on the assumption that short-period
expectations were always fulfilled; and then have a subsequent chapter
showing what difference it makes when short-period expectations are
disappointed . . . The main point is to distinguish the forces
determining the position of equilibrium from the technique of trial
and error by means of which the entrepreneur discovers where the
position is' (Keynes, 1973b, pp. 181–2).

22 Point E in figure 5.3 is a position of short-period equilibrium. Not
only is saving equal to investment (which it must be because of
Keynes's definition of these terms) but saving is in the desired relation
to income and actual investment is equal to planned investment for
the period.

23 Equilibrium is understood here to denote a position of rest for the
variable under consideration (cf. Asimakopulos, 1973).

24 Cf. Wells (1979), Weintraub (1974) and Leijonhufvud (1974).

25 Keynes was very emphatic in a 1933 draft chapter of *The General
Theory* that the inverse relationship between the real wage rate and
the level of employment should not be confused with a labour demand
curve. '. . . we may well discover empirically a correlation between
employment and real wages. But this will occur, not because the one
causes the other, but because they are both consequences of the same

cause . . . If, for example, the working classes were persuaded to put more of their earnings into the savings bank, real wages would rise and employment would diminish: but it would be misleading to call the rise in real wages the cause of the unemployment for *both* would be consequences of the increased propensity to save' (Keynes, 1979, p. 100).

26 For Keynes marginal costs include not only labour costs but also other factor and user costs (Keynes, 1936, p. 55 n.1, pp. 70–1). In the Appendix to chapter 19 he refers 'to the fallacious practice of equating marginal wage-cost to marginal prime cost' and goes on to note that 'the results of an analysis conducted on this premise have almost no application, since the assumption on which it is based is very seldom realized in practice. For we are not so foolish in practice as to refuse to associate with additional labour appropriate additions of other factors in so far as they are available, and the assumption will, therefore, only apply if we assume that all factors, other than labour, are already being employed to the utmost' (p. 272n.).

27 The word 'determines' in Keynes's statement that 'For every value of N there is a corresponding marginal productivity of labour in the wage-goods industries: and it is this which determines the real wage' (Keynes, 1936, p. 29) should thus not be confused with 'equals'.

28 From the equality $P_n = MC_n \equiv (w\Delta N_n + \Delta OPC)/\Delta Q_n$, we can derive $w/P_w = (\Delta Q_n/\Delta N_n)(P_n/P_w) - (\Delta OPC_n/P_n\Delta N_n)(P_n/P_w)$, where the subscript n identifies a non-wage-goods industry.

29 Our derivation of the aggregate supply function makes clear that firms choose, on the basis of expected prices, points on their supply curves for output and, if these expectations are fulfilled, they are on their supply curves no matter what the level of involuntary unemployment. Patinkin's statements (1965, chapter XIII) about firms being 'off' their supply curves in a situation of involuntary unemployment has no foundation in Keynes's model (or in Patinkin's model of perfect competition) unless it refers to situations where actual prices differ from expected prices. Patinkin (1965, p. 324, n. 10) noted that this notion of firms being off their supply curve is not that of Keynes. Malinvaud (1977, pp. 31–2) defines 'Keynesian unemployment' as a situation with excess supply in markets for goods as well as for labour, but he too notes that this is probably not an accurate portrayal of the model in *The General Theory*.

30 Cf. Patinkin (1979, pp. 69–70).

31 This accomodation of the aggregate demand function to the aggregate supply function could come about through various ways. For example, a marginal propensity to spend out of wages and other factor incomes equal to unity, with entrepreneurs as a group increasing their

expenditures on consumption and investment to match the anticipated increase in the gross profits they foresee when money wage rates are lower, would produce this result. In his review of *The General Theory* Robertson gave a possible defence for the 'classical theory' along these lines. He raised the possibility that the expectations that led to an increase in output, which would appear to be mistaken when an equilibrium aggregate demand function with a given volume of investment is compared with the aggregate supply function, may turn out to be justified when allowance is made for induced investment. 'But perhaps, as output grows . . . consumption breeds investment, as well as investment consumption. The mistake will turn out not to have been a mistake after all' (Robertson (1936), reprinted in Robertson (1940, p. 115)).

32 This conclusion differs from those which emphasize only the demand side of Keynes's analysis. For example, Hawtrey (1954, p. 835), in commenting on de Jong (1954) wrote 'Mr. de Jong is therefore right when he says that according to Keynes, employment is "determined by a one-sided demand theory".'

6

Keynes and Sraffa: Visions and Perspectives

Piero Sraffa's *Production of Commodities by Means of Commodities* has stimulated the writing of numerous articles and books, as economics theorists have tried to come to grips with the implications of this seminal work. It has led to the reconsideration of other approaches 'to economic theory, and the demonstration of the absence of a theoretical basis for '*any* notion of capital as a measurable quantity independent of distribution and prices' (Sraffa, 1960, p. 38) was a critical element in the 'reswitching' arguments of the 1960s (Pasinetti et al., 1966; Harcourt, 1972). Sraffa's subtitle for his book was 'Prelude to a Critique of Economic Theory', with the theory referred to being the neoclassical or marginalist explanation of prices and distribution that was developed from the 1870s. Keynes's theory of employment, presented in *The General Theory of Employment, Interest and Money*, also represents a fundamental criticism of this neoclassical approach,[1] since he tries to establish that the equilibrium position in the economy is not one of full employment. Even though they both provide the basis for fundamental critiques of the neoclassical approach to economics, these works of Sraffa and Keynes focus on different questions. The former is concerned with the determination of relative prices, given technology and final output, and the latter with the factors determining output and employment. On the surface the two appear to be, at least potentially, compatible, since Sraffa's work leaves open the question of the determination of the level of output, it has been argued that 'his system is compatible . . . with Keynes's theory' (Roncaglia, 1978,

p. xviii). It has also been argued (Garegnani, 1979a, p. 79) that the replacement of the marginalist elements in Keynes's analysis by Sraffa's explanation of relative prices will provide a much firmer basis for Keynes's critique of the view that the 'normal' level of employment in a capitalist economy is one of full employment.

Attempts to 'marry' the Sraffa and Keynes approaches to economic theory overlook the fundamental differences between them – the difference in the role of time and the visions of the operations of capitalist economies implicit in these theories. That this is, at least partly, recognized by those who are trying to combine the two theories is evident in the attempt to interpret Keynes's *General Theory* as being concerned with 'long-period' output and employment (Eatwell, 1979; Milgate, 1982). This chapter will deal mainly with Keynes's General Theory, and the position taken is that its short-period setting is a critical feature of this theory that must be part of any attempt to consider its implications for developments over time. For purposes of contrast it is useful to begin with a brief statement of what appears to be the economic basis of Sraffa's approach to the determination of prices.

Sraffa's prices of production

Sraffa's system of production is set in a particular period of time, a year (Sraffa, 1960, p. 3), in which the technical relations of production and the total amount to be produced of each commodity are fixed. These technical relations show (in part I of the book where there are only single-product industries) the amounts of each of the commodities and labour (which for purposes of simplification is taken to be homogeneous) required to produce the specific output of each commodity. It is assumed in the main body of the book that the system produces a surplus – more of at least one of the commodities is produced in the year than is required as an input, and at least enough of all the other commodities is produced to replace the amounts used as inputs. In order to determine the prices of production in such a system it is necessary to know how the surplus is to be divided between wages and profits. Sraffa asserts that in his system there will be an equal rate of profits in all industries. There is no attempt to justify this assumption; he simply states when setting out his price equations 'we add the rate of profit (which must be uniform for all industries)' (Sraffa, 1960, p. 6). If the share of the surplus going to wages is then given, prices and this equal rate of profits can be determined. For different shares of surplus going to wages, relative prices as well as the rate of profits will, in general, differ.

Sraffa obtains in this way an explanation of relative prices that depends only on technical relations of production and distributive shares. The commodity composition of the surplus is taken as given in all the comparisons of differences in prices, and there is no investigation of the effect of differences in demand on prices. If the assumption of constant returns to scale in each industry were added, then demand could be said to have no effect on relative prices, but Sraffa makes no such assumption. He noted in his Preface that 'No changes in output . . . are considered, so that no question arises as to the variation or constancy of returns' (Sraffa, 1960, p. v). The question of whether demand could affect the prices of production in a complete economic system,[2] of which Sraffa's system of production is a part, is thus left formally open even though the general thrust of Sraffa's work implies that demand is not important in this context or, at least, that its influence on price is 'not comparable' with those of labour and material inputs.[3]

Sraffa (1960, p. v) writes that the 'standpoint' of his investigation 'is that of the old classical economists from Adam Smith to Ricardo', and his prices of production have thus been identified with the 'natural' or long-period prices of the classical economists (Garegnani, 1979b, p. 185). These prices are viewed as 'centres of gravitation' for actual market prices (Garegnani, 1976, pp. 26–9; Milgate, 1982, p. 20). Sraffa's system of production and the specification of distributive shares only allow for the mathematical derivation of prices of production; there is nothing in his analysis to justify the treatment of prices of production as values towards which actual prices tend to move. He does not deal with dynamic processes of adjustment.[4] The only 'time' in the system is the 'year' during which production takes place, and there is no linking of 'years' – even in an informal manner – in order to indicate the possible relationship between the prices of production and actual prices.[5]

With Keynes's *General Theory* we are in a very different analytical environment, even though relatively little attention is paid to dynamic processes. The focus is on the factors affecting the determination of output and employment in the short period, with some consideration being given as to whether there would be reliable forces at work tending to move the economy to a position of full employment over time. The conclusion is a negative one, with no weight being given to the possibility of attraction being exerted by long-period equilibrium values.

Keynes's theory of employment

Keynes's analysis of the factors determining the level of output and employment in an economy is set in a Marshallian short period. 'We take as given the existing skill and quantity of available labour, the existing quality and quantity of available equipment, the existing technique. . .' (Keynes, 1936, p. 245). His theory is concerned, in a formal sense, with the equilibrium level of output and employment in such a period, and in a less formal sense with whether over time – over a sequence of short periods – automatic forces would be set in motion to move the economy towards a position of full employment. In the one-paragraph first chapter of *The General Theory*, Keynes explains why he is 'placing the emphasis on the prefix *general*' (p. 3) in the title of his book. He states that the postulates of what he calls the 'classical' theory are 'applicable to a special case only and not to the general case, the situation it assumes being a limiting point of the possible positions of equilibrium'. The implication is that his theory is concerned with the general case, where equilibrium with full employment is only one of many possibilities.[6] The term 'equilibrium' as used by Keynes refers to a position of rest for the variable of interest (employment in this case) given the values of the parameters, and not necessarily one where there is no change in the values of other variables (Asimakopulos, 1973; Patinkin, 1982, p. 14). Equilibrium for Keynes in this book does not refer to a situation where prices and quantities transacted are such that all individuals are on their demand and supply curves.

The critical decision-makers in Keynes's model are the entrepreneurs. They decide on the levels of employment and output in the short period in the light of short-term expectations of prices and costs, and they determine investment on the basis of long-term expectations. The setting for Keynes's model can be viewed as a particular 'moment' in historical time, a 'moment' whose characteristics have been determined by decisions and actions in the past; in fact, this moment is defined by the 'existing quality and quantity of available equipment, the existing technique. . .' (Keynes, 1936, p. 245). This is one reason for its identification with Marshall's short period, to which a calendar dimension of 'a few months or a year' (Marshall, 1920, p. 379) is given. Changes in equipment and techniques are, of course, taking place in a progressive economy even within such a period, but the effects of these changes are small relative to those of the initial conditions, and it is not unreasonable to ignore them.[7] Keynes concentrates on equilibrium situations in these short periods; he does not deal with the process of adjustment to equilibrium positions or the time required to reach a new equilibrium position after a change in the values of the parameters. Although Keynes's analysis is in 'historical time' from the point of view of its setting and his emphasis on the expectational basis of decisions and actions, it is 'out of time' in terms of its limitation to situations of equilibrium.[8] With its use of given equipment and techniques, Keynes's short period must occupy a relatively brief span of time in a economy where there is net investment, but the time required to reach a position of equilibrium after a change may be greater than this interval.[9] Keynes simply concentrates on positions of short-period equilibrium, presumably to contrast his conclusions with the equilibrium results of 'classical' theory.[10]

Given his aim of dealing with the factors determining the level of aggregate output, Keynes had to adapt Marshall's short-period supply curves for individual goods to serve this purpose. He distrusts measures and comparisons of aggregate output, because 'the community's output of goods and services is a non-homogeneous complex which cannot be measured. . .' (Keynes, 1936, p. 38). He thus relies 'on the general presumption that the amount of employment associated with a given capital equipment will be a satisfactory index of the amount of resultant output' (p. 41). The employment in any period is the result of decisions that depend on short-term expectations that are 'concerned with the price a manufacturer can expect to get for his "finished" output at the time when he commits himself to starting the process which will produce it' (p. 46). These individual expectations of prices – together with the cost conditions of the individual firms – are then turned into expectations of proceeds for purposes of aggregation. The profit-maximizing competitive firms produce outputs that equate these expected prices and marginal costs, and their short-term expectations of proceeds are the proceeds they would receive if they sold these outputs at the expected prices. Since these proceeds are measured in dollar terms, they can be aggregated over the economy, and for each set of expected prices they provide (once user costs are deducted) a point on the aggregate supply function.[11]

Keynes emphasized the importance of expectations in a theory of employment: 'The expected results are not on a par with the *realised* results in a theory of employment. The *realised* results are only relevant in so far as they influence the ensuing expectations in the next production period' (Keynes, 1973b, p. 179). He could thus have gone on from this perspective to define effective demand as the value of proceeds at the point on the aggregate supply curve corresponding to the short-term expectations of proceeds of entrepreneurs, since in this theory it is this value that determines the amount of employment offered by firms. But Keynes concentrated on situations of short-period equilibrium where the short-term expectations of firms are borne out by events – he identifies the aggregate demand function[12] with the value of proceeds that would be received by firms at alternative levels of employment in the economy – and he defines effective demand as the value 'of the aggregate demand function, where it is intersected by the aggregate supply function. . .' (Keynes, 1936, p. 25). The proceeds on the aggregate demand function are also taken to be equilibrium values. The consumption expenditures that are included in this function are assumed to be in the desired relation to income, and the investment expenditures are equal to those that firms planned to make in the period.

The factors underlying the aggregate demand and supply functions thus explain the determination of equilibrium employment in the particular short period of the economy. This equilibrium was stable – given the level of investment – because, at a value for employment higher (lower) than this equilibrium level, the aggregate supply price would lie above (below) the aggregate demand price. This relationship was assumed to hold because 'The psychology of the community is such that when aggregate real income is increased aggregate consumption is increased, but not by so much as income' (p. 27). Although, in the statement of the 'essence' of his general theory of employment,[13] Keynes gives equal emphasis to the role of the propensity to consume and to the volume of investment, it is to the latter that he keeps referring for an explanation of why employment could be less than full. For example, '. . . to justify any given amount of employment there must be an amount of current investment sufficient to absorb the excess of total output over what the community chooses to consume when employment is at the given level. . . It follows . . . that, given what we shall call the community's propensity to consume, the equilibrium level of employment . . . will depend on the amount of current investment' (p. 27). In his 1937 reply to reviewers of *The General Theory* in the *Quarterly Journal of Economics*, Keynes referred to investment as the '*causa causans*' of the economic system, because of the unreliability of the factors 'which determine the rate of investment . . . since it is they which are influenced by our views of the future about which we know so little' (Keynes, 1973b, p. 121).

Keynes's central message in *The General Theory* is thus twofold. There is first the theory of effective demand – output and employment for the economy are determined by the intersection of aggregate demand and supply curves – and second the unreliability of the factors determining investment, which explains why aggregate demand will be variable and often less than sufficient to ensure full employment.[14]

The determination of investment in Keynes's theory

Keynes presents two seemingly different approaches to the determination of investment – one in chapter 11 of *The General Theory*, and the other in chapter 12 as well as in his 1937 *Quarterly Journal of Economics* paper. The first approach emphasizes the inverse relationship between the rate of interest and investment, while the second, although not excluding the possibility of such a relationship, looks primarily to states of mind and attitudes in the face of an uncertain future as the major factors underlying investment decisions.[15]

The presentation in chapter 11 implies the existence of a stable downward-sloping investment demand schedule with investment being pushed to the 'point on the investment demand-schedule where the marginal efficiency of capital in general is equal to the market rate of interest' (Keynes, 1936, p. 137). It is from such a schedule that an IS curve can be derived (Hicks, 1937). The reason Keynes gives for a diminishing marginal efficiency of capital schedule as investment increases is not consistent with the framework of his analysis, as Kalecki pointed out in his 1936 review of *The General Theory* (Targetti and Kinda-Hass, 1982). The marginal efficiency of capital is expected to be lower, the higher is the investment in Keynes's short period, because of the higher price of capital goods, which are produced under conditions of increasing costs. This argument contains both *ex ante* and *ex post* features. The expectations of profitability, of future quasi-rents from the purchase of capital goods, are *ex ante*, but the higher prices of capital goods which are required to make the marginal efficiency of capital schedule downward-sloping would only be experienced as a result of a general increase in investment. If such an increase occurred, prices of other goods and profitability in general would also increase, so that it would not be reasonable to assume that the expectations of future quasi-rents would be unchanged (Asimakopulos, 1971).

In chapter 12 the viewpoint shifts from the dependence on the calculation of yields to recognition of 'the extreme precariousness of the basis of knowledge on which our estimates of prospective yield have to be made. Our knowledge of the factors which will govern the yield of an investment some years hence is usually very slight and often negligible' (Keynes, 1936, p. 149). Estimates made on such a basis are subject to large margins of error and to substantial change in the light of current events. Keynes thus backs away from the idea of a stable investment demand schedule that can be acted on by monetary policy. '. . . it seems likely that the fluctuations in the market estimation of the marginal efficiency of different types of capital, calculated on the principles I have described above, will be too great to be offset by any practicable changes in the rate of interest' (p. 164).

With investment being subject to fluctuations for the reasons given above, the short-period equilibrium levels of employment, determined by these fluctuating investments, will also fluctuate. There is no reason to expect from Keynes's analysis that these fluctuations will be around some full-employment level – there are no 'normal' long-period values that serve as centres of gravitation for actual values in Keynes's theory.[16]

Long-period employment in *The General Theory*

The present interpretation of the General Theory has emphasized its short-period framework. This theory concentrates on what has been referred to here as 'short-period equilibrium employment'. This is the level of employment corresponding to a situation where actual investment is equal to planned investment and consumption is in the desired relation to income. In this equilibrium situation the short-term expectations of proceeds held by entrepreneurs are borne out by events in this short period. The proceeds of capital goods producers (equal, in this case, to their short-term expectations) come from investment expenditures, and they thus depend on the long-term expectations of investing firms. These long-term expectations may have been held at different times in the past, since the time lags in the investment process are such that investment expenditures in any short period are the result of decisions taken at different times. The actual investment in any period is thus, in general, the result of more than one state of long-term expectations. Keynes looks briefly at a very special case where *all* the investment in a short period is the result of a particular state of long-term expectations. The resulting level of employment is 'called the long-period employment corresponding to that state of expectation' (Keynes, 1936, p. 48). Keynes added a footnote to this definition:

> It is not necessary that the level of long-period employment should be *constant*, *i.e.* long-period conditions are not necessarily static. For example, a steady increase in wealth or population may constitute a part of the unchanging expectation. The only condition is that the existing expectations should have been foreseen sufficiently far ahead.

The level of employment being referred to in all these cases is, of course, short-period employment, but short-period employment based on investment guided by identical long-term expectations. If these expectations are that stationary conditions will prevail, then this employment would be that corresponding to zero net investment.[17] But the unchanging expectations may be of a steady increase in demand over time, with the rates of investment generated by these expectations increasing over time. The corresponding long-period employment would then also be increasing from one short period to the next.

The relationship between Keynes's long-period (equilibrium) employment and his short-period (equilibrium) employment bears a superficial resemblance to the relationship between Marshall's long-period equilibrium and short-period equilibrium for competitive industries (Asimakopulos, 1984–5). A situation of long-period equilibrium must also be one of short-period equilibrium in both cases. For Marshall, long-period equilibrium values tend to attract short-period values,[18] but there is not even a hint in Keynes's presentation of long-period employment serving as a centre of attraction for actual values.[19]

Long-period interpretations of *The General Theory*

Eatwell and Milgate have argued for an interpretation of Keynes's theory of output and employment as one concerned with 'the long-period level of output' (Eatwell, 1979, p. 98; Milgate, 1982, pp. 84–91). This view differs from the one taken here, which is consistent with statements made by Keynes's close associates. Joan Robinson has always emphasized the short-period framework of Keynes's analysis and she noted, for example, that 'Keynes hardly ever peered over the edge of the short period to see the effect of investment in making additions to the stocks of productive equipment' (Robinson, 1978b, p. 14). Lord Kahn has recently reaffirmed this position with his statement: 'The *General Theory* is short-period in the Marshallian sense' (Kahn, 1984, p. 122). The bases for the long-period interpretation advanced by Eatwell and Milgate are a few statements in *The General Theory*. They give a special reading to Keynes's listing of the factors he takes as given when he comes to restate his General Theory in chapter

18, and they then attach great weight to Keynes's reference to "'natural" tendencies' which 'are likely to persist' in the final paragraph of that chapter.

Eatwell argues that 'the fixed composition of the capital stock which defines Marshall's short period plays no role in Keynes's theory of employment – unemployment is, according to Keynes, not due to the shortage of a particular capital good, but to a lack of effective demand' (Eatwell, 1979, p. 97). This position is based on a misinterpretation of the use of Marshall's short period in Keynes's analysis. The composition and quantity of capital equipment is taken as given, with the focus being on the degree of utilization, on average, of that equipment. It is not inconsistent in a macroeconomic analysis to overlook, for purposes of arriving at a general characterization of the situation in the economy, the possibility that an industry may have insufficient productive capacity to meet demand, even though plant in most other industries is operating at less than full capacity. This does not deprive the macroeconomic analysis of its short-period status. Keynes's recognition that, even in a short period, changes in equipment are taking place does not make his analysis a long-period one. The effects of these changes are ignored by Keynes because within the time period of his analysis they are small relative to initial values. Keynes's aggregate supply function, an essential element of his theory of effective demand, is based on the assumption of given productive capacity. Keynes incorporated in his theory the inverse relation between the real wage rate and the level of employment, a relation based on 'the familiar proposition that industry is normally working subject to decreasing returns in the short period during which equipment etc. is assumed to be constant. . .' (Keynes, 1936, p. 17). If Keynes were dealing with long-period output, as Eatwell and Milgate contend, then he would have had no basis for this inverse relation.

Eatwell interprets Keynes's statement qualifying the assumption of given equipment, 'This does not mean that we assume these factors to be constant; but merely that, in this place and context, we are not considering or taking into account the effects and consequences of changes in them' (Keynes, 1936, p. 245), as ruling out 'changes in the dominant and persistent forces' (Eatwell, 1979, p. 97) which Marshall classified as affecting secular movements in normal prices.[20] An alternative reading of Keynes's statement that is consistent with Marshall's three periods for the analysis of normal prices – 'short', 'long' and 'secular' – is that Keynes in *The General Theory* was, in the main body of this work, abstracting from the effects of changes in productive capacity that are the concern of long-period analysis. A formal treatment of long-period output would have required the explicit and careful consideration of the effects on productive capacity of investment. Such a treatment – a theory of accumulation – is absent in *The General Theory*.[21]

There is also the matter of the interpretation to be given to Keynes's statement at the end of chapter 18:

> . . . the outstanding features of our actual experience; – namely, that we oscillate, avoiding the gravest extremes of fluctuation in employment and in prices in both directions, round an intermediate position appreciably below full employment and appreciably above the minimum employment a decline below which would endanger life.
>
> But we must not conclude that the mean position thus determined by 'natural' tendencies, namely, by those tendencies which are likely to persist, failing measures expressly designed to correct them, is, therefore, established by laws of necessity. The unimpeded rule of the above conditions is a fact of observation concerning the world as it is or has been, and not a necessary principle which cannot be changed (Keynes, 1936, p. 254).

Eatwell takes the above statements to mean that 'The *persistent* forces establish the long-period level of output; it is these forces and that level which Keynes's theory is designed to explain' (Eatwell, 1979, p. 98).[22] Keynes's statements, however, should be interpreted in the light of his views on investment. He did not believe that investment, determined by entrepreneurs in a capitalist economy subject to change, would settle down at a level that would result, given the propensity to consume, in full employment. In fact, there is nothing in his vision of the capitalist system that would lead him to believe that the economy would be attracted to some other 'persistent' level of employment. The variability of conditions and uncertainty that affect the outcome of investment decisions would be reflected in the variability of investment, output and employment. The 'intermediate position' around which fluctuations occur, referred to by Keynes, is some average value indicated by 'our actual experience' and 'observation' rather than a 'centre of gravitation'.

For Keynes the time path of output and employment depends on the pattern of long-term expectations held over a sequence of periods, because of their effect on investment. Those who argue 'that the whole of the innovative core of the *General Theory* is best regarded as dealing with the "centre of gravitation" of the system' (Milgate, 1982, p. 90) concentrate on Keynes's theory of effective demand,[23] i.e. the adjustment of desired saving to investment as a result of changes in income. They treat his statements on the importance of the variability of long-term expectations in the face of uncertainty as part of his criticism of the neoclassical theory of interest (Garegnani, 1976, pp. 39–42), rather than as an integral part of his theory of employment in a capitalist economy. However, Keynes wrote, in setting out the basis of his theory of employment, 'Express reference to current long-term expectations can seldom be avoided' (Keynes, 1936, p. 50).It is reference to short-term expectations that is often omitted, on the assumption that they are subject to constant revision in the light of realized results, and Keynes tends to identify them with actual values. In the short-period equilibria on which he focused, the short-term expectations are equal to actual proceeds. It is with reference to this category of expectations that Keynes wrote in his 1937 lecture notes '. . . the theory of effective demand is substantially the same if we assume that short-period expectations are always fulfilled' (Keynes, 1973b, p. 181).[24]

The theory of effective demand in the short and long period

Production and employment always occur in a short-period context, with given equipment and technique being utilized. This short-period context never disappears even though the focus of attention is on long-period developments. In considering the latter, one is dealing, at least implicitly, with a succession of short periods as investment and technical progress alter productive capacity and techniques. If, as in *The General Theory*, the analysis concentrates on situations of short-period equilibrium, then employment (in a closed economy with no government economic activity) in each period will be determined by the level of investment and the economy's propensity to consume.[25] The nature of the theory of effective demand is not altered by extending the analysis to a sequence of short periods. The path traced by the short-period equilibrium output and employment over time depends – assuming that the consumption function is stable – on what happens to investment, i.e. on how long-term expectations and financial conditions change. A variety of possible growth paths can be deduced, each reflecting different assumptions about the drive of entrepreneurs, the degree of thriftiness in the economy, financial policies, trade union actions etc. (Robinson, 1962, pp. 52–9). Recognition of the infectious nature of good and bad news, and the financial system's propensity to facilitate the capitalization of expected profits (Minsky, 1982), lead to the conclusion that growth paths will be disturbed by cyclical movements and interrupted by crises. In fact, cyclical and long-term factors influence one another and are so intertwined that the separation of the two is problematic. In Kalecki's words '. . . the long run trend is but a slowly changing component of a chain of short run situations; it has no independent entity. . .' (Kalecki, 1971b, p. 165). There is no reason to expect – certainly in the type of world visualized by Keynes – that 'in the long period', if this is taken to be some time in the future, productive capacity will become adjusted to demand. The consequences of this occurring – and continuing to hold – for a stretch of time can be examined. But in a changing world such a situation would *not* be a 'centre of gravitation' for actual values. In making investment decisions, firms try, of course, to anticipate future demand and not be caught with too much or too little productive capacity, but this route takes us back to the importance of long-term expectations in determining investment, with employment in any short period then depending on this investment.

Conclusion

Keynes and Sraffa were concerned with very different questions in their two major works under consideration here. The former dealt with the factors determining the level of output and employment and the latter dealt with those determining prices of production, given output and employment. There was a further important difference between them, in the character of the 'equilibrium' implicit in each of their approaches.

Keynes's analysis was centred on a Marshallian short period, and the prices implicit in his model are those determined by the intersection of demand and short-period supply curves. The intersection of his aggregate demand and supply functions is a macroeconomic representation of the intersections of the large number of competitive industry demand and supply curves in his model. Macroeconomic changes would affect the level of costs when, for example, an increase in employment increases money wage rates, and thus the prices of individual commodities, but this could be readily incorporated in a Marshallian analysis. But Marshall's long-period equilibrium, where productive capacity is adjusted to demand, has no place, even implicitly, in Keynes's analysis. Long-period values can be defined for any given situation of technical knowledge and demand but in a changing economy such values would be in a continual state of flux so that they do not serve as the basis of investment decisions and thus do not act as a reliable force of attraction for actual prices. In Keynes's approach investment decisions are based on expected conditions in future time periods and, in the final analysis, after allowing for all the calculations based on current and past data and informed estimates, these long-term expectations are subjective.

Sraffa's analysis is concerned with the prices of production – prices based on equal rates of profits in all industries – where investment in the different industries has resulted in productive capacity in each that is appropriate to demand. For these prices to serve as centres of gravitation for actual prices, conditions must be changing relatively slowly so that mistaken investments are relatively minor, with actual prices tending towards the prices of production. Investment decisions in this case – although formally they can be said to be determined by long-term expectations – are basically determined by objective factors. Such a vision of a capitalist economy in the twentieth century is different from that held by Keynes.

Notes

1 Keynes expected his book to have a profound effect on economic theory. He wrote to George Bernard Shaw at the beginning of 1935 'that I believe myself to be writing a book on economic theory which will largely revolutionise . . . the way the world thinks about economic problems' (Keynes, 1973a, p. 492).

2 As Robinson (1965, p. 9) stated in her 1961 review of this book, 'we are given only half of an equilibrium system to stand on'.

3 I had written to Sraffa in 1971 and had observed that his theoretical framework did not permit any conclusions about the effects of demand on prices unless the assumption of constant returns to scale were added. He responded in a letter dated 11 July 1971: 'You say "I don't see how demand can be said to have no influence on . . . prices, unless constant returns. . .". I take it that the drama is enacted on Marshall's stage where the claimants for influence are utility and cost of production. Now utility has made little progress (since the 1870ies) towards acquiring a tangible existence and survives in textbooks at the purely subjective level. On the other hand, cost of production has successfully survived Marshall's attempt to reduce it to an equally evanescent nature under the name of "disutility", and is still kicking in the form of hours of labour, tons of raw materials, etc. This rather than the relative slope of the two curves, is why it seems to me that the "influence" of the two things on price is not comparable.'

4 Newman (1962, p. 63) has written that Sraffa's assumption that the rate of profits should be the same in each industry 'is obviously the equilibrium condition (in a world of certainty) for a dynamic process in which each capitalist tries to maximize his profits'. Similarly, Carvalho (1983–4, p. 274) has argued that the view of prices of production as centres of gravitation 'clearly involves the idea of a process and of a time span necessary for the production prices to emerge and assert themselves'. In a later work he stated that implicit in the view of prices of production as a centre of gravitation is a theory of investment where investments 'must be determined by *current* differences in rates of profit while mistaken investments do not lead to the loss of the capital value invested. Thus, firms are able to reorient their resources from less to more profitable sectors without significant capital loss' (Carvalho, 1984–5, p. 219).

5 Roncaglia (1978, p. 219) has argued that in contrast with neoclassical theories that 'are placed in an atemporal context as a consequence of the attempt to identify an equilibrium position for the values of the variables of the economic system under consideration . . . it would

seem more correct to say that Sraffa's analysis is not static, but rather that it represents a "photograph" of a particular moment of a system's development . . . time is taken into account by the fact that any particular moment of time is determined by its past history, and serves as the determining factor of the next moment in time.' Prices of production can, of course, be derived for any 'particular moment of time', but there is nothing in Sraffa's analysis to indicate the relationship between actual prices and these prices of production. There is no 'movement' from one 'moment' to the other, or any movement within a 'moment'.

6 Another explanation for the use of the word 'general', a concern with aggregate output, is given by Kahn. He refers to Keynes's February 1939 preface to the French edition of *The General Theory* where the latter wrote 'I have called my theory a *general* theory. I mean by this that I am chiefly concerned with the behaviour of the economic system as a whole. . .', in support of this explanation rather than the one contained in chapter 1. Kahn concludes that 'This is a far more fruitful exposition of the meaning of the word "general" – the result of three years of discussion and thought' (Kahn, 1984, p. 121). But this interpretation is best viewed as an additional justification for the use of the word 'general', since Keynes was not maintaining in his book that the early classical writers had no concern 'with the behaviour of the economic system as a whole'.

7 Keynes notes, when specifying that equipment and technique are taken as given, that 'This does not mean that we assume these factors to be constant; but merely that, in this place and context, we are not considering or taking into account the effects and consequences of changes in them' (Keynes, 1936, p. 245).

8 'A state of equilibrium, by definition, is a state in which something, something relevant, is *not* changing; so the use of an equilibrium concept is a signal that time, in some respect at least, has been put to one side' (Hicks, 1976, p. 140).

9 Hicks has noted the difficulty of reconciling the time intervals implicit in Keynes's analysis. 'It is one of the major difficulties of the Keynes theory (a difficulty that was acutely felt by its first readers, though it has now been lulled to sleep by long familiarity) that it works with a *period* which is taken to be one of equilibrium (investment being equal to saving, saving that is a function of *current* income), and which is nevertheless identified with the Marshallian "short period", in which capital equipment (now the capital equipment of the whole economy) remains unchanged. The second seems to require that the period should not be too long, but the first requires that it should not be too short; for the *process* of getting into the equilibrium in

question (the multiplier process) must occupy a length of time that is by no means negligible. It is not easy to see that there can be any length of time that will adequately satisfy both of these requirements' (Hicks, 1965, pp. 64–5).

10 Keynes tended to identify these equilibrium values with actual values. For example, he stated that 'except in conditions where the consumption industries are already working almost at capacity so that an expansion of output requires an expansion of plant and not merely the more intensive employment of the existing plant, there is no reason to suppose that more than a brief interval of time need elapse before employment in the consumption industries is advancing *pari passu* with employment in the capital-goods industries with the multiplier operating near its normal figure' (Keynes, 1936, pp. 124–5).

11 For the derivation of the aggregate supply curve from industry short-period supply curves, see Asimakopulos (1982).

12 Parrinello (1980), Casarosa (1981) and Asimakopulos (1982) have pointed out that Keynes's first definition of the aggregate demand function is not consistent with the competitive microfoundations of his theory. Lord Kahn has reminded us that 'Keynes had no systematic education in economics' (Kahn, 1984, p. 50), and the occasional slip in matters of detail should not be surprising.

13 '. . .the volume of employment in equilibrium depends on (i) the aggregate supply function. . . (ii) the propensity to consume. . . and (iii) the volume of investment. . .' (Keynes, 1936, p. 29).

14 Patinkin (1982, p. 30) argues that only the first of the two components given above is Keynes's 'central message', but Kahn (1984, p. 142) is in agreement with the position taken here.

15 Shackle presents the difference between these two approaches as follows: 'Chapter 11 shows us the arithmetic of the marginal efficiency of capital and its relation with interest-rates, a matter for actuaries and slide-rules. Chapter 12 reveals the hollowness of all this. The material for the slide-rules is absent, or arbitrary. Investment is an *irrational* activity, or a non-rational one. Surmise and assumption about what is happening or about to happen are themselves the *source* of these happenings, men made history in seeking to apprehend it. This is the message of *The General Theory*, and that is the only part of it which Keynes troubled to reproduce when in the *Quarterly Journal of Economics* for February 1937 he brushed aside the painstaking detail of his critics' incomprehension and attempted a final penetration of their minds' (Shackle, 1967, p. 130).

16 Recall that Keynes did not believe that falling money wages in times of unemployment could be relied on to increase investment and bring about full employment. 'There is. . .no ground for the belief that a

flexible wage policy is capable of maintaining a state of continuous full employment' (Keynes, 1936, p. 267).

17 This is the case examined by Robinson (1937a, pp. 105–38).

18 Marshall recognized that this attraction depends on the stationarity of conditions. '. . .the normal, or "natural", value of a commodity is that which economic forces tend to bring about *in the long run*. It is the average value which economic forces would bring about if the general conditions of life were stationary for a run of time long enough to enable them all to work out their full effect' (Marshall, 1920, p. 347).

19 Vicarelli has emphasized that in Keynes's view of the capitalist system 'there is absolutely no mechanism to guarantee that investment will stabilize at some long-term norm, or that its variation over time adheres to a regular law' (Vicarelli, 1984, p. 177).

20 Milgate, in a similar manner, uses a quotation from Keynes's discussion of the factors possibly influencing the propensity to consume to interpret his 'given equipment' assumption as an attempt 'to allow the analysis to proceed without the need to consider [the effects of secular progress]' (Milgate, 1982, p. 90).

21 Garegnani (1979a, 1979b), who has argued for the development of a theory of output in the long period that builds on the critique of the neoclassical conception of capital, recognizes the short-period character of Keynes's writings. Eatwell and Milgate in their preface to a collection of papers that include these and other papers by Garegnani raise the question '. . .does Keynes's principle of effective demand provide a new long-run theory of output. . .?' (Eatwell and Milgate, 1983). A footnote attached to this question reports on a letter from Garegnani containing an argument with which they are not in agreement. Garegnani writes:

The meaning of 'long run' cannot but be partly different when used in connection with a theory of aggregate output than when it is used for the theory of relative output. While the meaning of given plant or productive capacity remains, what is relevant for Marshall is the lack of congruence between relative capacity and relative demand in the several industries. What is relevant for a theory of aggregate output like that of Keynes is the lack of congruence between aggregate capacity and aggregate demand. . . When this distinction is made it should be clear that Keynes is concerned with a short period analysis of aggregate output (the determination of the level of capacity utilisation) and that a long period analysis of aggregate output, *i.e.* an analysis of the reciprocal adaptation of aggregate supply and aggregate demand is one and the same thing as a theory of accumulation.

This is absent from Keynes apart from some hints we find in the first two sections of chapter 24 of the *General Theory*.

22 Milgate states that the preceding quotation from Keynes 'bears all the hallmarks of the traditional long-period method: the choice of the term "natural" to describe the tendencies of a market economy and of the term "persist" to describe their long-period character is the standard fare of the traditional method. The idea that the system oscillates around such a position completes that picture' (Milgate, 1982, p. 88).

23 This view of the theory of effective demand – divorced from his views on the variability and unreliability of investment – as Keynes's 'central message' is, as noted above, shared by Patinkin (1982), but he accepts the short-period nature of Keynes's theory. The theory of effective demand was *The General Theory*'s main addition to Keynes's analysis of the determination of employment. But to understand the 'central message' of that work it is important to consider this feature in conjunction with Keynes's views on investment. As Vicarelli wrote '. . .*The General Theory* is nothing more than the culmination of Keynes's vision of capitalism' (Vicarelli, 1984, p. 182).

24 Milgate (1982, p. 90) uses this quotation in support of his position that the 'fundamental proposition of *The General Theory* . . .is entirely independent of the existence of uncertainty and expectations', but he omits the adjective 'short-period' that qualifies 'expectations' in the quotation. An unwary reader might be misled by the context to assume that Keynes was referring to long-term expectations (cf. Harcourt and O'Shaughnessy, 1983, p. 16n).

25 Recall that, for Keynes, 'long-period employment' is not something that tends to occur 'in the long run'. It is employment in a particular short-period situation where all investment expenditures in that period are determined by the same set of long-term expectations.

7

Kalecki and Keynes on Finance, Investment and Saving

For both Kalecki and Keynes the key element in the determination of the level of economic activity in any short period in a capitalistic economy is the rate of investment that firms have decided to implement. Kalecki, with his concentration on profits (which are positively related to the level of economic activity), expressed this dependence in the following way:

> Thus capitalists, as a whole, determine their own profits by the extent of their investment and personal consumption. In a way they are 'masters of their fate'; but how they 'master' it is determined by objective factors, so that fluctuations of profits appear after all to be unavoidable (Kalecki, 1971b, p. 13).

Keynes's own summary of his theory in the *Quarterly Journal of Economics* in 1937 when he responded to some reviews of *The General Theory* is

> the level of output and employment as a whole depends on the amount of investment. I put it in this way, not because this is the only factor on which aggregate output depends, but because it is usual in a complex system to regard as the *causa causans* that factor which is most prone to sudden and wide fluctuation. More comprehensively, aggregate output

I am grateful to L. G. Ascah and J. C. Weldon for comments on an earlier draft, but they are not responsible for any errors nor for the interpretation of writings in this chapter.

depends on the propensity to hoard, on the policy of the monetary authority as it affects the quantity of money, on the state of confidence concerning the prospective yield of capital assets, on the propensity to spend and on the social factors which influence the level of the money wage. But of these several factors it is those which determine the rate of investment which are most unreliable, since it is they which are influenced by our views of the future about which we know so little (Keynes, 1973b, p. 121).

These similarities have led Joan Robinson, among others, to claim that Kalecki 'had already published some articles in Polish (the first in 1933) outlining the main points of what afterwards became known as Keynes' theory . . .' (Robinson, 1973, p. 87). Kalecki himself had noted in his 1936 review of *The General Theory* for a Polish periodical that his 1933 study of the business cycle had emphasized the important role of investment in determining total output in a manner similar to that of Keynes. An early reference to this similarity, in English, is to be found in a footnote to his 1942 paper on 'A Theory of Profits' where he writes 'The theory of profits presented here is closely allied to Mr Keynes' theory of saving and investment. It has been, however, developed independently of Mr. Keynes in [reference is made to Kalecki (1935a, 1935b)]' (Kalecki, 1942, p. 258, n.1). A more forthright claim is made in the introduction to his *Selected Essays on the Dynamics of the Capitalist Economy: 1933–1970*: 'The first part includes three papers published in 1933, 1934 and 1935 in Polish before Keynes' *General Theory* appeared, and containing, I believe, its essentials . . .' (Kalecki, 1971b, p. vii). This claim has not gone without challenge, and Patinkin (1982) in his latest book has concluded that the General Theory was not an example of multiple discovery, in part because of his view of the 'central message' of the General Theory – the possibility of unemployment equilibrium – as contrasted with Kalecki's emphasis on the business cycle. What appears to have been overlooked in this literature is the extent to which Keynes's treatment of the finance required for an increase in investment was foreshadowed in Kalecki's 1935 papers, the first of which was published in French (1935a) and the second in English (1935b). Keynes's reference to the 'revolving fund' nature of finance, when he came to consider this question in his

1937 *Economic Journal* papers, is similar to Kalecki's image of 'the circle [of finance] will close itself' (Kalecki, 1935b, p. 343).

The availability of finance for firms was seen as an important precondition by both Kalecki and Keynes for the independence of investment from saving, an independence that was at the centre of their visions of the factors determining the levels of output and employment. In Joan Robinson's words, it is '. . . the central thesis of the *General Theory*, that firms are free, within wide limits, to accumulate as they please, and that the rate of saving of the economy as a whole accommodates itself to the rate of investment that they decree' (Robinson, 1962, pp. 82–3). Their treatments of finance should thus be seen as integral parts of their theories of the factors that can change effective demand, even though Keynes did not write on this question in connection with his theory of effective demand before 1937. Both Keynes and Kalecki emphasized that it was investment, through its effects on income (and for Kalecki in particular the distribution of income), that resulted in the equality between planned investment and saving that was in the desired relation to income. As we shall see below, neither writer paid sufficient attention to the time required for this equality to be achieved, i.e. for the full multiplier effects of a higher level of investment to be worked out. Keynes even appeared at times to confuse the definitional equality between saving and investment with the equilibrium relation between the two.

Keynes's justification for the use of the adjective 'general' in the title of his book was that it dealt with the general case of possible short-period equilibrium positions for the economy. As a result of the investment decisions of firms and the propensities to save, these positions could often be accompanied by involuntary unemployment, while 'the postulates of the classical theory are applicable to a special case only and not to the general case, the situation which it assumes being a limiting point [a position of full employment] of the possible positions of equilibrium' (Keynes, 1936, p. 3). Our examination of Keynes's treatment of finance, which shows it to be based on 'special' conditions, does not in any way limit the 'generality' of his theory in so far as it refers to the possibility of the economy becoming 'stuck' in situations with less than full employment. What it does is indicate that the complete independence of investment from saving, assumed by Keynes and Kalecki, may be related to the economic conditions at the time of writing of *The General Theory*, thus limiting the 'generality' of this aspect of their theories and the policy prescriptions to be derived from them.

Kalecki on finance and investment

Kalecki was the first to write on the relation between finance and investment in connection with the theory of effective demand,[1] but it is not clear from the written evidence (in English) when he first presented his views on this relation. In the foreword to *Studies in the Theory of Business Cycles: 1933–1939*, which contained translations of his pathbreaking 1933, 1934 and 1935 papers, Kalecki noted that he supplemented the first paper 'by a short passage concerning the problem of the money market taken from [Kalecki, 1935a]' (Kalecki, 1966, p.1). He did not make any reference there to his paper presented at the Econometric Society meeting in Leyden on October 1933, which in its published form (Kalecki, 1935b) also contained a section on finance. Three of the five paragraphs in that section (which will serve as the main source for our examination of Kalecki on this subject) are translations of the material in Kalecki (1935a). There is no indication in the final version that these paragraphs were added after the presentation of the paper at Leyden, but the discussion of Kalecki's paper at the Econometric Society meeting points to their absence in the original version.[2]

Kalecki points out that 'credit inflation' – by which he means an increase in the money supplied by the banking system – is required if there is to be an increase in investment and in economic activity. It is required both to provide funds to finance an increase in investment and to meet the higher transactions demand resulting from the consequent increase in economic activity and prices. On the first requirement Kalecki writes:'When giving an investment order, the entrepreneur has to provide some corresponding fund, out of which he will currently finance the filling of that order' (Kalecki, 1935b, p. 144). Because Kalecki assumes that the current level of investment activity '"finances itself"', i.e. is reflected in realized profits that are available for repeated investment at that level, 'new' credit is only required for the increment in the value of investment decisions over the current level. On the second requirement Kalecki notes: 'Another reason for the inflation of credit is the circumstance that the increase in the production of capital goods or in the consumption of capitalists . . . calls forth a rise of the general level of production and prices. This has the effect of increasing the demand for means of payment under the form of cash or current accounts, and to meet that increased demand a credit inflation becomes necessary' (p. 144).

Kalecki argues that the finance or credit advanced to entrepreneurs for investment is part of a circular flow that not only returns to the banking system within a year but that restores the banks' initial liquidity position. He writes:

> Imagine . . . that some capitalists . . . borrow that amount at the Central Bank, in order to invest it in construction of some additional equipment. In the course of the same year that amount will be received by other capitalists under the form of profits (since, according to our assumptions, workers do not save), and put again into a bank as a savings deposit or used to pay off a debt to the Central Bank. Thus, the circle will close itself (Kalecki, 1935b, p. 343).

The model in Kalecki's 1935 *Econometrica* paper is the same as the one in his 1933 paper on the business cycle, reprinted in English translation in the first chapter of Kalecki (1971b), and the notation employed in the latter will be used here (this model was also published in French in Kalecki (1935a)). In that model there is no saving by workers and the consumption of capitalists is given by $C = B_0 + \lambda P$, where B_0 is positive, λ is a small positive fraction and P is the level of profits. The short-period equilibrium level of profits is given by the equation $P = (B_0 + A)/(1 - \lambda)$ where A is the rate of actual (and planned) investment. Saving is, of course, equal to this rate of investment ($S = P - B_0 - \lambda P = A$), and Kalecki's position is that this saving is available to continue financing a rate of investment equal to A in subsequent periods. If firms want to make investment decisions I that are greater than A, then an extension of credit by the banking system that is equal to $I - A$ ($= \Delta I$) is necessary in order to provide the required finance for this increase of planned investment. It will be assumed, in line with Kalecki's suggestion, that the finance required for an increase in investment is obtained from the central bank, but nothing essential in the argument would be changed if it were to be obtained from commercial banks.

At the beginning of the period (year) in which investment is to be increased, there is an increase in the assets of the central bank of ΔI (debt notes of financing firms) and an increase in liabilities of ΔI (the increase in the chequing accounts of the financing firms).[3] Kalecki's argument that the spending of this finance for investment will result in the restoration of the initial liquidity position of the banking system – the circle will close itself – requires that the increase in assets and liabilities (or the change in their composition) be reversed. If debts are paid off equal to ΔI then the initial position would certainly be restored. (In all this we are ignoring the increased demand for money due to the transactions motive.) This is what the reference to 'pay off a debt to the Central Bank' means in Kalecki's statement quoted above referring to the 'closing' of the circle of finance. Kalecki also referred to the possibility of the capitalists financing the increase of investment by drawing down their savings deposits. There would thus initially be a change in the liquidity position of capitalists as a group, and not in that of the banks (unless the required reserve ratios for savings and cheque accounts differed). The initial situation would once again be restored if saving increased by the amount of the increase in investment and it was 'put again into a bank as a savings deposit . . .' (Kalecki, 1935b, p. 343).

For it to be possible that debts equal to the value of ΔI be paid off, saving – *desired* saving – must be increased by this amount. This eventuality requires the full operation of the multiplier, i.e. the achievement of short-period equilibrium with the new level of investment. Using Kalecki's notation, we find the short-period equilibrium difference in profits to be $\Delta P = \Delta I/(1 - \lambda)$. The desired increase in saving, ΔS, is equal to $(1 - \lambda)\Delta P$, which is equal to ΔI. Since Kalecki assumes that the increase in saving is equal to the increase in planned investment by the end of the year, he is assuming that the full multiplier effect is completed within that period. If this increase in saving is used to increase savings deposits, when the investment finance was obtained through an extension of bank credit, then there has not been a restoration of the bank's pre-increase in investment loan liquidity position. The pay back of bank debt is essential for this. In order for Kalecki's 'circle' to 'close itself', when investment finance is obtained through bank credit, it is thus necessary for both the operation of the full multiplier *and* the retirement of bank debt equal to the initiating credit to have occurred.

Kalecki's analysis dealt with a comparison of positions of short-period equilibrium, and he did not pay sufficient attention to the time required for the operation of the full multiplier in order to 'restore' the liquidity position of the banking system. In his statement of the multiplier he noted that it attains its full value 'eventually', even though he provided no analytical justification for the use of this adverb. '*The general level of production and prices must rise, eventually, so as to provide for an increment of the real profit equal to the increment of the production of capital goods and of the consumption of capitalists*' (Kalecki, 1935b, p. 343). In other contexts, however, he tended to forget the need for the time lapse. For example, in discussing the effects of an imposition of an increase in tax on capitalists' income in 1937 he writes 'the immediate result of an increased income tax is a rise of gross profit . . . by the amount of the increment [in taxation]' (Kalecki, 1971b, p. 39). This is *not* the immediate result but the new short-period equilibrium position that would be reached after the multiplier had worked itself out.[4]

Kalecki's treatment of finance, investment and saving was also flawed because of his neglect of the need for long-term financing. Investing capitalists should replace their bank loans by long-term bonds that are a better 'match' for the expected life of the capital assets that they have acquired. Borrowing 'short' to invest 'long' can be very dangerous for a business enterprise. A reference to bonds in relation to financing investment is found only in a 1954 publication in a chapter on 'The Determinants of Profits'. 'If additional investment is financed by bank credit, the spending of the amounts in question will cause equal amounts of saved profits to accumulate as bank deposits. The investing capitalists will thus find it possible to float bonds to the same extent and thus to repay the bank credits' (Kalecki, 1954, p. 50). An earlier version of this chapter was published in the *Economic Journal* (Kalecki, 1942), and there is no reference there to the use of bonds to obtain the funds to repay bank loans.

Keynes on finance and investment

Keynes did not mention the finance requirements of an increase in investment decisions in his *General Theory*. He returned to this topic[5] in a June 1937 paper on 'Alternative Theories of the Rate of Interest' in response to comments by Ohlin (1937a) and Robertson (1936). Keynes noted that he had not previously given sufficient emphasis to the fact 'that an investment *decision* (Professor Ohlin's investment *ex ante*) may sometimes involve a temporary demand for money before it is carried out, quite distinct from the demand for active balances which will arise as a result of the investment activity whilst it is going on' (Keynes, 1973b, p. 207). Keynes thus makes explicit reference to the two reasons Kalecki gave for the need for an increase in bank finance if investment is to be increased.

Keynes goes on to note that 'unless the banking system is prepared to augment the supply of money, lack of finance may prove an important obstacle to more than a certain amount of investment decisions being on the tapis at a certain time'. He sees this possible restraint on investment as being divorced from saving, since he argues that '"finance" has nothing to do with saving' (Keynes, 1973b, p. 209). Keynes then continues in a way that is also reminiscent of Kalecki. 'It is to an important extent, the "financial" facilities which regulate the *pace* of new investment. . . . But if the banking system chooses to make the finance available and the investment projected by the new issues actually takes place, the appropriate level of incomes will be generated out of which there will necessarily remain over an amount of saving exactly sufficient to take care of the new investment' (p. 210). That is, Keynes introduces investment finance into his system while still maintaining 'that it is not the rate of interest, but the level of incomes which ensures equality between saving and investment' (p. 212).

Comments on this article by Ohlin, Robertson and Hawtrey appeared in the *Economic Journal* for September 1937, and Keynes replied in the December 1937 issue in an article entitled 'The "Ex Ante" Theory of the Rate of Interest'. In this paper he restricted himself to the matters raised by Ohlin because he appeared to recognize the crucial nature of 'finance' for his analysis. He wrote of Ohlin: 'He has compelled me to attend to an important link in the causal chain which I had previously overlooked, and has enabled me to make an important improvement in my analysis' (Keynes, 1973b, pp. 215–16). Keynes emphasized the key role of 'finance' in investment decisions, and even provided a definition of this term ('In what follows I use the term "finance" to mean the credit required in the interval between planning and execution' (Keynes, 1973b, p. 216n.)), but he kept repeating that this finance is independent of planned saving. For example, 'Surely nothing is more certain than that the credit or "finance" required by *ex ante* investment is not mainly supplied by *ex ante* saving' (p. 217). He also recognizes that the availability of short-term finance is not sufficient for a favourable investment decision. 'The entrepreneur when he decides to invest has to be satisfied on two points: firstly, that he can obtain sufficient short-term finance during the period of producing the investment; and secondly, that he can eventually fund his short-term obligations by a long-term issue on satisfactory conditions'. But apart from noting parenthetically in the following paragraph that 'the terms of supply of the finance required by *ex ante* investment' include 'some element of forecast on the part of the entrepreneur as to the terms on which he can fund his finance when the time comes' he then implicitly assumes that the current long-term interest rate can serve as a proxy for this forecast of the future rate that will rule when entrepreneurs go to the new issues market to obtain funds to repay their bank loans. His general position is: 'Broadly speaking, therefore, the rate of interest relevant to *ex ante* investment is the rate of interest determined by the *current* stock of money and the *current* state of liquidity preferences at the date when the finance required by the investment decisions has to be arranged' (pp. 217–18). If this is the long-term rate of interest (cf. Graziani, 1984), then Keynes implicitly assumed an unchanged structure of interest rates, as well as unchanged short-term rates for bank loans. He subsequently refers only to the availability of bank loans, with the banks being able to keep 'the existing rate of interest' unchanged if they 'are ready to lend more cash. . .' (Keynes, 1973b, p. 222).

In the remainder of the paper Keynes is concerned with maintaining his liquidity preference theory of the determination of the rate of interest as opposed to one that sees it as determined by saving and investment. He uses a simile that recalls Kalecki's 'circle' of finance by referring to 'a revolving fund of liquid finance', but this 'revolution' now takes place in an 'interim period' that is much shorter than Kalecki's 'year'. 'For "finance" is essentially a revolving fund. It employs no savings. It is, for the community as a whole, only a book-keeping transaction. As soon as it is "used" in the sense of being expended, the lack of liquidity is automatically made good and the readiness to become temporarily unliquid is available to be used over again. Finance covering the interregnum is, to use a phrase employed by bankers in a more limited context, necessarily "self-liquidating" for the community taken as a whole at the end of the interim period' (Keynes, 1973b, p. 219). From this perspective Keynes argues (as did Kalecki) that a flow of new finance is only required when the rate of investment is to be increased since the current rate of investment is releasing finance equal in value to itself. This leads to what Keynes terms 'the most fundamental of my conclusions within this field':

> in general, the banks hold the key position in the transition from a lower to a higher scale of activity. If they refuse to relax, the growing congestion of the short-term loan market or of the new issue market, as the case may be, will inhibit the improvement, no matter how thrifty the public purpose to be out of their future incomes. On the other hand, there will always be *exactly* enough *ex post* saving to take up the *ex post* investment and so release the finance which the latter has been previously employing. The investment market can become congested through shortage of cash. It can never become congested through shortage of saving. This is the most fundamental of my conclusions within this field' (p. 222).

Our examination of Kalecki's treatment of the relations between finance, investment and saving shows that Keynes's position is based on very special assumptions, assumptions that are even more extreme than those made by Kalecki. In stating that 'the lack of liquidity is automatically made good' as soon as the investment expenditure is made, Keynes is assuming implicitly that the full multiplier operates instantaneously, with a new situation of short-period equilibrium being attained as soon as the investment expenditure is made. Such a situation is a necessary, even though not a sufficient, condition for the initial liquidity position to be restored. It is not enough to have *ex post* saving equal to *ex post* investment (this equality holds, of course, at all times as a result of the national accounts identities) in order for saving to be potentially available to repay the bank loans which made possible the increase in investment. To illustrate this, let us consider situations where investment has increased and short-period equilibrium has not yet been achieved.

(i) The increase ΔA in actual investment is less than the increase ΔI in planned investment, due to mistaken short-term expectations that result in inventories that are lower than expected as a result, for example, of unexpectedly high sales. Therefore, the increase ΔS in saving is less than the initiating increase in bank finance. (We have $\Delta S = \Delta A$, but $\Delta S < \Delta I$ since $\Delta A < \Delta I$.) It is thus insufficient to retire the full increase in bank loans. The firms whose inventories have been unexpectedly drawn down by the higher sales have more cash (including bank deposits), but they will use this unexpected increase in liquidity to replenish inventories in order to carry on with their businesses and not to repay bank loans. The initial liquidity position of the banks is thus not 'automatically made good' even if the total increase in saving is directed to repaying bank debt.

(ii) $\Delta A = \Delta I$, but saving is not in the desired relation to income because consumption has not caught up with the increase in income (the full multiplier effect has not yet been achieved). This increase in saving (even though $\Delta S = \Delta I$) is not *all* available to pay back debts, since some of this saving is temporary (or 'disequilibrium' saving) which individuals intend to use as soon as possible for consumption purposes.

The definitional equality between saving and investment can thus provide no support for Keynes's position that 'there will always be *exactly* enough *ex post* saving to take up the *ex post* investment and so release the finance. . .' (Keynes, 1973b, p. 222). The position he takes might indicate a confusion between the equality of *ex post* investment and saving and the conditions for short-period equilibrium.[6]

Finance, investment, speculation and saving

The examination of the similar treatments by Kalecki and Keynes of the relation between finance, investment and saving has made clear that they underestimated the time required before it would be possible for the banks' liquidity position to be restored (abstracting from the increase in credit required to satisfy a higher transactions demand for money) after an increase in bank loans to finance an increase in investment. Keynes's position on this point was even more extreme than Kalecki's since he stated that the investment expenditure itself would be sufficient to release the finance tied up by the increase in investment decisions.[7] As we have seen, such a 'release' requires that there be an increase in desired saving equal to planned investment and this saving must be used, directly or indirectly, to retire bank debt. The achievement of a higher level of investment thus requires the banking system to become less liquid (to increase its current account liabilities, balanced by IOUs from investing firms) and to maintain a less liquid position at least until the full multiplier has operated and the increase in desired saving has caught up with the increase in planned investment. A constant rate of increase in the level of investment over time will require banks to continue expanding their current liabilities, even if the resulting increases in desired saving are used to retire bank debts.

There is the further, complementary, point about the long-term financing required by firms to match their long-term commitments in their investment projects. These firms must be assured about the availability of long-term, as well as short-term, finance before committing themselves to investment decisions. There is scope here for the activities of intermediaries ('speculators') who are prepared to adjust their relative holdings of long- and short-term securities. They could thus provide the investing firms with long-term finance *before* the full multiplier effects of the increase in investment have been completed by purchasing their long-term bonds with the proceeds of short-term loans from the banks. Such activity does not, of course, restore the initial liquidity position of the banks since one set of loans is replaced by another, but it does permit the investing firms to go ahead with their investment plans. After the full multiplier has operated, following a maintained

increase in the rate of investment, there is an increase in desired
saving that, if directed to the purchase of long-term securities,
can relieve the pressure on these intermediaries (speculators) to
support this higher rate of investment. In such a case banks will
then no longer be required to keep increasing their loans. There
is, however, the question of the terms at which speculators, and
eventually those whose savings increase, would be willing to
purchase long-term securities. Is the spread between the short-
and long-term rates that they require sufficiently small not to
discourage investment?

Kaldor, in his important 1939 paper on 'Speculation and
Economic Stability', pointed out that Keynes's General Theory
'in so far as it concerns his theory of the rate of interest and the
theory of the multiplier, is rather in the nature of a "special case"'
(reprinted in Kaldor (1960, p. 52)), since it depends on the
stabilizing influence of speculation on the price of long-term bonds
being infinite. By this he meant that it was based on the implicit
assumption that speculators would absorb the new issues of long-
term securities (obtaining the necessary funds by borrowing at
short term) until the increased saving became available for this
purpose, without any noticeable change in the term structure of
interest rates. Kaldor illustrates the role of speculative activity by
means of a numerical example in which the increase in investment
is financed by the sale of long-term securities. The increase in
desired saving is assumed to flow, directly or indirectly, to the
purchase of long-term securities but, since it is not increased until
after the investment has been made, the securities making possible
the higher rate of investment are purchased by those who are
prepared to increase their speculative commitments. Kaldor
assumes that there is a one-'week' lag in the consumption function,
i.e. $C_t = C(Y_{t-1})$, and a marginal propensity to save of one-quarter.
In order to make possible a £1 million increase in the 'weekly'
rate of investment, speculative resources must absorb an increase
in long-term securities of £4 million. The formula showing the
relation between the required total increase in long-term securities
purchased out of speculative resources and the propensity to save
s, and the increase ΔI in investment per 'week' is $\Delta I/s$. (In the
first week the total increase ΔI in investment must be financed
by speculators. In the second week the increase in desired saving
is $(1 - c)\Delta I$, where c is the marginal propensity to consume, and

thus speculators are only required to absorb $c\Delta I$. In the third week, the increase in desired saving over its initial level is equal to $(1 - c^2)\Delta I$, and speculators are required to absorb additional securities equal in value to $c^2\Delta I$. The total amount that they must absorb until the full multiplier effect is completed is thus equal to $\Delta I(1 + c + c^2 + \ldots)$, or $\Delta I/(1 - c) = \Delta I/s$.) This amount is also the total increase in their bank loans.

The increase in speculative commitments (and the corresponding increase in bank loans) thus ceases once the full multiplier effect of a maintained increase in the rate of investment is completed. Kaldor concludes

> . . . the contribution which the speculative resources of the market have to make is limited. Provided that the total required increase in the size of speculative stocks is not too large relatively to the resources of the market (i.e., provided it does not impair the degree of price stabilising influence) there will be no pressure on the price of securities (i.e. no tendency for the rate of interest to rise) either in the long run, or in the short run' (Kaldor, 1960, p. 50).

Kaldor introduces an important exception to this conclusion when he considers an open economy, as we shall see below, but his conclusion for a closed economy is more 'special' than he allows. He writes

> . . . if we abstract from the case of foreign exchange under a gold standard or quasi-gold-standard regime, it is true that the degree of price-stabilising influence, though not perhaps infinite, is very much larger in the case of long-term bonds than for any other commodity; and this means that the Keynesian theory, though a 'special case', gives, nevertheless, a fair approximation to reality' (p. 52).

Kaldor's judgement here reflects economic conditions ('reality') at the time at which his article was written. There was then still considerable unemployment, idle productive capacity, ample stocks of raw materials and stable prices and money wage rates. But in situations where prices have been increasing, and there are fears of further increases, there may very well be downward pressures on the prices of long-term securities even if the banks are prepared to increase their short-term loans, because savers find that other assets become more attractive to hold. The possible constraints on the ability of firms to increase their rates of investment under such circumstances should be recognized in a 'general' theory. An increase in the propensity to save in this case might make it more likely that an increase in investment could be accommodated without an increase in prices, and this could facilitate the financing of that investment by affecting expectations about future long-term interest rates. Such an increase in the propensity to save would also, if directed to long-term securities, relieve some of the pressures placed on speculators to facilitate an increase in investment since, as we have seen, the amount of long-term securities that speculators are called on to absorb when investment is increased is inversely related to the marginal propensity to save. The independence of investment, and the finance that makes investment possible, from saving is not as robust as Keynes stated. The investment market *can* become 'congested through shortage of saving' even in a closed economy.

An open economy

Consideration of an open economy strengthens the position that the treatments of finance by Kalecki and Keynes are based on conditions that are more special than is indicated by their statements. In an open economy the increase in imports following an increase in investment dampens the subsequent increase in income, and thus limits the increase in desired saving. The increase in domestic saving, even in short-period equilibrium, would be smaller than the increase in investment, with the decrease being substituted for by foreign saving. Only if the latter is directed to domestic long-term securities, at an unchanged term structure of interest rates, would we be in a situation similar to that of short-period equilibrium in a closed economy when the increase in desired saving is used to purchase such securities. If the increased deficit is financed by accommodating short-term loans (or by a decrease in the holdings of gold or foreign currencies), then the term structure would have to change to allow the increase in long-term debt to be absorbed by speculators. Such an increase in long-term interest rates could have an adverse effect on investment. The necessity for an increase in long-term rates under these conditions, and its import for casting doubt on Keynes's assertion that 'the investment market can be congested on account of a shortage of cash. It can never be congested on account of a shortage of savings' (Keynes, 1973b, p. 222) was pointed out by Kaldor. 'The long-term rate rises *relatively* to the short-term rate simply because, owing to a shortage of savings, speculators are required to expand continuously the size of their commitments; and there are limits to the extent to which this is possible' (Kaldor, 1960, p. 51). He went on to note that 'Temporarily, the banks might prevent the long-term rate from rising by *reducing* the short-term rate; but however much they inundate the system with cash, sooner or later the long rate must rise' (p. 52n.).

Government expenditure and taxation

The introduction of government expenditure and taxation into the model of a closed economy has some formal similarities to the opening of an economy to foreign trade, since the condition for short-period equilibrium in a model with government activity is that desired saving be equal to the sum of planned investment and the government deficit. If the structure of government expenditure and taxation is such that the government deficit is a decreasing function of the level of income in the economy, then the increase in saving generated by an increase in investment will be less than this increase in investment. The consequent decrease in the government deficit dampens the multiplier effects of the increase in investment in a manner similar to the increase in imports in an open economy. In this case, however, the increase in domestic saving potentially available to fund the short-term credits financing the increase in investment is equal, at the conclusion of the multiplier process, to that increase, because less is required to finance the government deficit.

Large government deficits, and the fear of possibly increasing deficits, may increase apprehensions about future long-term interest rates. In such circumstances firms might be reluctant to increase investment, even if short-term finance could be obtained, because of concern over being able to fund these credits at reasonable interest rates. Speculators might be unwilling to absorb additional long-term securities without substantial increases in long-term rates.[8] In such an environment an increase in the propensity to save – although taken by itself it would have adverse effects on effective demand – would lessen the depressing effects on financial markets of any given level of the government deficit. It might thus make it easier for firms to proceed with plans to increase investment.

Conclusion

Both Kalecki and Keynes emphasized the importance of an increase in bank loans in permitting firms to increase the rate of investment. For both it was the subsequent changes in income (as well as the distribution of income for Kalecki) that brought desired saving into equality with the increase in investment. They both underestimated the time required before the initial liquidity position of the banking system could be restored after banks increased their loans to finance an increase in investment (the position of Keynes in this regard is susceptible to even more criticism than is Kalecki's). There was also insufficient attention given to the requirement for long-term finance (or at least confidence about its availability) in order for firms to proceed with their investment plans (and in this case it is Kalecki's position that is weaker than Keynes's).

Keynes concluded his 1937 *Quarterly Journal of Economics* paper by drawing a distinction between the general nature of his 'diagnosis' of the factors affecting the level of output and employment and his 'suggestions for a cure'. The latter, he noted, 'avowedly, are not worked out completely, are on a different plane from the diagnosis. They are not meant to be definitive; they are subject to all sorts of special assumptions and are necessarily related to the particular conditions of the time' (Keynes, 1973b, pp. 121–2). We have seen, however, that an important aspect of his diagnosis, his view of the general independence of investment from the propensity to save and the 'revolving nature of finance', can be shown not to be definitive but to be based on special assumptions, some of which are '. . . related to the particular conditions of the time' of composition of *The General Theory*.

None of these criticisms affect the conclusions of Kalecki and Keynes on the critical role of the rate of investment in determining effective demand, on the possibility of equilibrium with involuntary unemployment and on the possibly large fluctuations in the rate of investment because of changing views concerning a future about which there is a great deal of uncertainty. What they do is to indicate that there may be limits, related in some way to the propensity to save, to the extent to which firms are in a position to increase their rate of investment even if short-term credit is available to finance such an increase.

Notes

1 Keynes had previously mentioned the importance of credit facilities in making possible changes in investment in his *Treatise on Money*. For example, '. . . the pace, at which the innovating entrepreneurs will be able to carry their projects into execution at a cost in interest which is not deterrent to them, will depend on the degree of complaisance of those responsible for the banking system' (Keynes, 1930, p. 96). Wicksell (1965, pp. 74–5) had earlier emphasized the importance of bank credit in enabling entrepreneurs to carry out their investment plans.

2 A comment by Fritz Machlup that is reported in the publication of the proceedings of this 1933 meeting makes sense only if Kalecki had neglected to draw attention to the requirements for finance. Kalecki is reported to have 'agreed with Fritz Machlup that a credit inflation was necessarily implied in his explanation of the business cycle' (Marschak, 1934, p. 194). This comment might have been the catalyst for the inclusion of an explicit reference to the need for finance in Kalecki's final version of the paper. I am grateful to Don Patinkin for drawing my attention to this discussion.

3 Commercial banks could have made the finance available by selling bills or bonds. If they are purchased by private entities, then there is no net change in the banking system's total assets and liabilities; there is a change only in their composition. The assets have become less liquid, with bank debts of the financing firms replacing the more liquid bills and bonds. If the bills or bonds are purchased by the central bank then there will be a net increase in the banking system's assets and liabilities equal to the increase in investment. Again, the system is less liquid than it was before this increase in finance.

4 In his 1937 paper 'A Theory of the Business Cycle' – a paper to which Keynes made reference in his June 1937 article on finance and investment – Kalecki implicitly assumed that the full multiplier effect was worked out within a short period, a period he gave as being 'equal to a few months' (Kalecki, 1937a, p. 82). In that paper Kalecki's

emphasis was on the liquidity position of the investing capitalists, with their exposure to risk growing with the level of their planned investments. It was this increase in risk that limited (neglecting possible credit restraints from the banking system) the value of investment decisions in any short period, even though the prospective rate of profit exceeded the rate of interest. New investment decisions, however, were seen as being made in the succeeding short period because the saving in that period, which is equal to the value of the investment decisions currently planned, restores the liquidity position of capitalists as a group. Here again is the completion of the full multiplier effect within the short period, this time of a few months' duration rather than a year.

5 See reference in note 1 to statements in his *Treatise on Money*.

6 It is interesting to note Robertson's warning on this point, born of experience in controversies concerning saving, investment and the rate of interest. 'In any position other than one of static equilibrium, confusion between a concept of saving in which it is definitionally identical with investment and a concept in which it is functionally related to income will give rise to trouble' (Robertson, 1951-2, p. 105). Another possible reason for Keynes's error is his presentation in *The General Theory* of the 'logical theory of the multiplier, which holds good continuously, without time-lag, at all moments of time' (Keynes, 1936, p. 122). In developing this approach he defines the 'marginal propensity to consume' without reference to a consumption function. It is defined to be equal to the ratio of the actual increment in consumption to the actual increment in income that occur during any time period (p. 115). As we have seen, it is not enough for the increase in saving to be equal to the increase in investment for the finance to be 'released'. The full multiplier must have worked itself out, with the increase in saving being in the desired relation to income and being used, directly or indirectly, to repay bank loans.

7 In connection with this stand taken by Keynes, Robertson wrote to Keynes in a letter dated 31 December 1937 (see also Robertson (1938, p. 315)): 'I cannot see that any revolving fund is released, any willingness to undergo illiquidity set free for further employment, by the act of the borrowing entrepreneur in spending his loan. The bank has become a debtor to other entrepreneurs, work people, etc., instead of to the borrowing entrepreneur, that is all. The borrowing entrepreneur remains a debtor to the bank and the bank's assets have not been altered either in amount or in liquidity' (printed in Keynes (1973b, pp. 28–9)).

Keynes's answer to Robertson appeared in the *Economic Journal* for June 1938 following Robertson (1938), and is reprinted in Keynes (1973b, pp. 229–33). Keynes tried to evade the issues raised by

Robertson by changing the questions. He stated that he used the term 'finance' to mean 'cash'. 'A large part of the outstanding confusion is due, I think, to Mr. Robertson's thinking of "finance" as consisting in bank loans; whereas in the article under discussion I introduced this term to mean *cash* temporarily held by entrepreneurs to provide against the outgoings in respect of an impending new activity' (Keynes, 1973b, p. 229). This statement contradicts what he had written in the article discussed by Robertson where we find: 'In what follows I use the term "finance" to mean the credit required in the interval between planning and execution' (Keynes, 1973b, p. 216, n. 1). Keynes also switched his position on the meaning to be attached to the significance of the expenditure of 'finance'. From 'As soon as it ["finance"] is "used" in the sense of being expended, the lack of liquidity is automatically made good and the readiness to become temporarily unliquid is available to be used over again' (p. 219); it became 'the demand for cash, due to the requirements of "finance", is automatically at an end as soon as the finance is expended' (p. 230). His retreat into this triviality is an implicit admission of the indefensibility of his earlier position.

8 The ability to obtain long-term finance for investment at rates not much above short-term rates depends very much on economic conditions in the present and in the recent past, because of their effects on expectations. For example, concern has been expressed in the United States that the Federal Reserve Board might be unable to bring down long-term rates sufficiently to stimulate investment. It was reported in the *New York Times* of 23 December 1982 that

> At the Federal Reserve Board, which has nervously tried to push down interest rates to get a recovery started, the chairman, Paul A. Volcker, is still worried that record deficits in 1984 and beyond could get in the way of a recovery at the beginning, by forcing interest rates up again.
>
> Mr Volcker, in an appearance in Mayfield, Ky., last week even wondered if the Fed's current policy was not already running into trouble. He noted that long-term interest rates, which reflect inflationary expectations, inched up slightly in the days following the latest cut in the Fed's discount rate to $8\frac{1}{2}$ percent.

8

Anticipations of Keynes's General Theory?

Don Patinkin's book *Anticipations of the General Theory? And Other Essays on Keynes*[1] is a scholarly and stimulating addition to the voluminous literature dealing with the writings of John Maynard Keynes. Part I, which occupies almost half of the book, examines the question of whether the 'central message' of Keynes had been anticipated by the writings of the Stockholm School or by Michal Kalecki. The chapters in parts II–IV of the book present a critique of Keynes's theory of effective demand, examine the relationship between Keynesian monetary theory and the Cambridge School, examine Keynes's role in the development of the multiplier, consider the evolution of his attitude to economic policy and conclude with an examination of the interaction between macroeconomic theory and the development of national income statistics in the inter-war period. The material in these chapters is based on previously published articles, but there have been substantial revisions in some, with additional notes and postscripts appended to others, often in response to comments made by those who were involved in the developments examined by Patinkin.

This book, written by a very conscientious scholar whose own contributions to macroeconomic theory are frequently cited, thus represents not only his carefully considered views on the most important aspects of Keynes's General Theory, but his 'reconsidered' views. They thus deserve serious attention and study. It is a book to be recommended to one's students and colleagues, even though one can argue, as can be seen below, with some of Patinkin's main conclusions.

The present review will concentrate on the first two parts of the book, those concerned with possible anticipations of *The General Theory* and with Patinkin's critique of Keynes's presentation of the theory of effective demand.

The 'central message' of the General Theory

The answer to the question of whether Keynes's General Theory[2] had been anticipated by others depends critically on what is taken to be the 'central message' of that theory. Patinkin argues that it is 'the theory of effective demand as a theory which depends on the equilibrating effects of the decline in output itself to explain why [and he then quotes from page 30 of *The General Theory*] "the economic system may find itself in stable equilibrium with N [employment] at a level below full employment, namely at the level given by the intersection of the aggregate demand function with the aggregate supply function"' (p. 11). In defence of this choice he points to Keynes's own emphasis in an August 1936 letter to Harrod, commenting on the latter's review article of *The General Theory*, on the importance for him of the 'psychological law, that when income increases, the gap between income and consumption will increase . . .' (Keynes, 1973b, p. 85). This 'law' means that, given the rate of investment, aggregate demand will increase by less than output so that an initial position of excess aggregate demand will tend to change to one of short-period equilibrium owing to the consequent equilibrating increases in output. This is certainly an important element of the central message of the General Theory, and Patinkin correctly points out the limited meaning of the term 'equilibrating' in Keynes's model. It does not mean 'that nothing in the economy tends to change' (p. 14), but rather that it is a position of 'rest' for the variable of interest (Asimakopulos, 1973). In this case it is the level of employment that does not tend to change. Patinkin's description of the central message is incomplete, however, because of its relative neglect of investment.

The importance that Keynes gave to the rate of investment in connection with his theory can be seen by the prominence he gave to it in his 1937 *Quarterly Journal of Economics* article. This was written in reply to a series of four articles on *The General Theory* that appeared in an earlier issue of that journal, and Keynes (in the words of the editor of this volume of his collected writings) 'tried again to set out his theory' (Keynes, 1973b, p. 108). Keynes wrote that his 'theory can be summed up by saying that, given the psychology of the public, the level of output and employment as a whole depends on the amount of investment. I put it in this way, not because this is the only factor on which aggregate output depends, but because it is usual in a complex system to regard as the *causa causans* that factor which is most prone to sudden and wide fluctuation (Keynes, 1973b, p. 121). Keynes's central message thus comprises not only the view that total output and employment are determined by aggregate demand and supply but also 'a theory of why output and employment are so liable to fluctuation'.

In support of his interpretation of the central message, Patinkin quoted, as noted above, from a letter Keynes had written to Harrod, with the preliminary comment that it 'largely repeats what Keynes had written Abba Lerner two months earlier' (p. 8). There is an important difference, however, between these two letters that supports the present interpretation. Keynes wrote to Lerner 'as income increases, the gap between income and consumption may be expected to widen. . . . A higher level of income will only be possible without loss to the entrepreneur, if the widening gap between income and consumption can be filled. This can only be filled by investment. Yet it is evident that the requisite volume of investment is not necessarily there' (Keynes, 1979, p. 215). The determination of the rate of investment, and the reasons why it might not be sufficient to result in full employment, are an integral and central part of Keynes's General Theory.

Patinkin, before stating his choice for the major contribution of *The General Theory*, dismisses as candidates 'the crucial role it gives the fluctuations in investment in generating business cycles' and 'its emphasis on the fact that economic decisions in the real world (and especially those related to investment) are made under conditions of uncertainty which are not subject to probability calculus' (p. 6). The reasons given are that the former theme 'is to be found at least as far back as the business cycle theories of Tugan-Baranowsky' and that the latter 'notion of uncertainty had already been forcefully presented many years before . . . by Knight in his classic 1921 work, *Risk, Uncertainty, and Profit*'. But this dismissal ignores the essential contribution of Keynes, which was to integrate an approach to investment with a theory of aggregate output and employment. It is this integration of various elements – traces of which can be found in earlier writings – into a general theory that is his major contribution.

The theory of effective demand interpreted narrowly as an explanation of the factors determining the short-period equilibrium level of employment, and the stability of that level given the rate of investment, is thus an incomplete statement of the central message of the General Theory.[3] This message also includes an explanation of this rate of investment, why it is potentially volatile, and why investment in any short period cannot, in general, be expected to have just the right value required to ensure full employment.

Anticipations of the General Theory – the Stockholm School?

Patinkin's main search for possible anticipations of the General Theory is in two directions: towards Swedish economists (the 'Stockholm School' (Ohlin, 1937a)) on the one hand, and towards the Polish economist Michal Kalecki on the other hand. In deciding whether the General Theory had been anticipated, Patinkin is looking for a clear statement of that theory. He notes 'that in studying a man's writings we must distinguish between that which was fully integrated into his conceptual framework and that which was not; between the systematic component of his thinking and the random component; between, if you wish, the "signal" – or what I have called the "central message" – the writer wished to convey and the "noise"' (p. 16).

The three Swedish economists to whose writings he pays particular attention are Erik Lindahl, Gunnar Myrdal and Bertil Ohlin. In each case he concludes that the central concern was not with the factors determining the equilibrium level of output and employment – a level that could be one of less than full employment – but rather with changes in prices, even though there were some references to changing output.   Lindahl's main work that is examined in this connection is a 1930 monograph, most of which was translated into English in his *Studies in the Theory of Capital*

(1939). Patinkin concludes that this work cannot be viewed as an anticipation of the General Theory, since his chief concern is with 'the determination not of output, but of prices . . .' (p. 44). Even though at one point it is assumed that initially there are unemployed resources, Lindahl 'does not analyze how the level of unemployment is determined and merely says that these unemployed resources make it possible for some expansion of output to take place before prices begin to rise' (p. 45). There is no recognition of the feedback effects of changes in output on demand and their role in establishing equilibrium between planned investment and desired saving.

Myrdal is 'also not seen as anticipating the General Theory, since his *Monetary Equilibrium* (1939) (basically a translation of an essay published in German in 1933) was concerned with the lack of theoretical support for Wicksell's contention 'that the equating of money and real rate of interest rates will also achieve equality between savings and investment as well as stability of the price level' (p. 51). Situations of unemployment appear in Myrdal's analysis in the consideration of downward movements due, for example, to an increase in savings,[4] but there is no clear statement of the equilibrating role of changes in output.

Ohlin's writings that have been pointed to as anticipations of *The General Theory* are a 1933 article, published in English translation in 1978, and a 1934 *Report* for the Government Committee on Unemployment (Steiger, 1976). Patinkin concludes that the central message of the former concerns the analysis of changes in prices, and there is 'no recognition of . . . the equilibrating role of changes in output' (p. 53). He notes that Ohlin recognized that an increase in the propensity to consume, through the favourable effect of higher consumption demand on investment may increase total saving as a result of the consequent increase in total output. But Patinkin argues that such a recognition 'does not differ fundamentally from Keynes' imprecise contention in *Can Lloyd George Do It?* (1929) that increased investment in public works will generate correspondingly increased savings – in part "by the very prosperity which the new policy will foster"' (p. 53). Richard Kahn's 1931 multiplier article provided a rigorous demonstration of this proposition, and Patinkin's position is that 'recognition of the multiplier did not constitute recognition of the General Theory' (p. 54). With respect to the 1934 *Report*, Patinkin concludes that 'though the ultimate concern of Ohlin's 1934 *Report* is unemployment, its central message (like that of his 1933 article) remains the analysis of prices, and not output' (p. 56).

Anticipation of the General Theory – Michal Kalecki?

Patinkin's summary of his consideration of Kalecki's pre-*General Theory* writings is that 'In his primary concern with quantities as against prices; in his concentration on national-income magnitudes and functional relations among them; and in his corresponding emphasis on analyzing the relationship between investment and other macroeconomic variables, Kalecki came significantly closer to the General Theory than did the Stockholm School . . .' (p. 77). But he does not consider

> Kalecki's theory to be an independent development of the General Theory . . . [because] Kalecki's central message has to do not with the forces that generate equilibrium at low levels of output, but with the forces that generate cycles of investment: more specifically, not with the feedback mechanism that equilibrates planned saving and investment via declines in output, but with cyclical behavior of investment on the implicit assumption that there always exists equality between planned savings and investment. (pp. 77–8)

There are various places in Patinkin's analysis of Kalecki's works where my interpretation would be slightly different, and I would have included a consideration of Kalecki's anticipation of Keynes's treatment of finance, but his conclusion appears to me to be warranted. Kalecki came very close to the General Theory, and although his framework of analysis can be used to reach Keynes's conclusions he did not do so in his early theoretical writings. The crucial role of investment was recognized (and it was part of Kalecki's main concern), but he did not deal explicitly with unemployment equilibrium. In large part this was because he was 'outside' the mainstream of economic theory in terms of his education (and his relative isolation in Poland would not have helped), so that the critical *theoretical* significance of an explanation of unemployment equilibrium would not have been obvious to him. Kalecki's approach to economics was very much affected by Marxian theory and national income accounting (p. 63), and with this background the theoretical explanation of the coexistence of equilibrium and involuntary unemployment would not be seen as a matter of central concern. Dealing with it would not have been for him, as it was for Keynes, 'a long struggle of escape . . . a struggle of escape from habitual modes of thought and expression' (Keynes, 1936, p. viii). The existence of involuntary unemployment – a reserve army of unemployed – was something taken for granted in his analysis,[5] which was concerned with the examination of the business cycle. He found the key to be the double-sided relationship between investment and profits and the time lags in the investment process.

Kalecki presented a situation of unemployment equilibrium and showed why it was stable given the rate of investment, even in the face of a reduction of money wage rates, in a 1935 article (reprinted in English translation in Kalecki (1966, pp. 26–33) and Kalecki (1971b, pp. 26–34)) published in a Polish semi-governmental weekly magazine devoted to economic commentary and reports. He argued that even if the initial effect of the wage reduction is to increase production and employment 'A precondition for an equilibrium at this new higher level is that this part of production which is not consumed by workers . . . should be acquired by capitalists . . . the capitalists must spend immediately all their additional profits on consumption or investment. It is, however, most unlikely that this should in fact happen' (Kalecki, 1971b, p. 27).[6] This is, of course, the conclusion that Keynes drew from his theory of effective demand.

Joan Robinson, in her contribution to *Essays in Honour of Michal Kalecki* (Kowalik et al. (1964), reprinted in Robinson (1965)), refers to this article in support of her claim, in comparing Kalecki and Keynes, that Kalecki 'found the same solution' (Robinson, 1965, p. 94). What this article shows is that the key elements in Keynes's theory could have been derived on the basis of Kalecki's analysis; however, Patinkin's position that Kalecki did not derive them in his professional writings appears to be correct: 'this theme of "unemployment equilibrium" receives little if any attention in Kalecki's professional writings during the pre-*General Theory* period. And lest I be misunderstood, let me emphasize that my point here is not that this theme appears in Kalecki's nonprofessional writings, but that it appears *only* there' (p. 72).[7] This fact is implicitly recognized in Robinson's

Introduction to a collection of Kalecki's studies that included his 1933 article. She wrote that Kalecki 'arrived at a general theory through a model of the trade cycle. It was probably for this reason that the significance of his ideas was not recognized by readers of his French publication in 1935. The problem of the trade cycle had always been regarded in the orthodox tradition as a special kind of conundrum, apart from the main body of doctrine. Keynes, on the other hand, attacked the main body directly and never really succeeded in getting out a coherent theory of the cycle' (Kalecki, 1966, p. x). It was this attack on the 'main body of doctrine' of 'orthodox tradition' that is at the core of the General Theory.

There is no discussion of short-period equilibrium in Kalecki's theoretical writings before the appearance of *The General Theory*.[8] It would seem that it appears in these writings only after he read *The General Theory*. It is given an important role in his 1937 *Review of Economic Studies* paper (Kalecki (1937a), which contains important sections of his 1936 review of *The General Theory*), where Keynes's two-part approach is used first to consider the determination of short-period equilibrium given the rate of investment and then to look at the determination of that rate. In his 1933 paper (and in the slightly different forms in which it appears in Kalecki (1935a, 1935b)) there is no indication of an awareness of the difference between the equality of gross profits and the sum of capitalists' consumption and investment as a definitional relation, and its equality as an equilibrium relation.

Kalecki explains the equality between profits and the sum of capitalists' consumption and investment, with which he begins his 1933 article, as a consequence of the national income identity between gross national product and gross national expenditure (Kalecki, 1971b, p. 1n.). But he then assumes that the consumption of workers and capitalists is in the desired relation to their incomes, i.e. all wages are consumed, and the consumption of capitalists is a linear function of current profits. When this assumption, along with his implicit one that actual investment is equal to planned investment, is incorporated into his profits equation, the latter becomes an equilibrium relation. With investment, output and profits changing throughout the cycle, the maintenance of short-period equilibrium in each 'unit of time' (whose length is not otherwise specified) is a very special case, but there is no indication in Kalecki's presentation of this problem.[9] This abstraction from the time required to reach short-period equilibrium, or any discussion of such a position, when investment is changing serves to support Patinkin's conclusion that Kalecki's central message concerned the cyclical process rather than the factors determining the short-period equilibrium levels of output and employment.[10]

It is easy, with the benefit of hindsight, to read the General Theory into Kalecki's writings, since his analytic framework can be readily used to derive it. Kalecki seemed to be on the verge of stating the theory of effective demand following his consideration of the cycle in his 1933 paper, when he turned to the fluctuations in aggregate production that accompany fluctuations in investment. He provides a statement of the conditions for a new short-period equilibrium position if investment increases: '*The aggregate production and the profit per unit of output will ultimately rise to such an extent as to assure an increment in real profits equal to that of production of investment goods and capitalists' consumption*' (Kalecki, 1971b, p. 12).[11] This statement implies recognition of the investment multiplier, and the need for the passage of time for the full multiplier to operate, but it does not take the further step required to turn it into the theory of effective demand.[12] Similarly, his conclusion from these reflections. 'Thus capitalists, as a whole, determine their own profits by the extent of their investment and personal consumption. In a way they are "masters of their fate"' would be a promising introduction to a statement of the theory of effective demand, but it goes on to make clear that the explanation of fluctuations were his main concern: 'but how they "master" it is determined by objective factors, so that fluctuations of profits appear after all to be unavoidable (Kalecki, 1971b, p. 13). An unequivocal statement of the theory of effective demand using his model only appeared after the publication of *The General Theory*: 'the level of spending of the capitalists (expressed in wage-units) is the chief determinant of the short-period equilibrium and particularly of employment and income" (Kalecki, 1937a, p. 79).[13]

Keynes's General Theory comprised the view that investment was independent of saving, with changes in the level of incomes ensuring equality between (desired) saving and the new level of investment. It thus assumes that entrepreneurs are able to obtain command of the finance required to increase investment, finance that the theory states is independent of saving. Kalecki, with his emphasis on the variability of investment, anticipated Keynes's treatment of this subject, a subject whose importance the latter realized after reading Ohlin's *Economic Journal* articles (Ohlin, 1937a, 1937b). Keynes stated in 1937 that Ohlin 'has compelled me to attend to an important link in the causal chain which I had previously overlooked, and has enabled me to make an important improvement in my analysis' (Keynes, 1973b, pp. 215–16). Kalecki first made explicit reference to the credit expansion required to facilitate an increase in investment in his 1935 *Revue d' économie politique* paper, and he then incorporated a consideration of it in the English translation of his 1933 paper (Kalecki, 1966, p. 1).[14] There are some differences in the treatments of this question by Kalecki and Keynes, but both emphasize the circular flow of investment finance and its independence from saving.[15] Kalecki writes about finance that within a year 'the circle will close itself' (Kalecki, 1935b, p. 343), while Keynes writes '"finance" is essentially a revolving fund' (Keynes, 1973b, p. 219).

Patinkin's critique of Keynes's theory of effective demand

There is an error in Keynes's presentation of his theory of effective demand – an error that is due to the inconsistency between Keynes's first definition of his aggregate demand function and the microfoundations of his theory – and the careful reader who already knows of this error will be able to spot it from Patinkin's critique. For others, however, it will be obscured by Patinkin's claim – which this writer feels is not warranted – that a serious problem with Keynes's presentation is his confusion between marginal and average concepts. This claim is based, in part, on a misinterpretation of some of Keynes's statements about his aggregate supply function and on some ambiguous statements in early drafts of *The General Theory*.

Patinkin finds chapter 3 on effective demand 'the most obscure chapter in *The General Theory*' (p. 123). An important reason for this would seem to be his unwillingness to accept Keynes's assurance to Robertson that the aggregate supply function 'is simply the age-old supply function . . . it is only a re-concoction of our old friend the supply function' (Keynes, 1973a, p. 513).

Once this is accepted, Patinkin's concerns with that function largely disappear. It is not accidental that Keynes used terms to describe his function that parallel Marshall's statements about supply curves. In his definition Keynes writes 'the aggregate supply price of the output of a given amount of employment is the expectation of proceeds which will just make it worth the while of the entrepreneurs to give that employment' (Keynes, 1936, p. 24). This echoes Marshall's definition of the supply price for a particular commodity: 'the normal supply price of any amount of that commodity . . . is the price the expectation of which will just suffice to maintain the existing aggregate amount of production' (Marshall, 1920, pp. 342–3). For Keynes, as well as for Marshall, the 'expectation' that is controlling the situation is based on the expectations of price that are held by individual entrepreneurs when they are deciding on their individual rates of output and employment (Keynes, 1936, p. 46).

Marshall's aggregation was limited to an industry, while Keynes went on to define an aggregate supply function for the economy. A price, since it relates to a specific commodity, cannot form the basis of Keynes's aggregation, and he thus went from the expected prices (which control output decisions) to the corresponding expected proceeds. The latter are obtained by multiplying the expected prices by the outputs (sales) the firms plan to produce (and sell), given these expected prices. Keynes could then, conceptually, sum these expected proceeds (after deducting user costs) across industries in order to obtain the point on the aggregate supply function that corresponds to the assumed set of expected prices. A different point on this curve would thus correspond to a different set of expected prices. The shape of the aggregate supply curve would thus depend on the shapes of the underlying supply curves and the weights used to combine them.[16]

As soon as the microfoundations of Keynes's aggregate supply function are recognized, it becomes clear that effective demand (and for Keynes 'Employment is determined *solely* by effective demand' (Keynes, 1973b, p. 180)) is the point on the aggregate supply function corresponding to the entrepreneurs' expected proceeds.[17] It is at this point, given expected prices, that entrepreneurs' expectations of profits are maximized. There is no room in this determination of employment for the only type of aggregate demand function that is permitted by Keynes's microfoundations, an aggregate demand function that shows the realized results at alternative levels of employment. For as Keynes wrote in the surviving rough notes for his 1937 lectures, 'the proceeds which entrepreneurs *expect* to receive . . . [are the only relevant ones] in a theory of employment . . . *realised* results are only relevant in so far as they influence the ensuing expectations in the next production period' (Keynes, 1973b, p. 178).

Keynes made a mistake in the first definition he gave of the aggregate demand function – a definition that had no basis in the microfoundations of his theory – by relating the proceeds entrepreneurs expect to receive (i.e. the prices they expect) to the employment they offer (Keynes, 1936, p. 25). Patinkin, among others,[18] has noted this problem: 'Marshall's representative firm in a competitive industry does not – and indeed by definition, cannot – perceive the demand curve for the industry as a whole. Instead it is confronted by a given demand price. In contrast . . . Keynes' firms do somehow perceive the aggregate demand curve' (p. 126). But because he perceives difficulties with Keynes's aggregate supply function – difficulties that are not there – Patinkin does not present a consistent and clear restatement of Keynes's theory of effective demand that observes the limits Keynes set for himself. He derives an aggregate supply function, not from the industry supply curves which are part of Keynes's microfoundations,[19] but from an aggregate production function, even though he notes Keynes's objection to the use of aggregate output. Further, he assumes that labour is the only variable input, while Keynes thought it highly unlikely that this would ever be the case.[20]

A possible explanation of Keynes's error in his definition of the aggregate demand function is his use, in the early formulations of his theory, of the concept of a single giant firm in the economy. Traces of such use continue to appear in *The General Theory*. Assumptions concerning the perception of the effects of changes in output on price, which would be reasonable for a giant firm, would not be valid for Marshall's (and Keynes's) competitive firms. That this concept, rather than Patinkin's supposition about a confusion between marginal and average concepts, lies at the bottom of the inconsistencies in Keynes's presentation of his theory of effective demand is supported by the following statement arising from Keynes's reflections on differences between his *Treatise on Money* and *The General Theory*.

As I now think, the volume of employment (and consequently of output and real income) is fixed by the entrepreneur under the motive of seeking to maximize his present and prospective profits (the allowance for user cost being determined by his view as to the use of equipment which will maximise his return from it over its whole life); whilst the volume of employment which will maximise his profit depends on the aggregate demand function given by his expectations of the sum of the proceeds resulting from consumption and investment respectively on various hypotheses (Keynes, 1936, p. 77).

Such an entrepreneur must, presumably, be in charge of the single giant firm in the economy, since his decisions are based (and *only* his decisions can be so based) 'on the aggregate demand function'. Further support is to be found in a letter Keynes wrote to Richard Kahn in 1934. He referred enthusiastically to a

> beautiful and important (I think) precise definition of what is meant by effective demand: –   Let W be the marginal prime cost of production when output is O.
> Let P be the expected selling price of this output.
> Then OP is effective demand.
> The fundamental assumption of the classical theory, 'supply creates its own demand', is that OW = OP *whatever* the level of O, so that effective demand is incapable of setting a limit to employment which consequently depends on the relation between marginal product in wage-good industries and marginal disutility of employment. On *my* theory OW≠OP for *all* values of O, and entrepreneurs have to choose a value of O for which it is equal: – otherwise the equality of price and marginal prime cost is infringed. This is the real starting point of everything. (Keynes, 1973a, pp. 422–3)

This letter shows the unsatisfactory mixture of Keynes's Marshallian competitive assumptions and his use of a single all-encompassing firm to clarify his ideas. The 'marginal prime cost of production' for the firm is that for the economy, with P being the firm's expected selling price for its output. The competitive assumptions then creep in, with the equilibrium output determined by the equating of expected price and marginal cost. There is no confusion here between marginal and average concepts – just an inability to see that his competitive assumptions are inconsistent with the use of a giant firm that can base its output on a perceived aggregate demand function that relates expected prices to employment offered. The only aggregate demand function that is consistent with Keynes's competitive assumptions is one that shows the relation between *realized* proceeds (which may in special circumstances be the proceeds of a short-period equilibrium situation, i.e. actual investment is equal to planned investment, and consumption is in the desired relation to income) and the level of employment. His competitive firms, whose expectations of prices and marginal costs determine effective demand, cannot, by definition, base their expectations on an aggregate demand function.

Keynes's occasional confusion between the aggregate schedules derived from the actions of his competitive firms and those that would exist if the economy were controlled by a giant firm can also explain his erroneous statements about the aggregate supply function in the footnote on page 55 of *The General Theory*, to which Patinkin refers (pp. 144–6). This footnote is attached to a paragraph in which Keynes is implicitly assuming a single economy-wide firm that equates 'marginal proceeds (or income) to the marginal factor cost' (Keynes, 1936, p. 55). Keynes makes two mistakes about the construction of his aggregate supply function in that footnote (Asimakopulos, 1982, pp. 26–7). The one that is of interest here is his failure to remember that profits, as well as labour and other factor costs, are included in the aggregate supply price, since profits on intra-marginal outputs are included in the industry short period supply curves on which the aggregate supply function is based. The aggregate supply function is *not* a cost curve for a single firm maximizing profits on the basis of that curve. It is a construct derived to represent the relationship between expected proceeds (i.e. sets of expected prices) and the level of employment to be offered. The marginal proceeds – the expectation of which is required to justify offering one more unit of employment – always contain a profits component, since the prices underlying these proceeds result in profits (the excess of revenues over average variable costs) for some firms. In order to obtain higher employment, the expected product prices on which actual employment decisions are made must be higher, and the resulting expected proceeds include profits that are also higher.

Even though I disagree with Patinkin's views on the source of the inconsistencies in Keynes's presentation of the theory of effective demand, and on what form a corrected statement of that theory should take, there are many of Patinkin's observations with which I agree, as for example his statements that Keynes's analysis was not based on the assumption that 'workers suffer from "money illusion"' (p. 137) and that 'the analysis of the *General Theory* as a whole does not depend on the assumption of absolutely rigid money wages' (p. 138). There is also agreement with his conclusion that the inconsistencies in Keynes's presentation (whichever explanation is accepted for their source) are not 'basic' (p. 153). They do not affect Keynes's important conclusions about the factors determining the short-period equilibrium level of employment, nor the latter's dependence on a rate of investment which is 'prone to sudden and wide fluctuations' (Keynes, 1973b, p. 121).

Conclusion

This is an important book, the result of a careful scholar's study over many years of *The General Theory* and the vast literature surrounding it. Readers might disagree with particular aspects of Patinkin's interpretations, but they cannot help but benefit from exposure to his scholarship.

Notes

1 (1982) *Anticipations of the General Theory? And Other Essays on Keynes* (Chicago: University of Chicago Press)
2 I shall follow Patinkin's convention and mean by the term 'General Theory', not italicized, the theory presented in Keynes's book, *The General Theory*. Further, all page references with no further identification are from Patinkin (1982).
3 Patinkin makes use of a textbook diagram to illustrate Keynes's theory of effective demand, even though he notes that 'this diagram does not exactly accord with the presentation in chap. 3 of *The General Theory*, it captures its essence' (p. 9n.). Patinkin's diagram, which is expressed in 'real' quantities of output and expenditure rather than in Keynes's aggregates of money proceeds and employment, hides the increase in prices that accompanies an increase in employment

(even when the money wage rate is constant) in Keynes's General Theory (Keynes, 1936, p. 17). The impression, given by Patinkin's diagram, and even in his text ('disequilibrium between aggregate demand and supply causes a change in output and not price' (p. 9)), is that only output is changing. Such a view is not consistent with Keynes's model. It is on the short-term expectations of *prices* that Keynes's entrepreneurs, who operate in competitive markets, base their output and employment decisions, and it is changes in these expectations (as a result of recent experience) that lead to changes in output and employment.

4 A typographical error occurs in a footnote Patinkin appends to a statement by Myrdal concerning the setting-off of a downward Wicksellian process due to increased saving. It is the real rate of interest that has thus fallen below the money rate and not, as the footnote reads, 'that the money rate has fallen below the real rate' (p. 48n.). There are a few typographical errors or slips that should be corrected in a second printing. Examples of these include the following: the first work of Kalecki's to which Keynes referred was Kalecki (1937a), not a 1938 *Econometrica* paper (p. 59); Kalecki's name is mentioned three times in volume XIV of Keynes's *Collected Writings* and not 'only twice' (p. 80); the last letter in the Kalecki–Keynes set was dated 12 April 1937, and not 22 April (p. 100).

5 In his discussion of the business cycle in the 1935 *Econometrica* paper he attaches a footnote that makes this assumption explicit: 'We take for granted that there is a reserve army of unemployed' (Kalecki, 1935b, p. 343n.). (This footnote is also found, in French, in Kalecki (1935a, p. 296) at a comparable place in the text.)

6 Kalecki refers to these 'additional profits' as though initially they are realized by entrepreneurs. This is not the case. The initial increase in production and employment he postulates must be due to entrepreneurial expectations of an '"improved" price–wage relation' (Kalecki, 1971b, p. 26). These expectations will turn out to be validated by events only if capitalists' expenditures increase sufficiently to maintain the level of prices in the face of lower wage costs and higher output. He concludes, as we have seen above, that such an increase in expenditures is 'most unlikely'. This means that firms will accumulate unwanted inventories of goods, which 'will sound the alarm for a new price reduction of goods which do not find any outlet. Thus the effect of the cost reduction will be cancelled.' Kalecki mistakenly assumes that in these circumstances increased profits will be realized and 'the immediate effect of increased profits will be an accumulation of money reserves in the hands of entrepreneurs and

in the banks' (Kalecki, 1971b, p. 27). There will, of course, be no
such accumulation of 'money reserves'. These 'increased profits' will
be at most 'book' profits, owing to the valuation of the increased
inventory at expected market prices; they will not become actual
profits, because the goods, as Kalecki argues, cannot be sold at these
prices.

7 There is also a discussion of the effects of a wage reduction during
a depression in Kalecki (1935a, pp. 301–3), but it only serves to
reinforce Patinkin's conclusion that Kalecki's central message concerned fluctuations and income distribution. Kalecki demonstrates
that with perfectly competitive markets the profit share in total output
is independent of the level of money wage rates, given capitalists'
expenditures. He goes on to show that, where cartels play an important
role, wage reductions would result in an increase in profit share and
a fall in the total real incomes of workers. These changes have
implications for production and employment, but these consequences
are not made the centrepiece of the analysis.

8 Specific reference is made here to his 'Outline of a theory of a business
cycle' (1933), and Kalecki (1935a, 1935b).

9 There is no discussion of the role of short-term expectations in
determining output decisions, and the possibility of these expectations
being mistaken, with actual and planned investment differing. He
writes *'For the sake of simplicity we assume that aggregate inventories
remain constant throughout the cycle'* (Kalecki, 1971b, p. 2), and this
assumption allows him to translate any increase in investment to an
increase in the production of capital goods. This is not a proxy for
the assumption of short-term expectations being correct, since the
justification he gave for it is 'in existing economic systems totally or
approximately isolated (the world, U.S.A.) the total volume of stocks
does not show any distinct cyclical variations. Indeed, while business
is falling off, stocks of finished goods decrease, but those of raw
materials and semi-manufactures rise; during recovery there is a
reversal of tendencies. From the above we may conclude that *in our
economic system the gross accumulation A is equal to the production of
capital goods'* (Kalecki, 1935b, p. 328).

10 Kalecki's analytic formulation of the multiplier is timeless, since he
assumes that workers' consumption is always equal to their wages and
capitalists' consumption is always in the desired relation to current
profits. In his texts he makes reference to the multiplier 'ultimately'
or 'eventually' reaching its full value, but his equations provide no
support for these adverbs. Kalecki falls into the trap of the timeless
multiplier specified by his equations, when he was trying to deal with
events that occupied real time in his 1937 *Economic Journal* paper on

the incidence of taxation (reprinted in Kalecki (1971b, pp. 35–42)). He writes, when considering the effects of an increase in tax on capitalists' income to finance an increase in dole payments, that 'the immediate result of an increased income tax [on capitalists' incomes, T_i] is a rise of gross profit . . . [equal to] the amount of the increment of T_i (Kalecki, 1971b, p. 39). This is, of course, not the immediate result, but the 'eventual' result after the full multiplier process has been completed. It is interesting to note from the Kalecki–Keynes correspondence on this paper, parts of which are reproduced in Patinkin (1982, pp. 96–100), that, although Keynes made remarks about this paper in his capacity both 'as editor' and as 'a private critic', he did not notice the errors about the 'immediate result'. (I am grateful to D.E. Moggridge for making the full texts of these letters available to me.)

11 The comparable statements in Kalecki (1935a, 1937b) mention explicitly that prices as well as production increase under these conditions. This explicit reference to prices may have been added because of Tinbergen's comment, on Kalecki's 1933 presentation of his theory of the cycle at the Econometric Society meeting, 'about prices which, remarkably do not appear at all in his theory' (Tinbergen, 1935, p. 270).

12 Patinkin writes about the italicized passage above that 'Kalecki seems to me in the preceding passage to be primarily concerned with demonstrating [that an increase in investment will increase output so as to generate a corresponding increase in savings] and not with analyzing the determination of the equilibrium level of output' (p. 68).

13 A similar statement was made in his review, in Polish, of the General Theory (Kalecki, 1936). For an English translation of this review see Targetti and Kinda-Hass (1982).

14 It also appeared in Kalecki (1935b, pp. 343–4).

15 A detailed examination of the positions of Kalecki and Keynes on finance, investment and saving is to be found in Asimakopulos (1983b).

16 Keynes noted this need for weights but stated that it 'belongs to the detailed analysis of the general ideas here set forth, which it is no part of my immediate purpose to pursue' (Keynes, 1936, p. 43n.).

17 It is defined in this way by Asimakopulos (1982).

18 In particular, Parrinello (1980), Casarosa (1981) and Asimakopulos (1982). Robertson (1936, p. 169) noticed the ambiguity in Keynes's aggregate demand function between its use to show 'what entrepreneurs *do* expect to receive' and 'what they can legitimately expect to receive, because that, whether they expect it or not, is what they *will*

receive'. He did not go on, however, to note that the first use is inconsistent with Keynes's competitive microfoundations.

19 For such a derivation see Asimakopulos (1982, pp. 22–7).

20 Keynes was critical of 'the fallacious practice of equating marginal wage-cost to marginal prime cost' (Keynes, 1936, p. 272n.), and he argued that 'the results of an analysis conducted on this premise have almost no application, since the assumption on which it is based is very seldom realised in practice. For we are not so foolish in practice as to refuse to associate with additional labour appropriate additions of other factors, in so far as they are available, and the assumption will, therefore, only apply if we assume that all the other factors, other than labour, are already being employed to the utmost' (Keynes, 1936, p. 273n.).

9

Joan Robinson and Economic Theory

When I came up to Cambridge (in October 1921) to read economics, I did not have much idea of what it was about. I had some vague hope that it would help me to understand poverty and how it could be cured. And I hoped that it would offer more scope for rational argument than history (my school subject) as it was taught in those days. (Robinson, 1978a, p. ix)[1]

Joan Robinson's approach to economics is reflected in the recollection quoted above. Her interest in the question of the distribution of income and her disdain for what she considered to be theories that tried to justify existing distributions of income never flagged. Her work is marked by a strong inclination for clear well-reasoned arguments that left no room for sloppy habits of thought. It touched many areas in economics, ranging from the theory of imperfect competition to the theory of international trade, and it included reflections on economic philosophy (1963), Marxian economics (1942) and a sketch of an economic interpretation of history (1970). The wide scope and quantity of Robinson's writings – in addition to many books there are six volumes of collected papers – make it difficult to present a critical evaluation

This is a shortened version of a paper published in French in *L'Actualité Économique*. I am grateful to H. Gram, G.C. Harcourt, A. Roncaglia and T.K. Rymes for comments on an earlier version of this chapter, but they are not responsible for any errors it might contain, or for its interpretations of various writings.

of her contributions within the context of even a lengthy chapter. This one will concentrate on her writings in five main areas: (i) the economics of imperfect competiton; (ii) the theory of employment; (iii) the theory of accumulation in the long run; (iv) the concept of capital and the production function; and (v) the problem of time in economics as reflected in her writings on the theme history versus equilibrium.

This separation of Robinson's writings into sections is done for convenience rather than in the belief that her contributions to economic theory can be placed in compartments. The problem of time is recognized in all sections, but in some it is set aside so that definite conclusions can be reached, while in others it comes to the fore and the limits it imposes on the possibilities for analytical development are stressed. There is also in each of the first four sections some consideration of factors affecting the distribution of income.

Robinson was a Cambridge economist, and as with all Cambridge economists of her day the influence of Alfred Marshall should never be overlooked. She wrote that as a student she was repelled by his moralizing and mystified by his 'representative firm', but later 'I took a more kindly view of Marshall. Though he fudged the problem of time, he was aware of it, and he took pains to avoid the spurious neoclassical methodology. It was Pigou who had flattened him out into stationary equilibrium' (1978a, p. xi). Cambridge was in many ways a self-contained world that supplied her with theories for criticism and development, and support in arriving at her own formulations. This world included J.M. Keynes and Piero Sraffa whose work provided great stimulation, and Richard Kahn who was a regular collaborator. Nicholas Kaldor arrived later, and discussions with him were important in the working out of an approach to accumulation in the long run. Roy Harrod, although at Oxford, should also be mentioned here, because it was to Keynes and Cambridge that he was sent for his studies in economics. There was a reaching out towards Knut Wicksell during the working out of her model of accumulation, when she was trying to make sense of accumulation within a given state of technical knowledge; however, the most important 'outside' influences on her work are Michal Kalecki and Karl Marx. She took over Kalecki's formulation of the theory of effective demand and the theory of income distribution, while from Marx she derived the concept of a capitalist economic system with its 'rules of the game' (1942).

The Economics of Imperfect Competition

> . . . the whole problem of time was fudged. There is no clear distinction in the book between short and long-period relationships or between the future and the past, . . . (1978a, p. x).

Robinson's first major work in economics was *The Economics of Imperfect Competition* published in 1933. The book, together with Chamberlin's *Theory of Monopolistic Competition*, which was also published in that year, were the key works in the 'imperfect competition revolution'. The analytical techniques they developed were to become standard items in textbooks on microeconomics. The two books were initially treated as two versions of the same theory, differing mainly in terminology, but there were important differences in the questions treated by the writers. In particular, Chamberlin paid much more attention to the problem of the definition of a determinate demand curve for an individual firm producing a differentiated product than did Robinson. Robinson recognized that for an industry 'in conditions of imperfect competition a certain difficulty arises from the fact that the individual demand curve for the product of each of the firms composing it will depend to some extent upon the price policy of the others' (1933, p. 21). This difficulty was then eliminated by the sweeping assumption that the individual demand curve shows 'the full effect upon the sales of that firm which results from any change in the price which it charges, whether it causes a change in the prices charged by the others or not'. Robinson also noted that in treating demand in two-dimensional diagrams, with price on one axis and quantity on the other, an important aspect of time is being overlooked, since the price charged may alter the position of the demand curve in the future. She saw no general and precise way of dealing with this problem and decided that 'these complications will be ignored, and we shall assume that it is legitimate to make use of a two-dimensional demand curve, without inquiring how it is drawn up' (p. 23). There is no recognition of this problem in Chamberlin's book. He treated the current period, for which price and output were determined, as being self-contained for the individual firm, without any acknowledgement of the very special nature of such an assumption for all but perfectly competitive firms. Short-period profit maximization (the equating of marginal revenue and marginal cost) for a firm in monopolistic competition was identified with profit maximization (e.g. Chamberlin, 1948, p. 193).

The starting point for Robinson's book, as she stated in her foreword, was Sraffa's 1926 *Economic Journal* article on 'The Laws of Return Under Competitive Conditions'. He had argued that the majority of firms producing manufactured goods worked under conditions of decreasing costs. The limitations on the firm's sales are set by a negatively sloped demand curve for that firm's output, with different groups of buyers being, more or less, attached to the products of different firms. Robinson then worked out the consequences of such curves for the determination of price and output with great singleness of purpose. As Shackle stated, 'the care and thoroughness of her statement of definitions and assumptions, the candour of her declaration about the abstract character of her analysis, the systematic organization which lets us know these things at the beginning and offers a formal explanation and training in the pure technique of average and marginal curves without, at that stage, giving these curves any specific content or interpretation, were at that date something new in economic reasoning' (Shackle, 1967, p. 53).

There are serious flaws in *The Economics of Imperfect Competition* if its purpose is to help explain the determination of prices of manufactured goods. It did not deal with the dynamics of product differentiation, selling costs, oligopoly, the uncertainty faced by firms in ascertaining their demand curves and the difference between short-period profit maximization and the profit maximization which would be the goal of a self-seeking firm whose interest was in survival and growth. Robinson became well aware of these shortcomings, and in a 1953 paper on '"Imperfect Competition" Revisited' she referred to the book as 'scholastic' and its assumptions as 'by no means a suitable basis for an analysis of the problems of prices, production and distribution which present themselves in reality' (1960a, p. 222). Its greatest weakness is judged to be its 'failure to deal with time' (p. 234). When writing this criticism she felt that no simple generalization could be usefully developed to explain the price policies of firms in manufacturing industries, a position she never really abandoned even though she made use of cost-based pricing in the *Accumulation of Capital*. She developed the notion of 'subjective-normal price', whose resemblance to some version of 'full-cost' pricing (of which she had been critical in earlier writings) was noted.[2] This price is obtained by adding a gross margin to prime cost 'calculated to yield a profit that the entrepreneurs concerned have come to regard as attainable (on the basis of past experience) with the productive capacity in the given short-period situation. Where fluctuations in output are expected and regarded as normal, the subjective-normal price may be calculated upon the basis of an average or standard rate of output, rather than capacity (1956, p. 186). Variation in demand relative to productive capacity could lead to actual prices deviating from subjective-normal prices, with prices tending to fall in buyers' markets and to rise in sellers' markets, where markets are competitive in the short period.

Use of cost-based pricing for analysing manufacturing industries was advocated in the preface to the second edition of the *Economics of Imperfect Competition*, with more emphasis being placed on the stability of prices relative to costs. 'The prices of manufactures in the nature of the case are administered prices. With short-period fluctuations in demand, prices vary little as long as money costs are constant. . . Movements of demand affect profits strongly, but prices hardly at all' (1969a, pp. vii–viii). But Robinson was always cautious about stating how the net profit component of the mark-up on prime costs was determined. She noted that the influence of demand or 'consideration of "what the traffic will bear"' (p. vii) could not be ignored.

There are two parts of this book that Robinson still approved of when the preface to the second edition was written. She felt that the analysis of price discrimination was 'still useful', and 'what was for me the main point, I succeeded in proving within the framework of the orthodox theory, that it is not true that wages are normally equal to the value of the marginal product of labour' (p. xii). This 'proof', however, was really a matter of definition, as long as the 'orthodox' assumption of a perfectly elastic supply of labour to the individual firm was maintained. Her analysis showed that in this case the wage in equilibrium would be equal to the value to the firm of the marginal product of labour. 'Exploitation' could be shown to have occurred in imperfect competition only if it was defined, as she did, as a situation where the 'wage is less than the marginal physical product . . . valued at the price at which it is being sold' (1933, p. 283).[3]

The Theory of Employment

Keynes . . . brought the argument down from the cloudy realms of timeless equilibrium to here and now, with an irrevocable past, facing an uncertain future (1971, p. 89).
On the plane of theory, the revolution lay in the change from the conception of equilibrium to the conception of history; from the principles of rational choice to the problems of decisions based on guess-work or on convention. . . . The other half of the Keynesian revolution was to recognize that, in an industrial economy, the level of prices is governed primarily by the level of money-wage rates (1980b, pp. 170, 173).

Robinson was one of a small group closely involved in the discussions leading up to the writing of *The General Theory*;[4] she was a careful reader of various drafts of this book[5] and an important contributor to the literature that expounded Keynes's theory[6] and that tried to extend its analysis. Initially her writings were closely related to the analytical structure and concepts appearing in the *General Theory*, but she then became more critical of some aspects of Keynes's presentation of his theory. Robinson, as the quotations given above indicate, tended in her later writings to consider her views about the importance of time to be part of the 'message' of *The General Theory*.[7] There is some support for this attitude in Keynes's summary of his theory in the *Quarterly Journal of Economics* in 1937, but Robinson herself did not make this a regular theme in her writings until the 1960s.

Keynes's theory is set within a Marshallian short period with given productive capacity.[8] This period was given a historical time dimension by Marshall, 'a few months or a year' (Marshall, 1920, p. 379), and Keynes's usage appears to imply implicit acceptance of this approximate time dimension. For Keynes, the level of employment depends on the short-term expectations of entrepreneurs about the prices they can get for their outputs and on their short-period supply curves. He assumed that manufactured goods were sold under competitive conditions, and these individual supply curves formed the building blocks for his aggregate supply function (cf. Asimakopulos (1982)). The prices entrepreneurs actually received, the proceeds they realized, depended, in his closed economy where government expenditures were ignored, on expenditures for investment and consumption. These realized results could differ from expected results and in so far as these differences led to changes in short-term expectations, there would be, within the short period, changes in the level of employment.[9] Keynes paid scant attention to this process of adjustment of expected to realized results, with the consequent changes in employment and degree of utilization of the given productive capacity. He concentrated on situations of short-period equilibrium where short-term expectations were borne out by events, actual investment was equal to planned investment and consumption was in the desired relation to income. His summary statement of his theory was '. . . the volume of employment in equilibrium depends on (i) the aggregate supply function. . . (ii) the propensity to consume . . . and (iii) the volume of investment. . . This is the essence of the General Theory of Employment' (Keynes, 1936, p. 29). Keynes argued that there was no reason to expect that, in general, the volume of investment and the propensity to consume would be such that the level of employment they determined would be equal to the full employment level.

The setting out of the relation between saving and investment so that the latter is the prime mover, is an important part of Keynes's theory. Saving must be equal to investment at all times, given the definition of these terms in *The General Theory*, but when this equality is part of an equilibrium relation, with saving in the desired relation to income, then Keynes (and Robinson) saw this as a causal relation where investment determines saving through its effect on output. As she wrote in considering an increase in investment: 'Investment causes income to be whatever is required to induce people to save at a rate equal to the rate of investment. . . The argument does not run in the reverse way. The desire to save does not promote investment' (1937b, p. 10). The first part of this quotation assumes a situation of short-period

equilibrium with the multiplier having its full value. But in general
it would take time before the full multiplier effects of an increase
in investment would be felt, and this did not receive adequate
recognition in *The General Theory*. The need for the passage of
time was obscured by Keynes with his 'logical theory of the
multiplier, which holds good continuously, without time lag, at
all moments of time' (Keynes, 1936, p. 122). This construct was
based on a very special definition of the marginal propensity to
consume, *viz.*, the ratio of the increment of consumption at any
moment to that moment's increment in income (Keynes, 1936, p.
115). Robinson recognized this problem when commenting in
1969 on her 1937 *Introduction to the Theory of Employment*, and
noted that implicit in the above quotation from her work was the
assumption of negligible time lags in the response of consumption
to income. 'The Multiplier represents the change in income
appropriate to a change in investment. When time lags are not
negligible, the income appropriate to one level of investment
cannot, in general, be reached before the level of investment has
changed, so that exact equality between the rate of investment
and the appropriate rate of saving would never be established'
(1969b, p. xiv).

There were two approaches to the determination of the rate of
investment in *The General Theory*. One was presented in chapter
11, and it makes investment dependent on a calculable marginal
efficiency of capital and the rate of interest. The second approach
was presented in chapter 12, and it emphasizes the fundamental
uncertainty concerning the outcome of investment decisions, which
makes all calculations of expected profitability, such as the marginal
efficiency of capital, suspect.

> Most, probably, of our decisions to do something positive,
> the full consequences of which will be drawn out over many
> days to come, can only be taken as a result of animal spirits
> – of a spontaneous urge to action rather than inaction, and
> not as the outcome of a weighted average of quantitative
> benefits multiplied by quantitative probabilities (Keynes,
> 1936, p. 161).

It was this latter approach that Keynes emphasized in his 1937
Quarterly Journal of Economics article, and that was the basis of
Robinson's approach to investment in her later writings. But

initially (for example, in her two books published in 1937) she used the marginal efficiency of capital to explain the determination of investment. Robinson's first published criticism (that I have found) of this approach appears in 1962 in 'A Model of Accumulation'.

> The formal structure of the *General Theory* embodies the proposition that the rate of investment tends to be such as to equate the marginal efficiency of capital to the rate of interest; this, it must be admitted, was in the nature of a fudge. For a scheme of investment to be undertaken, the profit expected from it must exceed its interest-cost by a considerable margin to cover the risk involved (1962, pp. 36–7).

In considering Robinson's contribution to the theory of employment it is important not to underestimate the influence on her writings of Kalecki's approach to the theory of effective demand and investment. Robinson incorporated in her work Kalecki's double-sided relation between investment and profits (traces of this are found as early as 1937 in her discussion of the trade cycle in Robinson (1937b)). Current investment is an important determinant of the current level of profits, while the latter affects the entrepreneurs' expectations of profits and thus current investment decisions and future investment. She also accepted, as her own, Kalecki's theory of distribution of income in the short period where 'the accumulation going on in a particular situation determines the level of profits obtained in it. . .' (1962, p. 47).

An area where Robinson's point of view did not change throughout her writings concerned the price implications of full employment in a capitalist economy. In discussing the labour market, she rejected the positively sloped supply curve of labour which formed part of Keynes's definition of full employment. Although she felt that the elasticity of the supply of labour with respect to real wages 'is likely . . . negative' (1937a, p. 12), a zero elasticity of supply was assumed in order to simplify the argument. This assumption of an inelastic supply of labour – subject to some minimum real wage rate at which conditions change drastically (the 'inflation barrier') and an 'irresistible demand for higher money wages makes itself felt' (1962, p. 42) – was to be found throughout her writings. The first of her 1937 *Essays* argued that given the general conditions of the labour market and the degree of union organization, an increase in effective demand will be favourable to a rise in money wages. Money wages increase, and at an increasing rate, as full employment is approached. 'The general upshot of our argument is that the point of full employment, so far from being an equilibrium resting place, appears to be a precipice over which, once it has reached the edge, the value of money must plunge into a bottomless abyss' (1937a, p. 24). Robinson judged that fear of inflation, abetted by rising imports in an open economy, would lead banking authorities to limit the increase in the money supply and raise interest rates before full employment is reached.

Robinson had cause to criticize (as in her 1967 review of Lekachman's book on Keynes) those who implied that the inflationary consequences of high levels of employment 'lay outside the scope of Keynes' argument. But the English Keynesians deduced from the General Theory, even while the slump was still with us, that a successful employment policy would lead to a chronic spiral of wages and prices. . . The incompatibility of continuous full employment with stable prices they saw as the unsolved problem of the future as, indeed, it still is' (1980b, p. 181). Some form of incomes policy appeared to her to be a necessary complement to a full employment policy, with the trade union movement accepting social changes and a say in the 'type' of output to be produced[10] in lieu of the rapid, but in the end futile, increases in money wages that their enhanced bargaining power could bring. She did not, however, specify how she saw such a policy being developed and implemented.

Robinson's attack on equilibrium theories, as in her 1953–4 paper on the production function and the theory of capital (1960a, pp. 114–31), was initially directed to those concerned with long-period equilibrium, but short-period equilibrium did not escape her criticism in later writings. In some of these she even appeared to deny the short period the historical time dimension to be found in Marshall and Keynes, as well as in her earlier works. *Economic Heresies*, published in 1971, can be taken to make the changeover. She begins her chapter on the short period with praise for 'an invaluable concept, which sharply distinguishes the Marshallian school of thought from the tradition of Walras – that is, the "short period" during which the stock of capital is unchanged while its utilization can be varied' (1971, p. 16). This parallels her treatment in the *Accumulation of Capital* where 'the *short period* in the analytical sense, is not any definite period of time, but a convenient theoretical abstraction meaning a period within which changes in the stock of capital equipment can be neglected. Within a short period the rate of output can alter, for it is possible to utilise given equipment more or less by employing more or less labour to operate it' (1956, p. 179). Although she does not attach a definite length to the short period here, it clearly encompasses some interval of time because it is long enough to enable decisions to be made and carried out to change the degree of utilization of the relatively unchanged productive capacity. In *Economic Heresies* the short period appears to lose its substance: 'Marshall's short period is a moment in a stream of time. . . It is better to use the expressions "short period" and "long period" as adjectives, not as substantives. The "short period" is not a length of time but a state of affairs' (1971, pp. 17–8). This is echoed in later writings, for example, 'A short period is not a length of time but the position at a moment of time' (1978b, p. 13). With this approach she takes away the setting for Keynes's theory since there is no time available to permit variations in the utilization of productive capacity in response to changing short-term expectations.

Robinson is thus going beyond a criticism of the automatic use of short-period equilibrium, and of the implicit assumption that there is a reliable and not very time-consuming process of adjustment to such an equillibrium. The logic of her position, if an attempt is made to include Keynes's analysis within its scope, requires a very special definition of 'equilibrium'. 'A state of expectations, controlling a given level of effective demand, is given only momentarily and is always in the course of bringing itself to an end. Perhaps it was a misnomer to describe such a position as equilibrium, but without a concept of the character of an existing short-period situation it is not possible to say anything at all' (1978b, p. 13). There is no indication in Keynes's analysis, or in Robinson's earlier writings, that the term 'equilibrium' in the theory of effective demand has this very special meaning. A particular set of short-term expectations might be 'given only momentarily' (or 'daily') but there is sufficient time in Keynes's short period for changes in these expectations in response to the experience of actual results. Output and employment would be adjusted within the short period, to the extent that it can be usefully done, given the changing short-term expectations and the fixed productive capacity. A situation of short period equilibrium would be a very special case, which might be of interest for analytical purposes to show the difference in results obtained with Keynes's model, as opposed to those to be deduced from the 'classical' model. That is, for Keynes a situation of less than full employment is not necessarily the result of short-run disequilibrium (cf. Kregel (1976, p. 213)).

Finally, mention should be made of Robinson's paper on 'The Long-period Theory of Employment' that was included in the 1937 *Essays*,[11] because it indicates how her later criticisms of equilibrium were directed at an approach that was reflected in her own work.[12] Robinson dealt with the special case of static conditions where the level of long-period employment resulting from an unchanging state of long-term expectations, was constant. Twenty years were to pass before she was to publish a major work, *The Accumulation of Capital*, that moved her long-period analysis from static conditions to changing conditions.

The Accumulation of Capital

Everything that happens in an economy happens in a short-period situation, and every decision that is taken is taken in a short-period situation, for an event occurs or a decision is taken at a particular time, and at any moment the physical stock of capital is what it is; but what happens has a long-period as well as a short-period aspect . . . Short-period decisions affect the utilisation of given equipment . . . long-period decisions affect the stock of productive capacity (1956, p. 180).

The short-period situation in existence to-day is like a geological fault; past and future developments are out of alignment. Only in the imagined conditions of a golden age do the strata run horizontally from yesterday to to-morrow without a break at to-day (p. 181).

The Accumulation of Capital must be given an important place in any consideration of Robinson's writings on economic theory.[13]

This is the work of a mature scholar that is centred around the analysis of the long-run development of a capitalist economy, and that touches on many aspects of economic theory. It is planned on a broad scale that combines statements full of insights on the purpose and scope of economic theory and the meaning of equilibrium, with a detailed and careful analysis of accumulation in the long run, the choice of technique, the evaluation of capital, and technical progress. She also devotes space to a consideration of the short period, the role of finance, the determination of relative prices, and international trade. The book concludes with a series of notes on various topics that include welfare economics, the neoclassical theory of wages and profits, Wicksell on capital, the natural rate of interest and the quantity theory of money. Many of the issues she raises in this book continued to appear in various forms in her later writings, such as the difference between analyses concerned with comparisons and those with changes. 'Throughout the argument it is necessary to distinguish *differences* from *changes*. The effect of having had in the past, and continuing to have, say, a higher rate of accumulation or a higher degree of monopoly, is not the same as the effect of a rise in the rate of accumulation or of an increase in monopoly' (1956, p. 71).[14]

The Accumulation of Capital is a valuable book – one which repays the student's effort to work through it with care – and yet it fails in its attempt to provide 'an extension of Keynes's short-period analysis to long-run development' (1956, p. vi), since the assumptions she makes in order to develop the theory represent a 'watering down' and even a denial, of what she considered to be essential elements of Keynes's theory. It may very well be that any such ambitious attempt is doomed to failure because no more than an indication of some possible lines of long-run development can be obtained if the essentials of Keynes's analysis are to be retained. A few years after the publication of this book she published a set of essays 'as an introduction . . . to my *Accumulation of Capital*' (1962, p. v), essays that showed her growing concern with the unsuitability of equilibrium concepts. These essays did not, however, avoid at critical points the contradictions between her views on the limitations of equilibrium, and her use of equilibrium in the presentation of her theory of economic growth.

There is in Robinson's treatment of accumulation the same characteristic boldness in the development of the analysis, that is to be found in the *Economics of Imperfect Competition*. She places at the core of her section on 'Accumulation in the Long Run' ('the central part of the work' (1962, p. ix)) the assumption of tranquillity – the development of the economy 'in a smooth and regular manner' – that eliminates uncertainty. 'In order to separate long-run from short-run influences it is a useful device to imagine an economy developing in conditions of tranquillity, and to postulate that the expectations about the future, held at any moment, are in fact being fulfilled. This yields results equivalent to assuming correct foresight. . .' (1962, p. 66). This makes it possible to deal with accumulation as part of an equilibrium story of steady growth. Entrepreneurs' long-term expectations – and thus the investment decisions based on them – turn out to be justified by events. Robinson follows Kalecki in assuming all wages are spent, and in her main model there is only workers' consumption since rentiers are excluded and the consumption of entrepreneurs, 'whose sole function and aim is to organize production and accumulate capital' (1962, p. 73), is negligible. Profits must thus be equal to investment.

Accumulation, determined 'by the energy with which entrepreneurs carry it out' (1963, p. 84), can proceed at a steady rate as long as there is sufficient labour available at the real wage rate permitted by technology and this equilibrium growth rate. There is an inverse relation between the real wage rate and the rate of accumulation (and thus the rate of profit), given the technique of production. Robinson brings this out by comparing different economies, with the same technique of production, but with different histories of steady growth. The economy with the higher rate of accumulation has the lower real wage rate.[15] If the two economies have the same money wage rate, then the price of consumption goods is higher in the economy with the higher rate of accumulation since there are relatively more workers employed in the investment sector competing for consumption goods. Robinson assumes that an 'inflation barrier', triggered by an irresistible demand for higher money wages when real wage rates are reduced to some minimum acceptable level[16] by rising investment and prices, limits the possible rate of investment in any situation. Within that limit the rate of accumulation (and thus the rate of profit) depends on the energy of entrepreneurs. Accumulation can proceed steadily with constant technique as long as the increasing amount of labour required to man the increasing productive capacity is available.

Technical progress is restricted in Robinson's model to changes in the methods of production, since the composition of the basket of consumption goods is assumed to remain unchanged through time. It can be introduced into the model without violating the conditions for steady growth, as long as output per head increases at the same rate in both consumption and investment sectors.[17] This type of technical progress is equivalent to Harrod's neutral technical progress, when accumulation is such as to keep the rate of profit constant. The real wage rate in this case will increase at the same rate as output per head, and thus the division of the labour force between the two sectors and income shares will be unchanged.

The economic system has difficulty in adapting to changes in the rate of technical progress, as well as to 'biased' changes since they destroy 'tranquillity'. Variations in the pace of technical progress disrupt equilibrium because they alter the rates of obsolescence of existing equipment from what firms had expected them to be on the basis of past experience. Technical progress is said to have a *capital-using bias* if output per man in the consumption sector increases at a faster rate than it does in the investment sector. It has a *capital-saving bias* if this increase in the investment sector is greater than it is in the consumption sector. If accumulation has been proceeding at a steady rate, then the introduction of capital-using technical progress means that productive capacity in the consumption sector is increased by less than output per man, thus leading to a fall in employment in that sector. Adjustment to such a change that maintains the level of employment (or its rate of growth) requires an increase in the rate of accumulation (and thus an increase in the rate of profit) with employment in the investment sector increasing relative to employment in the consumption sector. The real wage rate would increase in this case by less than the increase in output per man in the consumption sector. Conversely, with capital-saving technical progress and a constant rate of accumulation, productive capacity in the consumption sector is growing faster than output per man. If it is to be fully utilized, employment must be increased in that sector relative to employment in the investment sector. Adjustment to capital-saving technical progress thus requires a falling rate of investment (and rate of profit) and an increase in real wage rates that is greater than the increase in output per man in the consumption sector.

A situation where technical progress is neutral and proceeding steadily, with normal productive capacity being utilized and growing at a rate sufficient to employ the available labour force, with the rate of profit constant and the real wage rate rising with output per man, is described 'as a *golden age* (thus indicating that it represents a mythical state of affairs not likely to obtain in any actual economy)' (1956, p. 99). This corresponds, as Robinson notes, to an equality between Harrod's *actual, warranted* and *natural* rates of growth. In her later 'A Model of Accumulation' (1962, pp. 22–87) she uses the term '*desired* rate of accumulation' to describe a situation corresponding to Harrod's warranted rate of growth where entrepreneurial investment decisions are justified by events; but in which there may be unemployment. In Robinson's work the possible differences between the warranted (or desired) and natural rates are less marked than in Harrod's because the rate of technical progress is not given independently of entrepreneurial energy and pressures exerted by rising wage rates:

My model is intended to show that when the urge to accumulate ('animal spirits') is high relatively to the growth of the labour force, technical progress has a tendency to raise the 'natural' rate of growth to make room for it, so that near-enough steady growth, with near-enough full employment may be realized (though even then uncertainty may give rise to short-run instability). In the converse case, the existence of a growing surplus of labour, though it may slow down technical progress, cannot be relied upon to bring the 'natural' rate of growth down to equality with the sluggish rate of accumulation (1965, pp. 50–1).

There is also an important difference in the assumptions about the number of possible equilibrium rates of profit in a particular economy since they affect the possible values for the average propensity to save in the economy, given the propensities to save out of wages and profits. For Harrod as well as Robinson, the propensity to save out of profits is greater than the propensity to save out of wages, but in his model there is only one possible warranted growth path, given technology and these propensities, because there is only one possible equilibrium distribution of income.[18] As we see above, the equilibrium rate of profits in Robinson's model, and thus the average propensity to save, depends (within the limits set by the inflation barrier) on the dynamism of the entrepreneurs.

Robinson made great efforts, and showed considerable ingenuity, in order to examine the choice of technique when the state of knowledge makes available a variety of methods that are feasible (that is, each of which may be the most profitable at some hypothetical real wage rate). This involved the comparison of equilibrium positions at different real wage rates and the general rule was that the higher the real wage rate, the greater the degree of mechanization of the technique chosen (as indicated by net output per unit of labour). Robinson recognized that there could be exceptions to this rule, since the rate of profit enters into the cost of capital goods. With a higher real wage rate (and consequently lower rate of profit) the cost of capital for a less mechanized technique may decrease relative to the cost for a more mechanized technique. This decrease may be sufficient to make the former more profitable. The possible reversal of the expected result[19] was labelled 'A Curiosum' and its exposition was described as 'a somewhat intricate piece of analysis which is not of great importance' (1956, p. 109n.). It did, however, assume considerable importance in the subsequent 'Cambridge Controversies in the Theory of Capital', since the 'backward switch' whose possibility she demonstrated, is a requirement for reswitching (Harcourt, 1972).

Equilibrium growth paths are clearly very special within the general framework of Keynesian theory, but their elaboration in the central part of *The Accumulation of Capital*, with reservations more in the nature of anecdotal comments, gives them undue importance. Robinson also tends to neutralize the effects of changing conditions, with equilibrium adjustments to them being made to seem plausible, by conducting the analysis of accumulation in the long run 'on the assumption that at every moment entrepreneurs expect the future rate of profit obtainable on investment to continue indefinitely at the level ruling at that moment; that they expect the rate of technical progress (which may be nil) to be steady; and that they fix amortisation allowances for long-lived plant accordingly. *When something occurs which causes a change, we assume that expectations are immediately adjusted, and that no further change is expected'* (1956, p. 67 (my italics)). It is only in a later section (clearly not the 'central part of the work') that uncertainty is introduced.

There is an improvement in presentation in 'A Model of Accumulation', since Robinson begins the analysis in a particular short period and deals first with short-period equilibrium before introducing some of the possible equilibrium growth paths. Situations that are described as, for example, a 'Limping Golden Age', a 'Leaden Age', a 'Bastard Golden Age', and a 'Galloping Platinum Age', are presented as a partial catalogue of possible growth paths. The weak point in this impressive essay is the method used to show the movement from a given short-period situation to the long-period equilibrium of the *desired* rate of accumulation. Both this 'movement' and the introduction of the rate of profit into a short-period situation are based on the question-begging assumptions of her earlier book on the formation of expectations when changes are occurring. The expected rate of return on investment is assumed to be 'estimated on the basis of current prices' (1962, p. 47) and this rate is then used to derive a value for the existing stock of capital, since it is assumed that it can provide a stream of net profits at the current level indefinitely.[20] This value is then used to turn the actual and planned rates of investment into rates of accumulation.

Entrepreneurs expect 'tomorrow' to be like 'today', even though their expectations keep being disappointed, until the 'desired' rate of accumulation, where the expected and the actual rates of profit are the same, is achieved. The diagram (1962, p. 48) she presents to illustrate the double-sided relationship between the rate of profit and the rate of accumulation is inappropriate according to her own methodological position, since outside of long-period equilibrium the rate of profit does not have any clear meaning (Asimakopulos, 1977, p. 382). There is even a characterization of the stability of the equilibrium positions given by the two points of intersection of the two curves in her diagram. But, as Robinson stated in the introductory section of this essay, when expectations are liable to be falsified, as they are at all points other than at the intersection points in that diagram, 'the out-of-equilibrium position is off the page. . .' (1962, p. 25).

Another feature of the analysis that is at variance with her general position is the assumption of competition (in the short-period sense) in the consumption good sector when she is considering short-period equilibrium. This assumption is thus implicitly made for all the growth paths she discusses subsequently, since they take as given the existence of short-period equilibrium. The assumption of short-period competition ensures the production of normal capacity output even when effective demand is weak (prices are then low relative to money wages), with employment in the consumption good sector being 'more or less closely determined by the available plant' (1962, p. 47). It would have been more in keeping with her view on the oligopolistic nature of manufacturing industry (see above) to have assumed fixed rather than variable mark-ups in the face of variations in effective demand.[21]

Robinson's presentation of her model of accumulation in the long run is thus not always consistent with her general views on economic theory, and students may be misled by certain sections. Another example of this is her introduction of the possibility of the rate of interest being equal to the rate of profit, even though elsewhere she makes clear that the distinction between the two is important (see, for example (1971, p. 30)). A possible reason for this may be the way she built up the analysis, with rentiers excluded from the main model in Book II of The Accumulation of Capital, and thus there is only one type of capital income in that model.

These lapses from the very high standards Robinson set for herself do not detract from the important contributions of her two major works on accumulation. They make clear the possible effects on the rates of accumulation of differences in the degree of thriftiness, the extent of competition, the organization and attitude of labour, rates of technical progress, and entrepreneurial energy, and thus they indicate features of some of the possible growth paths. Robinson clearly recognized the limits on the ability of economic theory to explain any actual rate of accumulation, since the complex factors at work cannot be captured by any investment function. 'We must be content with the conclusion that, over the long run, the rate of accumulation is likely to be whatever it is likely to be' (1956, p. 244). Her position is thus similar to Kalecki's 'the rate of growth at a given time is a phenomenon rooted in past economic, social and technological developments rather than determined fully by the coefficients of our equations. . .' (Kalecki, 1971b, p. 183).

Capital and the production function

The real dispute is not about the *measurement* of capital but about the *meaning* of capital (1975b, p. vi).

Robinson's investigation of the theory of capital and the production function can be seen as initially having a constructive as well as a critical purpose. Its constructive purpose was to find acceptable ways of dealing with the process of accumulation, given the state of technical knowledge, a process that leads to a 'deepening' of the capital stock. Its critical purpose was to expose the inadequate theoretical foundations for the neoclassical production function that has capital as one of its factors of production. She later repudiated the analysis of accumulation within a given state of technical knowledge (1975c, p. 34), but she held firmly to her criticisms of the neoclassical theory of capital and distribution.

Robinson's definitive statement of accumulation and the production function is probably to be found in a 1959 *Economic Journal* article with the title 'Accumulation and the Production Function' (reprinted in 1960a, pp. 132–44). An important difference between this attempt to deal with this problem and that found in *The Accumulation of Capital* is that she no longer attempts to provide any plausibility to an equilibrium growth path. 'But why try to make it seem plausible, when we know that in real life nothing like it ever happens? Let us take it simply as an exercise, and postulate that accumulation does take place in this way for no other reason than that is what we choose to postulate' (1960a, p. 133). In this exercise she examines the neoclassical problem of accumulation occurring in an economy where both the labour force and the state of technical knowledge are unchanged. This accumulation results in a falling rate of profit and a rising real wage rate. Robinson makes use of the adjective 'Keynesian' for the manner in which she investigates this neoclassical problem, but 'Kaleckian' would be more appropriate, since the theory of distribution she uses is Kalecki's.

The very special nature of this exercise is made clear by her language. 'The Keynesian freedom of entrepreneurs to invest as they please has . . . been sacrificed . . . to the postulate that equilibrium is never ruptured' (p. 134). In this state of equilibrium, the value of capital per unit of labour is continuously rising, while the movement of income shares depends on the relation between real wages and output per head. Accumulation in this economy generally increases both of these, with constant relative shares being observed 'when the rise in output per head happens to be exactly proportional to the rise in wages associated with it, the ratio of investment to income is constant and consumption is increasing at the same rate as total net income' (p. 139). A situation where a small rise in real wages leads to the adoption of a more mechanized technique, with a much higher value of output per man, will cause the share of profits to rise under equilibrium conditions. Conversely, when a substantial rise in wages results in the adoption of a technique with only a slightly higher output per head, then the share of wages would increase under equilibrium conditions. Robinson identifies the first case as one of high substitutability of capital for labour, and the second with very low substitutability. She concludes: 'Thus, broadly speaking, easy substitutability causes the share of profits to rise as capital accumulates, and sticky technical relations cause the share of wages to rise' (p. 140). (It should be emphasized again that technical progress is kept out of this exercise. Its introduction could alter the equilibrium relation between accumulation, the rising degree of mechanization and the falling rate of profit.)

The opening shot in Robinson's attack on the use of capital in the neoclassical production function was made in her 1953 article 'The Production Function and the Theory of Capital' (reprinted in 1960a, pp. 114–29). She asked the critical question, if C is the quantity of capital that appears in a production function 'in what units is C measured'? (p. 114). It is not a question that neoclassical theorists have been able to answer satisfactorily. In the short period, capital can be taken to stand for the specific list of all the goods in existence at that point in time, but then it is possible to regard labour 'as the sole factor of production, operating in a given environment of technique, natural resources, capital equipment and effective demand' (Keynes, 1936, p. 214). The neoclassical approach can thus not find any support in a short-period situation, but it also faces problems when confined to long-period equilibrium situations, since the measure of the quantity of capital (a value) is *not* independent of the rate of profit. This point was recognized in Robinson's 1953 paper, but its expression became much sharper after the 1960 publication of Sraffa's *Production of Commodities by Means of Commodities*. In her 1961 review of that book Robinson emphasized that what Sraffa 'demonstrates decisively . . . is that there is no such thing as a "quantity of capital" which exists independently of the rate of profit' (1965, p. 13). This means 'that the contention that the "marginal product of capital" determines the rate of profit is meaningless' (1973, p. 144).

Robinson, and others, made use of the concept of a 'pseudo-production function' in the 'reswitching' controversy (Samuelson, 1966). This function is based on the idea of 'a book of blueprints specifying all possible techniques for producing a flow of net output of a given composition with a given labour force' (1978a, p. 121). The techniques have different net outputs per unit of labour, and the rates of profit they allow can be determined once the share of wages in net output is given. For each share the technique (or techniques) that provide the highest rate of profit can be said to be included in the pseudo-production function at that wage share (or for the corresponding rate of profit). This function may be represented diagrammatically by the wage rate of profit frontier. For each technique there is an inverse relation between the wage share and the rate of profit, which can be represented by a wage rate of profit curve, and it is the envelope of the set of all such curves for the techniques covered by the 'book of blueprints' that is called the wage rate of profit frontier. Each technique (assuming inferior techniques have been eliminated) provides a point (or points) to the frontier corresponding to the wage share (or shares) at which it allows the highest rate of profit. A technique providing the highest rate of profit (given the wage share) can be said to be 'eligible' at that rate of profit. Each point on this frontier represents a steady-state growth path in which the corresponding technique is reflected in the who's who of capital goods, and where the rate of profit, the expectation of which led to this choice to technique, is being realized. There may be stretches on this frontier where only a single technique is eligible and others where many techniques are to be found. A particular technique may appear at one point on the frontier and then reappear on another section (this is what is meant by 'reswitching'). When adjacent points on the frontier are compared, there is no necessary inverse relation between the values of net output per man of the techniques they represent, and the rates of profit at which they are eligible. (There could also be substantial differences in the types of capital goods that are employed by these adjacent techniques.) The more mechanized technique may be eligible at a higher rate of profit. It is this possibility, due to the impossibility of valuing capital independently of the rate of profit, that undermines the foundations of the neoclassical approach to capital and the production function.

The pseudo-production function is obviously a very artificial construct, which Robinson was only prepared to use for the sole purpose of making a critique of neoclassical theory. It involves the comparison of isolated economies, each of which is in long-period equilibrium, but some of the other economists using it left the impression that one could move from one point on this function to another. Robinson's continuing emphasis on the fundamental difference between analyses dealing with comparisons and those dealing with changes, as well as her appreciation of the very special nature of long-period equilibrium, were the main features in her writings of the last several years of her life, and it is to these that we now turn.

Time and equilibrium

As soon as the uncertainty of the expectations that guide economic behaviour is admitted, equilibrium drops out of the argument and history takes its place (1974, p. 48).

Long-period equilibrium positions can be defined on the basis of given technical conditions of production, the state of competition, tastes and incomes. They describe situations in which all market participants are in their chosen positions, given the values of the parameters. Producers have the capital equipment they would choose to have under current circumstances, and their plants are being operated at normal productive capacity, with prices being such as to provide a normal rate of profit on the values of their investments. Robinson's growing distrust of analyses that use these positions as 'centres of attraction' for the actual values in an economy led to disputes with some of those who were her allies in the 'capital controversies'. The direction of Robinson's thinking was indicated in her 1953 article on the production function and the theory of capital, where she was critical of the neoclasical view of a long-period equilibrium position as one towards which the economy is tending to move as time goes by.[22] This view is critically dependent on the assumption of stationary conditions, whose very special nature for anyone concerned with analysing actual events had been pointed out by Marshall.

> But in real life . . . the demand and supply schedules do not in practice remain unchanged for a long time together, but are constantly being changed; and every change in them alters the equilibrium amount and the equilibrium price, and thus gives new position to the centres about which the amount and the price tend to oscillate.
>
> These considerations point to the great importance of the element of time in relation to demand and supply . . . the normal, or 'natural', value of a commodity is that which economic forces tend to bring about *in the long run*. It is the average value which economic forces would bring about if the general conditions of life were stationary for a run of time long enough to enable them all to work out their full effect.
>
> But we cannot foresee the future perfectly. The unexpected may happen; and the existing tendencies may be modified before they have had time to accomplish what appears now to be their full and complete work. The fact that the general conditions of life are not stationary is the source of many of the difficulties that are met with in applying economic doctrines to practical problems (Marshall, 1920, pp. 346–7).

Robinson believed that entrepreneurs' expectations which guide their investment decisions in a world where future conditions can only be guessed at, are not focused on anything that can be covered by the term 'long-period equilibrium' values. She sometimes expressed her position on this point by distinguishing between 'logical time' and 'historical time'. What may have been her first published statement of this position is to be found in the introduction to the 1962 'A Model of Accumulation'. Consider a model that consists of a set of equations, sufficient in number to determine the equilibrium values of its variables. These equations may determine a path through time for these values, 'but the time through which such a model moves is, so to speak, logical time, not historical time' (1962, pp. 23–4), since nothing is allowed into the model that may disturb equilibrium. Robinson gives as an example of such a model her own exercise on accumulation and the production function referred to in the preceding section. It was assumed there, for the sake of the exercise, that entrepreneurial expectations were always borne out by events as accumulation proceeded in a constant state of knowledge and with a constant labour force. The disturbances and miscalculations that occur in any actual economy are ruled out by the self-contained world of the system of equations. The nature of the equilibrium path between any two points of time can be inferred by projecting 'forward' from its values in 'earlier' periods of time, or by projecting 'backward' from its values in 'later' periods of time. The fundamental difference between the past and future of historical time disappears since all aspects of the 'future' are foreordained by the 'past', and vice versa. There is no sense to the question of the 'stability' of such an equilibrium path. If an actual position were not on the path, then the equilibrium equations would not apply, and a tougher kind of model that allows for uncertainty and the disappointment of expectations must be used.

A model set in historical time will normally not be in equilibrium. 'To construct such a model we specify the technical conditions obtaining in an economy and the behaviour reactions of its inhabitants, and then, so to say, dump it down in a particular situation at a particular date in historic time and work out what will happen next. The initial position contains, as well as physical data, the state of expectations of the characters concerned (whether based on past experience or on traditional beliefs). The system may be going to work itself out so as to fulfil them or so as to disappoint them' (1962, pp. 25–6). This type of model does not furnish the wide range of precise results readily provided by equilibrium models, but this relative paucity is a reflection of the limits of economic theory as a guide to the intricacies of economic events. Only within the context of such a model, which of necessity must be 'loose-jointed' (1960a, p. 27) can the effects of changes, with the resultant disappointment of expectations, be analysed.

All that equilibrium models can provide are comparisons of equilibrium positions.

Robinson's rejection of equilibrium models as guides to the understanding of actual events is also reflected in her view of the 'unimportance of reswitching' (1975c). The discussion of this phenomenon was carried out using a pseudo-production function and, as we saw in the preceding section, this function is built up from the comparison of different economies experiencing steady-state growth. They all share the same technical knowledge, but they differ in the rates of accumulation and propensities to save. The whole purpose for Robinson of such a construct was a negative one, to show that the concept of the marginal productivity of capital has no meaning. With that established she wants to leave behind models that give an important place to positions of long-period equilibrium in order to come to grips with a process of accumulation going on through time. 'There is no such phenomenon in real life as accumulation taking place in a given state of technical knowledge' (1975c, p. 39).

Finally, it should be noted that Robinson's emphasis on the essentially 'negative' importance of Sraffa's *Production of Commodities by Means of Commodities*[23] has led to differences with those economists, such as Garegnani (1976, 1979a, 1979b), who want to build theoretical analyses on the basis of Sraffa's model. Her position reflects extreme caution about the possible significance of anything that might give precision to long-period concepts (1979b).

Conclusion

Robinson was a Cambridge economist whose work falls within the Marshallian tradition. Her writings, such as those on imperfect competition, the theory of employment and the accumulation of capital were motivated by a desire to extend economic theory. The high quality of her contributions was recognized by the economics profession as witnessed, for example, by the inclusion of her articles in the series of readings sponsored by the American Economic Association.[24] But she will probably be remembered best as a critic of the present-day drift of much of economic theory towards an excessive formalism which leaves out essential elements of economic reality. Her strong grasp of economic theory and deep understanding of how it can be constructed and manipulated sometimes led her to note 'that the Emperor had no clothes' (1975a, p. vi). Careful study of her writings will richly repay students for the time and effort devoted to them. There is as well the special quality of the person which is difficult to convey. Brus and Kowalik recall that the first time they met Robinson was at an official function for a group of visiting economists in Poland the day after the events of June 1956, when workers in Gdansk and Poznan had risen up against the authorities and provoked bloody reprisals. The atmosphere was heavy with unexpressed thoughts about the events, but only vacuous comments about the value of exchanges of views were being made – Robinson could not let things stand without stating the need to find out what had happened and why. 'Until that time we had thought of Joan Robinson as a left Keynesian bent on confronting Marxism with difficult questions. But at that moment she acquired a moral authority which she retained all her life. Joan Robinson was a person who awakened conscience and asked questions which disturbed complacency whether it be the complacency of academic or of Marxist orthodoxy' (Brus and Kowalik, 1983, p. 244).

Notes

1 All references, where only the date is given, are to Robinson's writings. Page references to articles appearing in the volumes of collected papers will be to the pages in those volumes, but the dates of original publication will be indicated either in the text or in the list of references. Harcourt has informed me that the date given by Robinson for her entry to Cambridge is incorrect; it should be October 1922.

2 She was probably influenced in this by Kalecki's use of 'cost-determined' prices for manufactured goods (Kalecki, 1943, 1971b, pp. 43–61), but she treated her 'debt' to Kalecki on a par with her debts to Keynes, Wicksell and Marshall, debts which did not always receive specific acknowledgement (1956, p. vi).

3 Cf. Chamberlin, 1948, pp. 177–90.

4 Robinson, Richard Kahn, James Meade, Austin Robinson and Piero Sraffa were key members of the 'Circus', a small group that met regularly during the period January–May 1931. The outcomes of

their discussions were relayed to Keynes by Kahn, and they influenced the former's subsequent work (Keynes, 1973a, pp. 373–43).

5 The correspondence between Robinson and Keynes in volume XIII of Keynes's *Collected Writings* makes clear her role as a sympathetic, and at times relentless, critic. She felt the need to write in a 1932 letter 'You must forgive my rough manners in controversy' (Keynes, 1973a, p. 378). In commenting on some of the galley proofs of Robinson's *Essays in the Theory of Employment*, Keynes wrote 'Your fierceness may quite possibly land you in trouble in some quarters. . .' (Keynes, 1973b, p. 147).

6 Robinson's considerable expository powers were also used in bringing members of her own generation to an acceptance of Keynes's theory. Abba Lerner was one who was influenced by her (1978a, p. xv). She could not help writing to Keynes, after Lerner's review of *The General Theory* in the *International Labour Review* for October 1936 had appeared, 'Don't you think Lerner is a credit to me?' (Keynes, 1973b, p. 148).

7 She shows herself to be conscious of the problem of time early on in the correspondence preceding *The General Theory* but, just as with the *Economics of Imperfect Competition*, it was left to the side. In a May 1932 letter to Keynes we find: 'There is a time element which perhaps cannot be treated on a 3rd dimension. But Time is a common enemy to us all' (Keynes, 1973a, p. 378).

8 Robinson made this point very vividly 'Keynes hardly ever peered over the edge of the short period to see the effect of investment in making additions to the stocks of productive equipment' (Robinson, 1978b, p. 14).

9 Keynes wrote that 'the behaviour of each individual firm in deciding its daily output will be determined by its *short-term expectations*' and in a footnote attached to 'daily' he added: *Daily* here stands for the shortest interval after which the firm is free to revise its decision as to how much employment to offer. It is, so to speak, the minimum effective unit of economic time' (Keynes, 1936, p. 47).

10 Robinson called the issues concerned with the *content* of employment 'The Second Crisis of Economic Theory' (the first crisis concerned the Depression of the thirties (Robinson, 1973, pp. 92–105).

11 Kregel (1983, p. 343n.) notes that Robinson's work on this concept arose out of her comments on page proofs of the *General Theory*, and concludes that this article, originally published in *Zeitschrift für Nationalökonomie* in 1936, was probably completed before publication of the *General Theory*.

12 She noted in the first footnote of this paper: 'The conception of equilibrium employed in this essay is the Marshallian conception of

a position of rest towards which the system is tending at any moment' (Robinson, 1937a, p. 106n.).

13 Harrod's (1939, 1948) writings on dynamic economics were important sources of stimulation for her, since both were working from a Marshallian as well as a Keynesian background (1956, p. vi).

14 This point, which underlies much of her later writings (see below), was one of the three methodological rules to which she drew attention in her *Exercises in Economic Analysis*. The other two rules mentioned are: 'A quantity has no meaning unless we can specify the units in which it is measured' and 'Technical and physical relations, between man and nature, must be distinguished from social relations between man and man' (1960b, p. v).

15 Caution must be exercised in drawing conclusions from these comparisons. Entrepreneurial 'energy' determines not only the rate of accumulation, but also the rate and nature of technical progress, and thus the comparison of economies with different rates of accumulation 'in the same phase of technical development' (1956, p. 90) is very special.

16 Within the spirit of the model, especially under conditions of oligopoly with fixed mark-ups, the 'inflation barrier' would be triggered by a fall in labour share in total output. Robinson, however, always refers to some minimum 'level' rather than to a minimum 'share'.

17 The equipment produced by the investment sector would tend to change with technical progress, but the measure of output in that sector is the productive capacity of the plant produced for the consumption sector where the type of output is unchanged over time.

18 In replying to a comment by Robinson on his model, Harrod wrote: 'I agree with Professor Robinson that, if there is more than one possible equilibrium profit share in a dynamic equilibrium, consistent with other dynamic determinants, there must be more than one equilibrium growth rate. I would not deny that a multiplicity of equilibrium profit shares and profit rates is a possibility; but it seems to me unlikely' (Harrod, 1970, p. 738).

19 Robinson noted that for this possibility 'I had picked up the clue from Piero Sraffa's Preface to Ricardo's *Principles*. . .' (1973, p. 145).

20 A telling criticism of this approach is to be found in Robinson's writings. 'In reality, to find the expected rate of return which governs investment decisions is like the famous difficulty of looking in a dark room for a black cat that probably is not there, and to give a true account of realised returns is like the famous difficulty of the chameleon on a plaid rug' (1956, p. 192).

21 Asimakopulos (1970) has worked out her model on the basis of mark-up pricing.

22 The timeless nature of long-period equilibrium is vividly conveyed by Robinson's statement: 'Long-period equilibrium is not at some date in the future; it is an imaginary state of affairs in which there are no incompatibilities in the existing situation, here and now' (1965, p. 101).

23 A change in her position can be discerned by comparing the 1961 review of this book (1965, pp. 7–14) and the 1975c and 1979a papers. In the review she was prepared to use the model to consider the effects of changes on the wage share, although even then she noted the very special nature of the term 'change' when used in connection with that model. In the later paper it is made clear that 'there is no movement from one position to another, merely a comparison of positions corresponding to different levels of the rate of profit. . .' (1979a, p. 5).

24 Two papers, 'The Foreign Exchanges', and 'Beggar-My-Neighbour Remedies for Unemployment', appeared in *Readings in the Theory of International Trade* (1950). 'The Classification of Inventions' was reprinted in *Readings in the Theory of Income Distribution* (1951), and the 'Rising Supply Price' was included in *Readings in Price Theory* (1952).

References

Asimakopulos, A. (1969) 'A Robinsonian growth model in one-sector notation.' *Australian Economic Papers* 8, June, 41–58.

Asimakopulos, A. (1970) 'A Robinsonian growth model in one-sector notation – an amendment.' *Australian Economic Papers* 9, December, 171–6.

Asimakopulos, A. (1971) 'The determination of investment in Keynes's model.' *Canadian Journal of Economics* 4, August, 382–8.

Asimakopulos, A. (1973) 'Keynes, Patinkin, historical time and equilibrium analysis.' *Canadian Journal of Economics* 6, May, 179–88.

Asimakopulos, A. (1975) 'A Kaleckian theory of income distribution.' *Canadian Journal of Economics* 8, August, 313–33.

Asimakopulos, A. (1977) 'Post-Keynesian growth theory' in S. Weintraub (ed.), *Modern Economic Thought* (Philadelphia: University of Pennsylvania Press).

Asimakopulos, A. (1982) 'Keynes' theory of effective demand revisited.' *Australian Economic Papers* 21, June, 18–36.

Asimakopulos, A. (1983a) 'A Kaleckian profits equation and the United States economy 1950–82.' *Metroeconomica* 35, February–June, 1–27.

Asimakopulos, A. (1983b) 'Kalecki and Keynes on finance, investment and saving.' *Cambridge Journal of Economics* 7, September–December, 221–33.

Asimakopulos, A. (1984–5) '"Long-period employment' in the

General Theory." Journal of Post Keynesian Economics 7, Winter, 207–13.

Asimakopulos, A. (1985) 'The role of finance in Keynes's General Theory.' *Economic Notes* 14, 5–16.

Asimakopulos, A. (1988) 'Kalecki and Robinson: an "outsider's" influence.' *Journal of Post Keynesian Economics* 10, Fall.

Asimakopulos, A. and J.B. Burbidge (1974) 'The short-period incidence of taxation.' *Economic Journal* 84, June, 267–88.

Bain, Joe S. (1956) *Barriers to New Competition* (Cambridge, MA: Harvard University Press).

Basile, Liliana and Neri Salvadori (1984–5) 'Kalecki's pricing theory.' *Journal of Post Keynesian Economics* 7, Winter, 249–62.

Brus, W. and T. Kowalik (1983) 'Socialism and development.' *Cambridge Journal of Economics* 7, September–December, 243–55.

Carvalho, Fernando (1983–4) 'On the concept of time in Shacklean and Sraffian economics.' *Journal of Post Keynesian Economics* 6, Winter, 265–80.

Carvalho, Fernando (1984–5) 'Alternative analyses of short and long run in Post Keynesian economics.' *Journal of Post Keynesian Economics* 7, Winter, 214–34.

Casarosa, C. (1981) 'The microfoundations of Keynes's aggregate supply and aggregate demand analysis.' *Economic Journal* 91, March, 188–93.

Chamberlin, E.H. (1948) *The Theory of Monopolistic Competition*, 6th edn (Cambridge, MA: Harvard University Press).

Davidson, Paul (1960) *Theories of Aggregate Income Distribution* (New Brunswick, NJ: Rutgers University Press).

Davidson, Paul (1978) *Money and the Real World*, 2nd edn. (London: Macmillan).

de Jong, F.J. (1954) 'Supply functions in Keynesian economics.' *Economic Journal* 64, March, 3–24.

Eatwell, John (1971) 'On the proposed reform of corporation tax.' *Bulletin of the Oxford University Institute of Economics and Statistics* 33, November, 267–74.

Eatwell, John (1979) 'Theories of value, output and employment.' *Thames Papers in Political Economy*, Summer. Reprinted in Eatwell and Milgate (1983), 93–128. Page references are to the latter.

Eatwell, John and Murray Milgate (eds), (1983) *Keynes's Economics and the Theory of Value and Distribution* (New York: Oxford University Press).

Eichner, Alfred S. (1973) 'A theory of the determination of the mark-up under oligopoly.' *Economic Journal* 83, December, 1184–1200.

Garegnani, Pierangelo (1976) 'On a change in the notion of equilibrium in recent work on value and distribution' in M. Brown, K. Sato and P. Zarembka (eds), *Essays in Modern Capital Theory* (Amsterdam: North-Holland, 1976), 25–45.

Garegnani, Pierangelo (1979a) 'Notes on consumption, investment and effective demand: II.' *Cambridge Journal of Economics* 3, March, 63–82.

Garegnani, Pierangelo (1979b) 'Notes on consumption, investment and effective demand: a reply to Joan Robinson.' *Cambridge Journal of Economics* 3, March, 181–7.

Graziani, A. (1984) 'The debate on Keynes' finance motive.' *Economic Notes* 13(1), 5–32.

Hall, R.L. and C.J. Hitch (1939) 'Price theory and business behaviour.' *Oxford Economic Papers* 2, May, 12–45.

Harberger, A.C. (1962) 'The incidence of the corporation income tax.' *Journal of Political Economy* 70, June, 215–40.

Harcourt, G.C. (1972) *Some Cambridge Controversies in the Theory of Capital* (Cambridge: Cambridge University Press).

Harcourt, G.C. (1977) 'Review of *Keynes' Monetary Thought: A Study of its Development* by Don Patinkin.' *Economic Record* 53, December, 565–9.

Harcourt, G.C. (1979) 'Robinson, Joan' in David L. Sills (ed.), *International Encyclopedia of the Social Sciences: Biographical Supplement*, Vol. 18 (New York: The Free Press), 663–71.

Harcourt, G.C. and T.J. O'Shaughnessy (1983) 'Keynes's unemployment equilibrium: some insights from Joan Robinson, Piero Sraffa and Richard Kahn.' University of Cambridge, Faculty of Economics and Politics, Research Paper Series 30.

Harrod, R.F. (1939) 'An essay in dynamic theory.' *Economic Journal* 49, March, 14–33.

Harrod, R.F. (1948) *Towards a Dynamic Economics* (London: Macmillan).

Harrod, R.F. (1970) 'Harrod after twenty-one years: a comment.' *Economic Journal* 80, September, 737–41.

Hawtrey, R.G. (1954) 'Keynes and supply functions.' *Economic*

Journal 64, December, 834–9.

Hicks, J.R. (1937) 'Mr. Keynes and the "Classics": a suggested interpretation.' *Econometrica* 5, April, 147–59.

Hicks, J.R. (1965) *Capital and Growth* (Oxford: Oxford University Press).

Hicks, J.R. (1974) *The Crisis in Keynesian Economics* (Oxford: Basil Blackwell).

Hicks, J.R. (1976) 'Some questions of time in economics' in A.M. Tang, F.M. Westfield and J.S. Worley (eds), *Evolution, Welfare, and Time in Economics: Essays in Honor of Nicholas Georgescu-Roegen* (Lexington, MA: Lexington Books), 135–51.

Hotson, John H. (1971) 'Adverse effects of tax and interest as strengthening the case for incomes policies – or a part of the elephant.' *Canadian Journal of Economics* 4, May, 164–81.

Kahn, R.F. (1931) 'The relation of home investment to unemployment.' *Economic Journal* 41, June, 173–98.

Kahn, R.F. (1959) 'Exercises in the analysis of growth.' *Oxford Economic Papers* 11, June, 143–56. All page references in the text are to the reprint in Kahn (1972).

Kahn, R.F. (1972) *Selected Essays on Employment and Growth* (Cambridge: Cambridge University Press).

Kahn, R.F. (1984) *The Making of Keynes' General Theory* (Cambridge: Cambridge University Press).

Kaldor, N. (1939) 'Speculation and economic stability.' *Review of Economic Studies* 6, October, 1–27. All page references in the text are to the reprinting in Kaldor (1960).

Kaldor, N. (1955) *An Expenditure Tax* (London: Allen and Unwin).

Kaldor, N. (1955–6) 'Alternative theories of distribution.' *Review of Economic Studies* 23(2), 83–100.

Kaldor, N. (1960) *Essays in Economic Stability and Growth* (London: Duckworth).

Kaldor, N. (1970) 'Some fallacies in the interpretation of Kaldor.' *Review of Economic Studies* 37(109), 1–7.

Kaldor, N. and J.A. Mirrlees (1962) 'A new model of economic growth.' *Review of Economic Studies* 29, June, 174–92.

Kalecki, Michal (1935a) 'Essai d'une théorie du mouvement cyclique des affaires.' *Revue d'économie politique* 49, 285–305.

Kalecki, Michal (1935b) 'A macrodynamic theory of business cycles.' *Econometrica* 3, July, 327–44.

220   *References*

Kalecki, Michal (1936) 'Pare uwag o teorii Keynesa' [Some remarks on Keynes's theory] *Ekonomista* 36(3), 18–26.

Kalecki, Michal (1937a) 'A theory of the business cycle.' *Review of Economic Studies* 4, February, 77–97.

Kalecki, Michal (1937b) 'A theory of commodity, income and capital taxation.' *Economic Journal* 47, September, 444–50. Reprinted in Kalecki (1971b).

Kalecki, Michal (1939) *Essays in the Theory of Economic Fluctuations* (London: Allen and Unwin).

Kalecki, Michal (1942) 'A theory of profits.' *Economic Journal* 52, June–September, 258–67.

Kalecki, Michal (1943) *Studies in Economic Dynamics* (London: Allen and Unwin).

Kalecki, Michal (1954) *Theory of Economic Dynamics* (London: Allen and Unwin).

Kalecki, Michal (1966) *Studies in the Theory of Business Cycles: 1933–1939* (New York: Augustus M. Kelley).

Kalecki, Michal (1971a) 'Class struggle and distribution of national income.' *Kyklos* 24(1), 1–8. Reprinted in Kalecki (1971b).

Kalecki, Michal (1971b) *Selected Essays on the Dynamics of the Capitalist Economy: 1933–1970* (Cambridge: Cambridge University Press).

Kaplan, A.D.H., J.B. Dirlam and R.F. Lanzillotti (1958) *Pricing in Big Business – A Case Approach* (Washington: Brookings Institution).

Keynes, John Maynard (1930) *A Treatise on Money*, Vol. II, The Applied Theory of Money (London: Macmillan).

Keynes, John Maynard (1936) *The General Theory of Employment, Interest and Money* (London: Macmillan).

Keynes, John Maynard (1973a) *The General Theory and After: Part I Preparation.* Edited by Donald Moggridge. Vol. XIII of the Collected Writings (London: Macmillan for the Royal Economic Society).

Keynes, John Maynard (1973b) *The General Theory and After: Part II Defence and Development.* Edited by Donald Moggridge. Vol. XIV of the Collected Writings (London: Macmillan for the Royal Economic Society).

Keynes, John Maynard (1979) *The General Theory and After: A Supplement.* Edited by Donald Moggridge. Vol. XXIX of the

Collected Writings (London: Macmillan for the Royal Economic Society).

Keynes, John Maynard (1983) *Economic Articles and Correspondence: Investment and Editorial.* Edited by Donald Moggridge. Vol. XII of the Collected Writings (London: Macmillan for the Royal Economic Society).

Keynes, John Maynard and Hubert Henderson (1929) *Can Lloyd George Do It? An Examination of the Liberal Pledge* (London: The Nation and Athenaeum).

Kowalik, T. et al. (1964) *Problems of Economic Dynamics and Planning: Essays in Honour of Michal Kalecki* (Warsaw: PWN – Polish Scientific Publishers).

Kregel, J.A. (1976) 'Economic methodology in the face of uncertainty: the modelling methods of Keynes and Post-Keynesians.' *Economic Journal* 86, June, 209–25.

Kregel, J.A. (1983) 'The microfoundations of the "Generalization of *The General Theory*" and "Bastard Keynesianism": Keynes's theory of employment in the long and short period.' *Cambridge Journal of Economics* 7, September–December, 331–42.

Kuh, E. (1960) *Profits, Mark-up and Productivity* (Washington: Study Paper No. 15, Joint Economic Committee Study of Employment, Growth and Price Levels).

Lanzillotti, R.F. (1958) 'Pricing objectives in large companies.' *American Economic Review* 48, December, 921–40.

Leijonhufvud, Axel (1974) 'Keynes' employment function: comment.' *History of Political Economy* 6(2), 164–70.

Lindahl, Erik (1939) *Studies in the Theory of Money and Capital* (London: Allen and Unwin).

Lydall, H. (1971) 'A theory of distribution and growth with economies of scale.' *Economic Journal* 81, March, 91–112.

Malinvaud, Edmond (1977) *The Theory of Unemployment Reconsidered* (Oxford: Basil Blackwell).

Mann, H.M. (1966) 'Seller concentration, barriers to entry and rates of return in thirty industries, 1956–60.' *Review of Economics and Statistics* 48, August, 296–307.

Marschak, J. (1934) 'Report on the meeting of the Econometric Society in Leyden.' *Econometrica* 2, April, 187–203.

Marshall, Alfred (1920) *Principles of Economics*, 8th edn (London: Macmillan).

Marty, Alvin (1961) 'A geometrical exposition of the Keynesian supply function.' *Economic Journal* 71, September, 560–5.

Mieszkowski, P.M. (1969) 'Tax incidence theory: the effects of taxes on the distribution of income.' *Journal of Economic Literature* 7, December, 1103–24.

Milgate, Murry (1982) *Capital and Employment: A Study of Keynes's Economics* (London: Academic Press).

Minsky, Hyman P. (1982) *Can "It" Happen Again?: Essays on Instability and Finance* (Armonk, NY: M.E. Sharpe).

Myrdal, Gunnar (1939) *Monetary Equilibrium* (London: W. Hodge).

Neild, R. (1963) *Pricing and Employment in the Trade Cycle* (London: Cambridge University Press).

Newman, Peter (1962) 'Production of commodities by means of commodities.' *Schweizerische Zeitschrift Fur Volkwirtshaft Und Statistik* 98, 58–75.

Nordhaus, William D. (1974) 'The falling share of profits.' *Brookings Papers on Economic Activity*, 169–208.

Nordhaus, William D. and Wynne Godley (1972) 'Pricing in the trade cycle.' *Economic Journal* 82, September, 853–82.

Nuti, D.M. (1970) '"Vulgar economy' in the theory of income distribution.' Reprinted in E.K. Hunt and Jesse G. Schwartz, (eds), *A Critique of Economic Theory* (Harmondsworth: Penguin, 1972).

Ohlin, Bertil (1937a) 'Some notes on the Stockholm theory of saving and investment.' *Economic Journal* 47, March, 53–69 and June, 221–40.

Ohlin, Bertil (1937b) 'Alternative theories of the rate of interest: a rejoinder.' *Economic Journal* 47, September, 423–7.

Ohlin, Bertil (1978) 'On the formulation of monetary theory.' *History of Political Economy* 10(3), 353–88.

Osiatyński, Jerzy (1987) 'A note on Kalecki and Keynes on unemployment equilibrium.' (mimeograph), presented at the Conference on 'The Notion of Equilibrium in Keynesian theory', Perugia, 13–14 March.

Parrinello, Sergio (1980) 'The price level in Keynes' effective demand.' *Journal of Post Keynesian Economics* 3, Fall, 63–78.

Pasinetti, L. et al. (1966) 'Paradoxes in capital theory: a symposium.' *Quarterly Journal of Economics* 80, November, 503–83.

Patinkin, Don (1965) *Money, Interest and Prices*, 2nd edn. (New York: Harper & Row).

Patinkin, Don (1976) *Keynes' Monetary Thought: A Study of Its Development* (Durham: Duke University Press).

Patinkin, Don (1978) 'Keynes' aggregate supply function: a plea for common sense.' *History of Political Economy* 10(4), 577–96.

Patinkin, Don (1979) 'A study of Keynes' theory of effective demand.' *Economic Inquiry* 17(2), 155–76.

Patinkin, Don (1982) *Anticipations of the General Theory? And Other Essays on Keynes* (Chicago: University of Chicago Press).

Patinkin, Don and J.C. Leith (eds) (1977) *Keynes, Cambridge and the General Theory* (Toronto: University of Toronto Press).

Riach, P.A. (1971) 'Kalecki's "degree of monopoly" reconsidered.' *Australian Economic Papers* 10, June, 50–60.

Roberts, David L. (1978) 'Patinkin, Keynes, and aggregate supply and demand analysis.' *History of Political Economy* 10(4), 549–76.

Robertson, D.H. (1936) 'Some notes on Mr. Keynes' General Theory of Employment.' *Quarterly Journal of Economics* 51, November, 168–91.

Robertson, D.H. (1938) 'Mr Keynes and "finance".' *Economic Journal* 48, June, 314–18.

Robertson, D.H. (1940) *Essays in Monetary Theory* (London: Staples Press).

Robertson, D.H. (1951–2) 'Comments on Mr. Johnson's Notes.' *Review of Economic Studies* 19(2), 105–10.

Robertson, D.H. (1955) 'Keynes and supply functions.' *Economic Journal* 65, September, 474–8.

Robinson, Joan (1933) *The Economics of Imperfect Competition* (London: Macmillan).

Robinson, Joan (1937a) *Essays in the Theory of Employment* (London: Macmillan).

Robinson, Joan (1937b) *Introduction to the Theory of Employment* (London: Macmillan).

Robinson, Joan (1937–8) 'The classification of inventions.' *Review of Economic Studies* 5, 139–42.

Robinson, Joan (1942) *An Essay on Marxian Economics* (London: Macmillan).

Robinson, Joan (1956) *The Accumulation of Capital* (London: Macmillan).

Robinson, Joan (1960a) *Collected Economic Papers*, Vol. II (Oxford: Basil Blackwell).

Robinson, Joan (1960b) *Exercises in Economic Analysis* (London:

Macmillan).

Robinson, Joan (1962) *Essays in the Theory of Economic Growth* (London: Macmillan).

Robinson, Joan (1963) *Economic Philosophy* (Chicago: Aldine Publishing).

Robinson, Joan (1964) 'Kalecki and Keynes' in Kowalik et al. (1964). Reprinted in Robinson (1965).

Robinson, Joan (1965) *Collected Economic Papers*, Vol. III (Oxford: Basil Blackwell).

Robinson, Joan (1966) 'Introduction' to Kalecki (1966).

Robinson, Joan (1969a) *The Economics of Imperfect Competition*, 2nd edn (London: Macmillan).

Robinson, Joan (1969b) *Introduction to the Theory of Employment*, 2nd edn (London: Macmillan).

Robinson, Joan (1969c) 'A further note.' *Review of Economic Studies* 36, April, 260–2.

Robinson, Joan (1970) *Freedom and Necessity* (London: Allen and Unwin).

Robinson, Joan (1971) *Economic Heresies* (New York: Basic Books).

Robinson, Joan (1973) *Collected Economic Papers*, Vol. IV (Oxford: Basil Blackwell).

Robinson, Joan (1974) 'History versus equilibrium.' *Thames Papers in Political Economy*. Reprinted in Robinson (1980b), 48–58.

Robinson, Joan, 1975a) 'Introduction 1974' to *Collected Economic Papers*, Vol. II, 2nd edn (Oxford: Basil Blackwell).

Robinson, Joan (1975b) 'Introduction 1974' to *Collected Economic Papers*, Vol. III, 2nd edn. (Oxford: Basil Blackwell).

Robinson, Joan (1975c) 'The unimportance of reswitching' and 'Reswitching: reply.' *Quarterly Journal of Economics* 89, February, 32–9 and 53–5.

Robinson, Joan (1978a) *Contributions to Modern Economics* (Oxford: Basil Blackwell).

Robinson, Joan (1978b) 'Keynes and Ricardo.' *Journal of Post Keynesian Economics* 1, Fall, 12–18.

Robinson, Joan (1979a) 'Misunderstandings in the theory of production.' *Greek Econimic Review* 1, August, 1–7.

Robinson, Joan (1979b) 'Garegnani on effective demand.' *Cambridge Journal of Economics* 3(3), 179–80.

Robinson, Joan (1980a) *Further Contributions to Modern Economics* (Oxford: Basil Blackwell).

Robinson, Joan (1980b) *Collected Economic Papers*, Vol. V (Cambridge, MA: MIT Press).

Roncaglia, Alessandro (1978) *Sraffa and the Theory of Prices* (New York: John Wiley and Sons).

Rothschild, Kurt W. (1971) 'Different approaches in distribution theory.' *Kyklos* 24(1), 10–29.

Samuelson, P.A. (1966) 'A summing up.' *Quarterly Journal of Economics* 80, November, 568–83.

Sawyer, Malcolm C. (1985) *The Economics of Michal Kalecki* (London: Macmillan).

Shackle, G.L.S. (1967) *The Years of High Theory: Invention and Tradition in Economic Thought, 1926–1939* (Cambridge: Cambridge University Press).

Sraffa, Piero (1926) 'The laws of returns under competitive conditions.' *Economic Journal* 36, December, 535–50.

Sraffa, Piero (1960) *Production of Commodities by Means of Commodities* (Cambridge: Cambridge University Press).

Steiger, Otto (1976) 'Bertil Ohlin and the origins of the Keynesian Revolution.' *History of Political Economy* 8(3), 341–66.

Targetti, F. and B. Kinda-Hass (1982) 'Kalecki's review of Keynes' *General Theory*.' *Australian Economic Papers* 21, December, 244–60.

Tarshis, Lorie (1979) 'The aggregate supply function in Keynes's General Theory' in M.J. Boskin (ed.), *Essays in Honor of Tibor Scitovsky* (New York: Academic Press).

Tinbergen, Jan (1935) 'Annual survey: suggestions on quantitative business cycle theory.' *Econometrica* 3, July, 241–308.

Trevithick, J.A. (1976) 'Money wage inflexibility and the Keynesian labour supply function.' *Economic Journal* 86, June, 327–32.

Vicarelli, Fausto (1984) *Keynes: The Instability of Capitalism* (Philadelphia: University of Pennsylvania Press).

Weintraub, E. Roy (1974) 'Keynes' employment function.' *History of Political Economy* 6(2), 162–4.

Weintraub, Sidney (1957) 'The micro-foundations of aggregate demand and supply.' *Economic Journal* 67, September, 455–70.

Wells, Paul (1960) 'Keynes' aggregate supply function: a suggested interpretation.' *Economic Journal* 70, September, 536–42.

Wells, Paul (1962) 'Aggregate supply and demand: an explanation of chapter III of *The General Theory*.' *Canadian Journal of Economics and Political Science* 28, November, 585–90.

Wells, Paul (1974) 'Keynes' employment function.' *History of Political Economy* 6(2), 158–62.

Wicksell, K. (1965) *Interest and Prices* (New York: Augustus M. Kelley).

Subject Index

Author Index